Praise for Welsh Fairies

"Much of the material contained in this work existed predominantly in the Welsh language and was unavailable to non-Welsh speakers.... Impeccably researched and written in Starling's delectable style, this book offers a new window into an Otherworld."
—KRISTOFFER HUGHES, Head of the Anglesey Druid Order, author of
 The Book of Druidry

"This is the book on Welsh fairies that the world has needed, a thorough exploration of who these beings are through the lens of the culture they come from."
—MORGAN DAIMLER, author of *A New Dictionary of Fairies and Fairy*

"This is by far the best book available to introduce Welsh fairy belief to practitioners of magic. It combines intelligence, generosity, excellent research, and long experience."
—RONALD HUTTON, historian and author of *Triumph of the Moon*

"I wish I had this book two decades ago when I first began walking a Celtic Pagan path."
—ANNWYN AVALON, author of *The Way of the Water Priestess*

"Mhara Starling not only explores the history and literature of the Welsh fairies and Otherworld but offers practical ways to work with them. *Welsh Fairies* is readable and personal ... giving access to little-known stories and traditions."
—ANDREW PHILLIP SMITH, author of *Pages from a Welsh Cunning Man's Book*

"An absolute treasure.... Perhaps this book's most valuable gift is the lovely, warm, and sincere guidance for building a ritual practice."
—MORPHEUS RAVENNA, author of *The Magic of the Otherworld*

"Mhara examines the multilayered relationship our ancestors had with the spirits of the Welsh landscape, its folklore, and its legends. The material in this book provides the reader with both the knowledge and the tools to strengthen their own connection to the spirits of place."
—VIKKI BRAMSHAW, author of *New Forest Folklore*

Welsh Fairies

About the Author

Mhara Starling (Chester, England) was born in North Wales, raised on the Isle of Anglesey, and is a native Welsh speaker. She is a transgender woman who has been practicing witchcraft from a very young age, and her witchcraft videos on TikTok have over a million views. Mhara is a celebrant and a tarot reader, and she runs moots, gatherings, and open rituals. She was featured in the BBC Wales documentary series *Young, Welsh and Pretty Religious*.

Visit her on TikTok @mhara_starling.

MHARA STARLING

Welsh Fairies

A Guide to the Lore, Legends,
Denizens & Deities of the Otherworld

LLEWELLYN
WOODBURY, MINNESOTA

FIRST EDITION
First Printing, 2024

Book design by R. Brasington
Cover design by Kevin R. Brown
Interior illustrations by Llewellyn Art Department

Llewellyn Publications is a registered trademark of Llewellyn Worldwide Ltd.

Library of Congress Cataloging-in-Publication Data (Pending)
ISBN: 978-0-7387-7774-0

Llewellyn Publications
A Division of Llewellyn Worldwide Ltd.
2143 Wooddale Drive
Woodbury, MN 55125-2989
www.llewellyn.com

Printed in the United States of America

Other Books by Mhara Starling

Welsh Witchcraft (2022)

Forthcoming Books by Mhara Starling

An Apostate's Guide to Witchcraft (September 2024)

Disclaimer

This book includes exercises that utilise plants, herbs, wood, and other natural ingredients. Before conducting any of the exercises, please be mindful of any possible allergens, and consult a medical professional if you have any reaction to the plants and herbs used in incenses and other exercises. When working with fire and incense, please ensure you are using a fireproof dish and a fireproof surface. Reaching out to the entities mentioned in this book is already a rather perilous task; approach exercises with care, and follow sensible measures to keep yourself and those around you safe and well. Perform the exercises at your own risk. Stay safe, and practice magic mindfully!

Acknowledgments

This book could not have fluttered its way into this world without the aid of some rather fabulous magical people in my life. When writing about a subject so near and dear to your heart, a subject that is a special interest, one would think the words would flow with ease. Alas, that was not the case. Many a sleepless night was spent worrying I would "get it wrong." It was thanks to very special friends that I pulled myself out of the pits of anxiety and self-doubt and did the work.

Thank you to Kristoffer Hughes for your wit, wisdom, and constant advice. To Brett Hollyhead and Moss Matthey, fabulous friends who listened to my constant ramblings and dealt with one or two spirals. To Bet Huws for helping me deal with the fact that when it comes to treigladau, I am an absolute terror! To Rachael and Steph, who helped me escape the stress of writing to have fun from time to time. To my teachers, who pointed me in the direction of Welsh folklore back when I was but a child, initiating this entire obsession. To my patrons for supporting me through it all. And, of course, most of all, to my love, Matthew Lewis, who is constantly there to help keep me grounded.

Diolch o galon i chi gyd.

Contents

Exercise List   *xiii*

Introduction: Who Are the Fairy?   *1*

The Otherworld   9

King of Fairy   37

The Denizens of the Otherworld   65

Goblins, Ghouls, and Phantom Fairies   95

Gods and Spirits of the Land   119

Fairy Flora and Fauna   145

Fairies and Magic   171

Conclusion: Fairies Today   *199*

Guide to Welsh Pronunciation   *209*

Welsh Glossary   *213*

Bibliography   *223*

Index   *231*

Exercises

Constructing a Shrine to Cerridwen   28

Creating a Maen Awenyddol–Inspired Stone   29

A Call to Gwyn ap Nudd   51

Dedicating a Shrine to the King of Fairy   62

An Offering to the Tylwyth Teg   90

Dedicating a Space to Give Offerings to the Household Fairy   109

Parting the Mists and Connecting to Rhiannon   124

Protective Rowan Rings   149

Heather-and-Fern Fairy Incense   151

Hazel Communication Wands   154

Cleansing Rite   185

Basic Ritual Outline   187

Sensory Deprivation Trance Journeying   191

Crystal Scrying   193

Crossroad Counsel   196

Introduction
Who Are the Fairy?

In the early seventeenth century, there lived a man in Caernarfonshire, North Wales, who went by the name Harry Lloyd. Harry came from a village called Llandygai, not far from Bangor, North Wales, and liked to refer to himself as a scholar. He was known by many across the region as a diviner, conjurer, and surgeon.[1] A vagabond, Harry would wander around various villages offering to help people via his magical talents.

He claimed that he could cure the sick, make poor men rich, and divine the whereabouts of items long lost. He did all of this, apparently, via magic utilising the aid of fairies.[2] He claimed that he would meet with the fairies at various times throughout the year, specifically on Tuesday or Thursday nights. His relationship with the fairies was emphasised as a qualification to how competent of a magical practitioner he was.

In the spring of 1636, Harry Lloyd would stand in court under accusations of using unlawful arts under the pretence of surgery or physick.[3] He is now remembered as a confidence trickster who preyed

. . . .
1. Suggett, *Welsh Witches*, 126–127.
2. Rüdiger, *Y Tylwyth Teg*, 187–189.
3. Suggett, *Welsh Witches*, 126–127.

1

on the naivety of vulnerable people and pretended to have relations with fairies. However, Harry Lloyd did indeed practice magic and may have truly believed that he was in relationship with fairies.

Harry is not the only person in Wales to have been taken to court on accusations of consorting with fairies or at least pretending to do so in order to con innocent people. Welsh folklore is also abundant with stories of cunning men, conjurers, wisewomen, and witches who work their craft against the enchantment of fairies or even make pacts with them. While deals with the devil in order to gain magical powers do not feature much in Welsh lore, the relationship between fairies and magicians is undoubtable.

These magicians and magical specialists were drawing upon a traditional cultural belief in beings who often interacted with mortals: beings who come from another world entirely, but interact with ours often; beings who are not limited by fickle mortal things such as corporeality and the linearity of time. This tradition stretches back into our oldest stories and legends. From the noble kings and regal ladies who rode upon horseback out of the mist to stories of goblin-like creatures wreaking havoc on men of the church, fairies have long been an integral aspect of the folkloric and mythic beliefs of Wales.

This book aims to explore those beliefs in detail. Who are the fairies? Where do they come from? Who rules over them? And are they friends or foes? All these questions and more will be explored in the following chapters. We will also explore the connection between magical practitioners and fairies and delve into methods of incorporating fairy beliefs into your own spiritual and magical practice.

More specifically, as the title suggests, this book aims to explore fairies and fairy lore within a Welsh cultural context. Fairies have been explored widely in a variety of books, encyclopaedias, and dictionaries. However, most of these books tend to look at fairies within a broader, almost homogenised "Celtic" lens. The word Celtic does not denote one homogenous cultural group where all belief, stories, and lore remain consistent.

Instead, Celtic should be understood as an umbrella term for a variety of different cultural groups. These individual cultures deserve to be examined individually so that unique beliefs are better represented. With that in mind, beyond a few sections where I might draw comparisons or where examination of other cultures may be needed to add context to a topic being discussed, all the information explored within this book is Welsh in nature.

Who Is This Book For?

Before we begin delving into fairy lore, I believe it is important to make clear who this book is written for. In order to explain that, I must quickly introduce myself. I grew up in a rural part of North Wales, in the coastal village of Aberffraw on Ynys Môn, the Isle of Anglesey. I have been captivated by fairy lore, folklore, and magic for as long as I can remember. This topic is one that is near and dear to my heart. I am also a modern-day Pagan and practicing Swynwraig, or witch.

The primary function of this book is to act as a guide to the fairy beliefs, traditions, and stories that come from Wales. Within the pages of this book, we will explore the concept of the Otherworld, the king of fairies, magic, mythology, and folk custom and belief within an entirely Welsh context. With that in mind, this book is for anyone who wishes to expand their knowledge of Welsh folklore and fairy lore.

However, as a modern-day witch, I am also someone who genuinely believes in fairies, and I incorporate that belief into my lived spiritual and magical practice today. As such, this book is also written with Pagans and witches in mind. Over the last few years, I have noticed interest in fairies growing among spiritual, occult, and magical communities. I attend various festivals, conferences, and Pagan events throughout the year, and it has been clear that people genuinely want to learn more about fairies.

My aim with this book is to provide an accessible and in-depth resource for those wishing to learn more about our fairy lore, beliefs, and traditions, as well as those who wish to incorporate said beliefs into their spiritual or magical practice today.

Throughout the book are various exercises. These exercises will act as a leaping board for those with a spiritual or magical interest in this subject to begin building and fostering their own relationships with the subject matter. If you are reading this book purely to learn more about folklore and have no interest in developing a magical or spiritual practice, then by all means skip these exercises and simply enjoy the exploration of myth and lore.

I would guess that many who have picked up this book are not currently living in Wales and as such may be wondering whether it is appropriate to partake in the exercises and practices outlined within its pages. As long as these practices are approached with respect toward the culture that inspired them, all are welcome to incorporate them into their own magical and spiritual practice. My personal recommendation would be to treat the exercises as starting points. Take what works, trial them and see if they fit into your practice, and then adapt them as you deem fit.

Many of these exercises are crafted with my own locale as the anchor. The plants worked with, spirits discussed, and methods are tailored to my practice, which is rooted in my square mile. You might need to adapt them to better suit your own locale.

What matters in magic is not whether a practice is ancient but whether it works. All the exercises outlined in these pages work for me. However, you are not me. Therefore, if you struggle with any of the exercises, I give you permission to use them as inspiration to craft your own methods.

A rather prominent piece of discourse lately in Pagan spaces seems to be whether or not fairies should be worked with in a magical context at all. On one hand, we have people who claim that fairies are inherently light and positive entities, which mirrors the popular cultural idea of fairies as small, gossamer-winged, flowery beings who flitter around with fairy dust and magic wands. This conception of fairies, as we will come to discover throughout this book, is a rather modern invention that cannot be found in older folklore and belief. On the other hand, many of those wishing to avert people from the misconception that fairies of older folk belief are not the glittery, pretty, dainty things we see in children's books and media have now caused the pendulum to swing to the complete opposite side of the spectrum.

Rather than perceiving fairies as dainty, delicate, pretty things, many now push the narrative that fairies of older lore are monstrous, dangerous, scary, and worthy of ignoring altogether. Both of these rather extreme views seem to miss the point. Yes, it is important to acknowledge that fairies are not as twee and whimsical as Victoriana would have us believe, and yet to say that fairies can *only* be dangerous and nasty creatures is also ignoring centuries of lore showing us that magical practitioners have long worked in reverent, respectful relationship with fairies.

This book aims to look at fairies with a more balanced perspective, acknowledging that fairies can indeed be dangerous and deadly, while also accepting that they are multifaceted entities just as complex and nuanced as human beings, if not more so.

Alongside folklore and mythology, we will explore ways in which people have interacted with fairies, whether that be ordinary people utilising folk magical techniques to ward away the fairies or the methods magical specialists such as cunning folk, charmers, and wisewomen employed in order to ally themselves with fairies for magical means.

fairy, faery, faerie, or fae?

One important thing to acknowledge from the beginning is why I choose to use the spelling fairy instead of the various alternatives available. Whenever I share work on the topic of Welsh fairy lore, I often receive criticism, usually from Pagans and witches, for using the spelling fairy. The reasoning for criticising this spelling is usually born of the notion that fairy is a more modern spelling, that the fair folk are offended by this word, and that words such as fae or the spelling faerie/faery is older and therefore more authentic.

Others have claimed that the fairy and fairies spellings are too reminiscent of the modern concept of fairies as twee winged beings, and using spellings such as faerie helps differentiate the fairies of pop culture from the fairies of older lore.

Let us briefly explore these ideas and part the mists as to the "correct" spelling and word to use when referring to the fair folk.

The earliest mention of the word fairy in the English language was in the early fourteenth century, likely evolving from the Old French fae or fay, which was used to describe beings with magical powers, anything inherently enchanting, or even the Otherworld itself.[4] English did not have standardised spelling for many centuries, meaning that we see variations in spelling throughout history—variations such as fairy, faerie, faery, fayri, and so on.[5]

What this tells us is that there is no real etymological difference between the spellings fairy and faerie or faery. All these spellings evolved from the same root and were used to mean the same thing. Therefore, the argument that any of these spellings is more authentic is simply incorrect.

On the subject of whether the word fairy is offensive to the beings referred to by that name, the discussion becomes somewhat more complicated. Euphemisms were used to describe fairies in various regions. For example, in Wales we refer to

. . . .
4. Williams, *The Semantics of the Word "Fairy,"* in Narvàez, *The Good People*, 463.
5. Williams, *The Semantics of the Word "Fairy,"* in Narvàez, *The Good People*, 459.

them as Tylwyth Teg, meaning the "fair family," or Bendith y Mamau, meaning "their mother's blessing." These names are not necessarily descriptors but rather euphemisms to appease and speak kindly of them lest they retaliate against you.[6] This idea will be explored in more detail in a later chapter.

However, this brings me to my main point. The native words we have for fairies in Wales are what we would usually use to refer to these beings. I am simply using the word fairy for ease and readability, as I am aware that many non-Welsh speakers will read this book.

Fairy, in all its spelling variations, has become a catchall umbrella term for the variety of beings we will discuss in this book. I prefer the spelling fairy as it is what I grew up using when conversing in English, and using a different spelling would feel strange when it is not the native term for these beings. The closest term to the English word fairy in vernacular Welsh dialects is verry, which was used in the southeast of Wales at one point in time but is not very common today. If I were to use an alternate spelling, I would choose that one. However, in my experience, most people in Wales today will say Tylwyth Teg or, when conversing in English, fairy.

This book is organised in a particular way. First, we will explore the lore of the land from which fairies are said to hail: the Otherworld. After dipping our toes into the Otherworld, we will then explore the ruler of the fair folk, Gwyn ap Nudd. It may seem odd that we start with the land and the king of fairies before we talk about the fairies themselves. However, there is reason for this format.

Much of the lore pertaining to the fairies themselves makes more sense when we have a greater understanding of the world from which they come and the rulers who govern over them. It is vital to understand that fairies are inherently "othered" in their nature. They are not quite like us. By understanding their world and the ways in which it operates, we are granted a better grasp of who they are on an intimate level. By studying the nature of their world and their enigmatic king first, we are better able to take in their otherwise complex, contradictory, and confusing nature.

· · · · · · · · · · · · · · ·
6. Rüdiger, Y Tylwyth Teg, 32.

Liminality

As we explore fairy beliefs and lore, you will notice one particular word appearing frequently. That word is liminality.

What does this word mean? And why does it show up so often when discussing fairies?

The Merriam-Webster dictionary defines liminal as something that is barely perceptible or capable of eliciting a response, or something that is in an intermediate state, phase, or condition—essentially, something that is in-between or transitional in nature.

Liminality can refer to something that is occupying a betwixt-and-between position. For example, if you stand in a doorway between the indoors and outdoors, you are in a liminal position. If you stand at the end of a pier, you are standing on a liminal structure that is connected to the land yet is technically out at sea. Twilight is often regarded as a liminal time of day because it is the meeting place between day and night. At twilight, it is neither entirely dark, nor is it completely light. The stroke of midnight could also be considered liminal because it is the middle place between yesterday and today.

Fairies, as we will come to discover, occupy a liminal state of existence. They move between two worlds, they can be perceived as both spirit and non-spirit, they are often conflated with the dead and yet are very much alive, they are visible yet invisible, and they are often associated with liminal places and times.

This is what I mean when I mention fairies as liminal in nature. They occupy a place in culture and lore that cannot easily be defined nor contextualised entirely. They are beings whom we are entirely aware of, and everyone has an idea of what you mean when you say fairy, and yet they are also unknowable, elusive, and shadowy. On top of this, the study of fairies is loaded with contradiction. For every piece of lore you find, there is another piece of lore that contradicts it. This will become all the clearer the further you journey into this book.

Diving Into the Deep

Fairies have always held a prominent place in my heart. I am not only a modern-day witch but an author, a teacher, and someone who delves into these stories and elements of our lore for a living. I cannot help but think that none of this would have happened if it were not for fairies.

I vividly remember my first day of primary school, when I told my teachers that, more than anything else in the world, I loved witches, fairies, and mermaids. They latched on to that fact and enthusiastically pointed me in the direction of books that held stories of these beings within our own landscape. Beyond the books, I was also captivated by local stories told by word of mouth.

In my eyes, fairies were not fantastical creatures from fantasy books who existed in faraway lands. The ellyll lived in the hills and hollows along the country roads behind my house. A pwca haunted the local burial chamber along the coastal path. A bwgan had been turned into stone along a dark road in a nearby town. These beings were part of my cultural heritage as well as my lived experience growing up in Anglesey.

This book is, in essence, a love letter to our magical lore. My hope is that you will be as captivated by these stories, legends, and magical beings as I was growing up. May we dive into the very depths of Annwfn together, hear the song of the Birds of Rhiannon, learn of a mermaid who rules over the waves of the sea, meet the king of fairies himself, and learn of magical practitioners who built relationships with fairies.

I warn you: these stories are initiatory in nature. Once you hear them, they may just stir and awaken something within you that has been sleeping for a long while. Like the fairy maidens who married mortal men, you will hear the call of the Otherworld beckon you. While there is danger involved in answering that call, great magic can come of it too.

May your journey into discovering the magic of fairies be as stirring as mine has been.

The Otherworld

Awen a Ganaf, o'r Dwfn y Dygaf.
Awen I sing, from the deep I conjure it.

In the depths of our world, one might find doorways that lead to strange, enchanting landscapes. Across the sea, strange islands that seem to move and vanish await the intrepid voyager. Beneath the glacial lakes in the tall mountainous regions are kingdoms gleaming with castles made of quartz and precious stones. This liminal, chthonic land is home to magical beings who seem to have a completely unique perception of both time and reality. This is the Otherworld.

In order to understand fairies at any depth, we must first understand the world they are said to originate from. Fairies are intimately linked with their otherworldly domain. Understanding this complex realm beyond our own allows us to better grasp the very nature of the beings who hail from there.

Countless Welsh legends and tales allude to the idea that the fair folk come from a world that exists adjacent to our own. The lore concerning the concept of an Otherworld spans across mythology, poetry, and folklore. In this chapter we will be exploring the Otherworld in its various guises, beginning with a look at the Otherworld and otherworldly motifs in the Mabinogion and other related myths, then moving on to the Otherworld of folklore and the bards.

The Otherworld in Mythology

In Welsh mythology, the Otherworld is a looming force that influences many of the core stories. Otherworldly characters act as initiators of great adventure, magical and tricksy protagonists, or cunning and calculated villains. Occasionally the influence of the Otherworld is overt and obvious. At other times the mystic forces of the world beyond our own sways the characters and arcs of the myths in subtle yet important manners.

The Otherworld of Welsh mythology is diverse and mysterious. Gloriously rich courts, timeless liminal islands, and castles that vanish into thin air all feature in the mythical landscape.

First, it is important to define what it is that I mean by mythology. When referencing Welsh mythology, I am referring specifically to the stories collected in Welsh medieval manuscripts: the four branches of the Mabinogi, the Native tales, and the romances (as they have come to be known). Specifically, I will be looking closely at the Otherworld as it has been portrayed in the four branches of the Mabinogi and in the stories beyond the four branches, such as "How Culhwch Won Olwen" and "The Tale of the Lady of the Fountain." This is not to say that these instances are the only times the Otherworld or otherworldly characters are present, but these are the stories I believe provide us with the most insight into the Otherworld within a Welsh cultural context.

Pwyll Pendefig Dyfed—Pwyll, Prince of Dyfed

In the first branch of the Mabinogi, Pwyll, the prince of Dyfed, encounters the king of Annwfn, Arawn. From the very first tale presented to us in the four branches, we are immediately thrust into the Otherworld's enigmatic and influential spirit. However, the Otherworld presented in the first branch deviates in a few ways to the Otherworld described in later texts.

When Pwyll enters the Otherworld alongside Arawn, there is no dramatic shift in location. They do not enter a portal; no ethereal mist envelops them; they do not enter the depths of the earth via a cave or body of water. Pwyll, escorted by Arawn, simply walks into the kingdom of Annwfn with ease. This element of the tale has led some scholars to believe that Annwfn exists as a land that is connected to or located within the ancient kingdom of Dyfed.[7] However, we must take into consideration the many otherworldly motifs that surround this encounter.

This story begins with Pwyll, prince of the kingdom of Dyfed, having an intuitive desire to go hunting. Dyfed is located in southwestern Wales, in an area that today is referred to as the counties of Sir Benfro (Pembrokeshire) and Sir Gaerfyrddin (Carmarthenshire). When the story begins, Pwyll is at one of his chief courts at Arberth. When he was pulled to go hunting, the area he wished to hunt in was a place known as Glyn Cuch. Just in the very first few lines of this tale we come across quite a few motifs associated with magic, supernatural contact, and otherworldly forces, though hidden in plain sight.

First and foremost, Pwyll feels the compulsion to go hunting. He is drawn as if by intuition or a divine call to venture out and hunt. The act of hunting is often employed in romantic and Celtic literature to signify that a supernatural or magical encounter is about to happen.[8] However, another important detail is not only the fact that Pwyll feels compelled to hunt, but also that he hunts at a specific location. Glyn Cuch is a valley that today runs along the border of Pembrokeshire and Carmarthenshire. Historically this place has always been a border or place of transition. The Afon Cuch, a river that is a tributary of the Afon Teifi, carves out this gloriously wooded valley.[9] This river historically acted as a boundary between two Welsh commotes known as Emlyn Is Cuch and Emlyn Uwch Cuch.[10] This means that Pwyll was drawn to hunt in a place that is liminal in nature: a boundary between places, a place betwixt and between, neither here nor there.

Once Pwyll has arrived at Glyn Cuch and is separated from his hunting party, he arrives in a vague and ambiguous part of the forest, and this is where he has his first encounter with the Otherworld.

The first glimpse we receive of the "other" comes in the form of hunting dogs. These dogs, known as the Cŵn Annwfn, have shining white fur all over their bodies except for their ears, which are a vivid shade of red. Pwyll witnesses these dogs chase and successfully hunt down a stag. As he watches the dogs eating the stag,

· · · · · · · · · · · · · · · · ·

7.   Davies, *The Mabinogion*, 228.

8.   Ford, *The Mabinogi and Other Medieval Welsh Tales*, 33.

9.   Afon is the Welsh word for river.

10. Commote is a word that refers to a secular division of land in medieval Wales; Shack, *Otherworld and Norman "Other,"* 176.

he eventually scares them away and sends his own dogs to eat from it. This small action will ultimately be the instigator to his otherworldly adventure.

From out of the thicket comes Arawn, dressed in light grey hunting clothes with a hunting horn hanging around his neck. He rides upon a dapple-grey horse and he speaks with authority and power. Upon arriving at the scene, Arawn refuses to greet Pwyll initially because he views what Pwyll just did as an insult. Eventually, Pwyll apologises for his lack of courtesy and asks this intimidating hunter if there is anything he can do to make it up to him. This is when he reveals that he is Arawn, king of Annwfn. He makes it clear even before this that he outranks Pwyll, a hint perhaps that either they are no longer in Pwyll's kingdom or that the noble class of Annwfn always outranks the nobles of the earthly kingdoms.

Arawn decrees that the only way Pwyll can make up for his transgression is by ridding him of an enemy, Hafgan. Arawn proposes that he and Pwyll switch places with one another: Arawn will live for a year in Dyfed, while Pwyll will live for a year in Annwfn. This will be done with one task in mind: that Pwyll will vanquish and kill Hafgan, a task Arawn has failed to do thus far. In order for the ploy to work, Arawn will enact a glamour upon himself and Pwyll so that they will look like one another and be able to live each other's lives. After a few questions, Pwyll ultimately agrees to take on this challenge. He will enter Annwfn and fight with Hafgan.

Annwfn

The name given to the Otherworld in this first branch of the Mabinogi is Annwfn. This is the name given to the Otherworld in most medieval Welsh texts, but what exactly does this word mean? There are numerous theories as to the meaning of Annwfn. Sioned Davies defines the word as "the in-world," essentially the world within our world, denoting that Annwfn exists somewhere within our own world.[11] The prefix An could indeed be understood as meaning "in" or "inside"; however, other theories regarding the meaning of Annwfn imply that An can also be an intensifying prefix, essentially meaning "very." With that, we have another definition for the term Annwfn: "the very deep." Finally, An can also be translated as meaning "not"; therefore, Annwfn could also be "the not-world" or, more specifically, "a world that is not our own."

. . . .

11.   Davies, *The Mabinogion*, 290.

The latter part of the word is generally understood to derive from dwfn, mean-ing "deep."[12] Therefore, when looking at the word and the various theories concern-ing its meaning, we get a general idea that the word is denoting a world that is not our own, a world that is deep within our own world, or a place underground or in "the deep." As will be made clear further into this chapter, this matches with ideas that the Otherworld is either chthonic in nature, being located underground, and with ideas that perhaps it is a place across or beneath water, or "the deep."

Attempting to translate this word is difficult. The Welsh language is a lan-guage of poetry and magic. The language itself developed from poetic, ceremonial language employed by bards in the processes of making monarchs.[13] Essentially, the Welsh language began its life as a language of artistry, poetry, and ceremony. Because of this, words in the language rarely have one singular definition or translation. Words like Annwfn cannot be adequately and succinctly boxed into one meaning; it is the "not-world," the "very-deep," the "other-world," and so much more. Every word in the Welsh language contains a multitude of layers. A single word can tell an entire story. And this is all rooted in the fact that it was poets who developed this language. It is important to keep this in mind as we approach more of our native Welsh terminology throughout this book.

A note on spelling: Some of you may be wondering why I spell it with an f and not in the way it is often spelled in modern Welsh, Annwn. Both Annwfn and Annwn are correct; however, Annwfn is an older, more formal spelling.[14] I person-ally prefer the spelling Annwfn due to the fact that it has the wfn found in the word dwfn, emphasising the fact that Annwfn is related to the concept of depth.

The name Annwfn, as previously mentioned, is a name given to the Other-world in various medieval texts and the name that carried over into folklore for the realm of fairies and the various Otherworlds of folk belief.

Hafgan and Arawn–Kings of Annwfn?
Arawn, when introducing himself to Pwyll, makes clear that he is the king of Annwfn, yet he also mentions Hafgan, another possible ruler of Annwfn: "A man

. . . .

12.   Rüdiger, *Y Tylwyth Teg*, 49.

13.   Conran, *Welsh Verse*, 18.

14.   Rudiger, *Y Tylwyth Teg*, 43–45.

whose territory is next to mine is forever fighting me. He is Hafgan, a king from Annwfn."[15]

This at first is confusing—how can there be two kings of Annwfn? First, it is worth noting that, in the previous quote, Hafgan is not referred to as king *of* Annwfn, but rather a king *from* Annwfn. Davies has translated this directly from the original medieval manuscripts. In *Llyfr Gwyn Rhydderch*, a medieval Welsh manuscript that includes some of the oldest written versions of beloved Welsh tales, such as those of the Mabinogion, Arawn introduces Hafgan as Hafgan urenhin o annwuyn.[16] Into modern Welsh, this is Hafgan frenin o Annwfn, which indeed implies he is a king *from* Annwfn, not *of*. This could imply that he is lord or king of another kingdom originating from Annwfn but fighting to dominate Arawn's domain, or perhaps that he is contesting Arawn's rulership in some manner. However, another explanation for having two kings in Annwfn may be that Annwfn reflects medieval Welsh culture.

While the exact dates of when these stories originate is essentially unknown, we can estimate that the manuscripts retaining the stories as we know them today were composed at a time when Wales was experiencing a time of great change and cultural shift: a time of colonisation; fluid, unstable borders; and wars among kingdoms. Wales in this period was essentially separated into various smaller kingdoms ruled by various princes and kings, both Welsh and Anglo-Norman.[17] It is likely that the Mabinogion reflects some of these cultural and political elements in the tales. Perhaps, then, Hafgan is a king of a smaller kingdom in Annwfn, and Arawn is another, though Hafgan's possible lack of claim to rule over Annwfn is emphasised by the fact he is referred to as a gormes. According to experts such as Rachel Bromwich, this word translates to "oppression," though it is usually used in medieval Welsh literature to imply an oppressive force from another land.[18] Therefore, in this context, Hafgan is essentially described as an oppressive force, and a foreign one at that, not native to the land that is Annwfn.

Regardless, the territory Hafgan rules over is next to Arawn's and they are battling for the dominant rule of the land. Arawn asks Pwyll to vanquish Hafgan,

· · · · · · · · · · · · · · · ·

15. Davies, *The Mabinogion*, 4.

16. Peniarth Manuscript 2, designated *Llyfr Gwyn Rhydderch* (*White Book of Rhydderch*), National Library of Wales.

17. Shack, *Otherworld and Norman "Other*,*"* 173–174.

18. For example, the Teir Gormes (three oppressions) mentioned in the Welsh triads. Bromwich, *Trioedd Ynys Prydein*, 90–93.

as Hafgan seemingly has a magical advantage whenever they battle. Arawn tells Pwyll that he must only strike Hafgan once, for if he strikes him more than once he shall be resurrected and the battle will continue. There is an implication in Arawn placing this task on Pwyll that he, an otherworldly character, cannot kill Hafgan, but Pwyll, an ordinary mortal, can.

Pwyll agrees to this, and he is escorted to Annwfn by Arawn.

Annwfn and Its People

We experience Annwfn through Pwyll's eyes as he spends his time there disguised as Arawn. His battle with Hafgan is not until a year after the day he met Arawn, and so he spends most of his days in this otherworldly kingdom hunting and having a jolly good time. Arawn's court is described as having the most beautifully adorned buildings. It is a place of luxury, opulence, and finery. As he is in the shape of Arawn, he is dressed by his servants in garments of golden brocaded silks. He enjoys abundant feasts, and he admires the copious amounts of jewels and golden vessels in the court. This place is almost a paradise, and yet the looming knowledge that kings battle for land here also implies that it is a place not unfamiliar with hostility and war.

The people of Annwfn are described as fair and beautiful. The most beautiful of all is the queen, who is also dressed in garments of golden silk. She is described as being incredibly gracious and very well spoken. Pwyll, assuming the shape of Arawn, enjoys her company in the court; they have rousing conversations together. The queen is never given a name in this tale. Despite viewing the queen as an incredibly intelligent and interesting individual, when Pwyll goes to bed with her at night, he turns his back to her and does not utter a word. He does this as a sign of respect to Arawn, and Arawn does indeed commend this choice later in the tale.

The battle between Hafgan and Pwyll in the shape of Arawn takes place next to a ford, a shallow stream or river that is easy to cross. While it is noteworthy to relate this fact to the liminality and otherworldly quality of water, historically battles seem to take place near fords quite often.[19]

Pwyll defeats Hafgan, and rulership of all Annwfn is granted to Arawn. Hafgan's death leads to Pwyll's departure from Annwfn, and from that day forth an

. . . .
19. Shack, *Otherworld and Norman "Other,"* 178.

alliance is formed between Arawn and Pwyll's kingdoms. This is significant, as this details a connection between the mortal world and the Otherworld, perhaps alluding to relations between mortals and the Divine.[20] Arawn and Pwyll send one another gifts in the forms of horses, hunting dogs, hawks, and various treasures. Upon the end of this tale, Pwyll's title Pendefig Dyfed (prince of Dyfed) is changed to Pen Annwfn (head of Annwfn). This solidifies Pwyll's connection to the Otherworld.

What we learn of the Otherworld from this tale is that Annwfn is accessible through liminal places, such as borders and ambiguous forest locations where people are easily lost. Arawn, king of Annwfn, escorts Pwyll to Annwfn, which may be why the transition from our world to the Otherworld is so very easy. Arawn acts as a bridge between our world and his own. The Annwfn Pwyll encounters is gloriously decadent and opulent. Gold is a colour deeply associated with this place; the noble people of Annwfn wear golden silk garments, and they are abundant in golden vessels and treasures. It is seemingly a paradise, and yet also surprisingly close to home. Wars still wage on, servants still exist, and it is a society not too dissimilar from medieval Welsh society. What makes this place othered are qualities such as its opulence and the obvious existence of magic.

The magic of Annwfn in this tale is subtle yet obvious. Arawn can change Pwyll's form with ease, placing a glamour upon himself and Pwyll to look like one another. Hafgan can resurrect if he receives more than one blow in battle. These are feats no mortal could ever achieve, and yet they are barely acknowledged in the text as anything incredibly remarkable. It is as though magic is an everyday occurrence in Annwfn.

A Place between Places

While not directly the Otherworld, there is one other location in the first branch that requires our attention: Gorsedd Arberth, a mound in the kingdom of Dyfed. After his time in the Otherworld, Pwyll ventures to Gorsedd Arberth due to a legend that surrounds it. It is said that whoever sits upon the mound will either be badly wounded or witness a wonder greater than anything they have seen before.[21]

. . . .

20.   Ford, *Prolegomena to a Reading of the Mabinogi*, 117.

21.   Jones and Jones, *The Mabinogion*, 9.

Among his trusted retinue, Pwyll does not fear an attack, and, therefore, he ventures up the mound in hopes of witnessing the wonder. Once atop the mound, Pwyll sees something tremendous: a woman more beautiful than he has ever laid eyes on prior. This woman is dressed in golden brocaded silks, echoing the type of clothing worn by the noble courts of Annwfn. She is striding upon a white horse, and though she seems to be idly trotting at a calm pace, none of Pwyll's men can catch up to her.

This woman is Rhiannon, a noblewoman who is the daughter of a highborn man named Hyfaidd Hen. Pwyll learns who she is when, after trying multiple times without success, he manages to catch up to Rhiannon after asking her to wait for him, after which Rhiannon says, "It would have been better for the horse if you had asked that a while ago!"[22]

In the initial description of Rhiannon, she is instantly identified as following similar motifs to the inhabitants of Annwfn. The way she is dressed, the colour of horse she rides upon, and the subtle yet obvious magic she seems to wield all point to her being not entirely mortal. There is a divine quality to her nature— something altogether fairy. We will explore Rhiannon a little more in the chapter Gods and Spirits of the Land.

It seems that Gorsedd Arberth is a magical place, perhaps a liminal space where the boundaries between our world and the Otherworld, if any exist at all, are weaker. Mounds are in and of themselves connected to the supernatural, and specifically to fairies.[23] We see a connection between fairies, the Otherworld, and supernatural occurrences in mounds beyond the folklore and mythology of Wales. In Ireland, the Otherworld is often viewed as a chthonic place that can be accessed via fairy mounds, or síd.[24] Perhaps Gorsedd Arberth is an inherently magical place due to its description as being a mound.

As we will discover later in this chapter, Gorsedd Arberth is a place that is rather important in the four branches as a space that is seemingly a midway between the ordinary, mundane, mortal world and the Otherworld. From here, magical things can be witnessed. The precise location of Gorsedd Arberth is disputed today in modern Wales. It seems that Arberth may be a reference to Narberth, a town situated in Dyfed, and so it is likely the mound is somewhere

. . . .

22. Davies, *The Mabinogion*, 10.

23. Sims-Williams, *Irish Influence on Medieval Welsh Literature*, 57–60.

24. Sims-Williams, *Irish Influence on Medieval Welsh Literature*, 57–60.

there. However, mounds are rather prominent across Wales. In close proximity to where I grew up on Ynys Môn, we had numerous prehistoric burial mounds that were rich with local folklore and superstition. Perhaps the importance of the mound in the four branches of the Mabinogi and its liminal, otherworldly nature is a signifier of how the people of Wales have always perceived these remnants of the ancient past dotted around our landscape.

Ynys Gwales—The Island Where Grief and Time Have No Effect

The tales of the second branch of the Mabinogi are tinged with a grief that the other branches do not hold. The second branch focuses on Branwen, the daughter of Llŷr, and her marriage to the king of Ireland, Matholwch.

Unfortunately, the union of Branwen and Matholwch was intended to form alliances between the Irish and the Welsh; however, this all goes awry. Branwen's half brother Efnysien cuts the tails and ears of the Irishmen's horses in a fit of anger during the wedding at Aberffraw. This act of violence angers the Irish, despite Brân, king of the Isle of the Mighty and brother to Branwen, apologising profusely by offering Matholwch and his retinue compensation in the form of horses, a rod of silver, a plate of gold, and a magical cauldron. The cauldron gifted by Brân to Matholwch is the Pair Dadeni, a cauldron that boasts the ability to resurrect the dead.

Unfortunately, despite the compensation, the Irish people are still unhappy with the disrespect shown toward their king and his retinue. This unrest ultimately leads to Branwen being sequestered to the kitchens of Matholwch's court and abused daily. Ireland cuts off ties with Wales so that news will not reach Brân of his sister's mistreatment. Branwen, however, befriends a starling and sends a message to Brân over the sea with this starling's aid.

When Brân discovers the truth of what is happening to his sister, he is overcome with rage. Brân was already implied to be a giant, but his rage allows him to swell in size, and he crosses the Irish Sea by foot with a fleet of ships by his side and the intention of saving Branwen. This situation leads to a great war where unfortunately Branwen's son is killed, and Brân is left fatally wounded. Brân is struck in the foot with a poisoned spear, and so he requests that his head be cut off and taken back to the Isle of the Mighty. This is where we begin to see elements of the Otherworld.

Upon arriving back at the Isle of the Mighty, Branwen dies. Brân's head is taken to Harlech where, under the enchantment of mystical birds known as the Birds of Rhiannon, the head is kept alive and feasts with his court for seven years.[25] Then, Brân's head is taken to an island known as Gwales. Upon the shores of this glorious island is a royal dwelling with a large grand hall. While on this island, no one suffers the ravages of time. No one ages, and grief dissipates. All the sorrows of their mortal life seem to slip away, and Brân's head does not decay. Instead, Brân delights his retinue with joyful tales, and it is as though he had never suffered any trauma or pain. They stay in this state of enchantment for eighty years, blissfully unaware of the long passage of time.

The island of Gwales's magic comes with a taboo. Within the feasting hall where Brân and his assembly enjoy one another's company, there are three doors. Two of these doors are open, but one, facing the mainland, is closed. Brân warns his men that the door must remain closed or else they will need to leave the island and all of the woes of everyday life will return to them. Unfortunately, a character named Heilyn one day allows his curiosity to get the better of him. Heilyn opens the third door, and all the grief, trauma, and pain of the war and loss they suffered comes flooding back to them. Brân's head begins to decay and die, and they know they must leave. Upon arriving back at the Island of the Mighty, they realise just how much time has passed and how much the world around them has changed.

The island of Gwales acts as a place of temporal distortion and infinite bliss. Simply being upon the island washes away all concern of mortal life. Pain, grief, and sorrow matter not here. It is a paradise of sorts, a place between places resting in a time between time. Time continues to move in the outside world and upon the mainland, yet those upon the otherworldly island are not affected by it. They do not age and are happy to stay in this welcoming, joyful place.

As we will come to discover in this chapter, islands become rather synonymous with the Otherworld, especially in later folklore. The island of Gwales is now identified as a real island off the coast of Pembrokeshire. For centuries in Wales and indeed across most of the Isle of the Mighty, or Britain, small islands off the coast became known as places of magic, where fairies dwell and enchantment abounds.[26]

. . . .

25. The Birds of Rhiannon will be discussed in more depth in a later chapter.

26. Davies, "Mythology and the Oral Tradition: Wales," 789.

The Vanishing Fort

As we continue examining the otherworldly elements of the four branches of the Mabinogi, we turn now to the third branch. This branch is arguably the most epic and fantastical. After the events of the second branch, Welsh heroes Manawydan (one of Branwen's brothers) and Pryderi (Pwyll and Rhiannon's son) return to the kingdom of Dyfed, where they join with Rhiannon and Cigfa, Pryderi's wife. Since the events of the first branch, Pwyll has died. He is not present in this branch, but Rhiannon is. Rhiannon marries Manawydan in this branch.

One day, while at Gorsedd Arberth, the four aforementioned characters witness a magical mist that seems to blanket the landscape around them. This mist extends across the entirety of the kingdom of Dyfed, and when it finally dissipates, the four realise that every person, building, and animal has vanished. They are alone in a land that has been hit by some form of otherworldly curse. The eerie silence and solitude of Dyfed leads to the four leaving and going to live and work in Hereford for a time.

Eventually the story returns the characters to Dyfed, where mysterious otherworldly forces seem to be at work. Pryderi and Manawydan venture out into the land to hunt, and during this hunt they come across a gleaming white wild boar. The appearance of this gleaming white boar is portentous: it seems to be a sign that magic and forces from the Otherworld are afoot. Think back to the gleaming white hounds that Arawn hunts with or the dapple-grey or white horses that Arawn and Rhiannon ride upon. White animals seem to be a common motif surrounding the Otherworld. This boar follows in the literary tradition of hunters being led toward a supernatural encounter by white animals, as happened to Pwyll in the first branch of the Mabinogi.

Manawydan and Pryderi follow the white boar to a large, towering, mesmerising fort. They note that this fort must have appeared seemingly out of nowhere, as if conjured by a spell. The boar runs into this glorious fort, and Manawydan and Pryderi's hunting dogs chase after it. The two men stand outside the fort, captivated by the sheer wonder of such a structure appearing out of nowhere. Eventually Pryderi decides to enter the fort to search for their dogs while Manawydan waits outside.

At this point in the story, we are given the details of what the interior of this glorious fort looks like. Within the walls of the fort, there are no people, nor are there living halls for people to dwell in. There is no sign of the dogs nor the white boar, and there is an eerie presence in the air. In the middle of this empty fort is a well adorned with marble, and near the well is a golden bowl held up by four chains over a marble slab. The chains holding up this glorious and large golden bowl extend up into the sky, with seemingly no end to how high they reach, suspended in the air.

Pryderi touches the golden bowl; as he does, he is frozen in place. His hands stick to the bowl and his feet cannot be pulled from the ground beneath him. He tries to call for Manawydan but is unsuccessful; he cannot speak. Hours go by, and Manawydan grows anxious awaiting Pryderi's return. Ultimately, Manawydan decides it is time to get help, so he runs to fetch Rhiannon.

When Rhiannon arrives at the fort, she finds Pryderi locked in place, still stuck to the bowl and unable to speak. In attempting to understand what has happened, Rhiannon touches the bowl. The same fate that befell Pryderi happens to her; she is frozen where she stands. Suddenly a blanket of mist envelops them and a most terrifying noise spews from the sky. In an instant, the fort, with Rhiannon and Pryderi still inside, is gone. Where once the fort stood is now simply forest, as though it had never been there to begin with.

A year goes by and Manawydan is now alone in Dyfed with Cigfa, both without their spouses. Eventually Manawydan discovers that this entire ordeal was the doing of one man. The mist that descended upon Dyfed, leaving it essentially a wasteland; the mysterious fort that vanished; the loss of Rhiannon and Pryderi—all of it was merely the petty revenge of a man named Llwyd ap Cilcoed.

While it is never clearly stated that Llwyd ap Cilcoed is an otherworldly character, many motifs surround him that seem to imply it. His name literally translates to "Grey, son of woodland retreat," and he employs magic that draws upon an ethereal mist.[27] He sent a white boar to attract Pryderi and Manawydan to a vanishing fort, and he had the power to change his shape similarly to Arawn. We also discover that Pryderi and Rhiannon had spent a year seemingly in an otherworldly court belonging to Llwyd ap Cilcoed, being essentially tortured and kept as prisoners. Pryderi had heavy chains that were attached to the court doors tied around his neck, and Rhiannon was forced to wear the collars of donkeys after they had been hauling hay. It is in this fact—that Llwyd's court is

---

27. Rüdiger, Y Tylwyth Teg, 141.

likely the vanishing fort in the tale—that we can tentatively ascertain he is indeed otherworldly.

While not directly referred to as the Otherworld or Annwfn, the third branch of the Mabinogi provides us with otherworldly motifs in the form of gleaming white animals, magical mist, a vanishing fort, and overt displays of magic that are seemingly commonplace.

Beyond the Four Branches

The fourth branch of the Mabinogi deals with magic in abundance; however, the magic presented there is for the most part rather earthly in nature. Now we shall move on to look at the Otherworld in other mythological sources. The four branches of the Mabinogi are usually published alongside seven other stories. These stories have been classified in a number of ways by translators and scholars in the past, though with great difficulty.[28] Five of these tales are often referred to as Arthurian simply because the legendary King Arthur is present in them. Only two of these additional tales that are often printed alongside the four branches do not feature Arthur in some capacity.

Nevertheless, a few of these seven stories do indeed feature elements of the Otherworld in some manner, and that is what we will be looking at now. I will be focusing primarily on two tales that have been dubbed "Culhwch ac Olwen" ("How Culhwch Won Olwen") and "Iarlles y Ffynnon" ("The Lady of the Fountain"). This is not to say that these two tales are the only ones that include otherworldly qualities, simply that these stories are where the Otherworld is more overt.

Let us begin with "Chwedl Iarlles y Ffynnon," "The Tale of the Lady of the Fountain." This tale is one of knights, giants, and epic quests. The protagonist of the tale, Owain, son of Urien, embarks on a quest that another of Arthur's men, Cynon, failed at. This quest involves journeying far away to a secret glade. Within this glade, an intimidating, powerful giant is warden, and he has power over all the animals of the woods. This giant can point those wishing to pursue a noble quest toward a clearing in the woods where a magical fountain sits.

This fountain is reminiscent of the scene inside the vanishing fort from the third branch of the Mabinogi. There is a glorious fountain beside a large marble slab, and chained to the fountain is a bowl. When a knight arrives at this fountain

. . . .
28.   Davies, *The Mabinogion*, x–xi.

and gathers water with the silver bowl to throw onto the marble slab, a terrifying knight riding a black horse appears to challenge them. When Cynon came here on a quest, he failed at defeating the knight. Therefore, Owain sneaks away from Arthur's court to embark on this quest himself.

Owain succeeds in defeating the knight, and thus he learns the secret of this mysterious place. It seems the fountain must be defended by a knight in order to protect the stability of a beautiful and seemingly magical nearby kingdom.

When Owain arrives at this kingdom, he comes across a large shining castle. The ladies of this castle are dressed in yellow brocaded silks, and magic is present. We see magic in many forms in this tale, from the magical fountain guarded by a knight, to a magical ring that can render the wearer invisible.

Though the terms Otherworld and Annwfn are not mentioned in this tale, we come across otherworldly motifs. From the golden brocaded silks worn by the ladies of the court, reminiscent of the court of Annwfn in the first branch of the Mabinogi, to the overt yet subtle inclusion of magic being weaved by the inhabitants of this opulent, gleaming castle, the very stability and safety of this kingdom rests entirely upon the preservation and protection of a magical well or fountain, as one of the ladies of the court states to the countess of the castle: "Unless thou canst defend the fountain, thou canst not defend thy dominions."[29]

If we are to tentatively consider the shining castle and opulent court of this tale as an otherworldly kingdom based on these motifs, it once again gives us a glimpse into a rich, decadent realm of magic and wonder. Yet, just as in the first branch, though the opulence and beauty of the place may emanate a sense of paradise, there is still death, grief, and violence present here. When Owain defeats and ultimately kills the knight of the well, the knight's wife, countess of the well, grieves his death, as does the entire court. This provides us once again with a rather consistent image of the Welsh Otherworld of mythology as being a place of beauty, grandeur, and magic, yet not all that far away or dissimilar to our own world.

In "How Culhwch Won Olwen," we are finally given a direct mention of Annwfn once again. Gwyn ap Nudd, whom we will look at in more depth in the next

. . . .
29. Jones and Jones, *The Mabinogion*, 168.

chapter, is said to be imbued with the nature of all the demons of Annwfn.[30] It is in this tale we begin to see Annwfn spoken of as though it is merely the Christian hell. Gwyn ap Nudd seems to be a gatekeeper or guardian who keeps the demons of Annwfn from causing chaos in the mortal world. Later in the story, we also see reference to the "very black witch," "daughter of the very white witch" who lives in the "valley of grief in the uplands of hell." If we are to consider hell and Annwfn to be almost synonymous in this tale, then according to the story, the Otherworld, or hell, can be accessed via a cave.

Annwfn seems to have become synonymous with the concept of the Christian hell at some point in history. The words for these places in Welsh share a similarity in that they both refer to something deep. Annwfn indeed could relate to an intense depth, whereas the Welsh word for the concept of the Christian hell, Uffern, refers to a pit or abyss.[31] In my personal opinion, it is likely that this convergence of the Christian hell and the mythological Otherworld of Wales likely came about due to the largely Christian culture of Wales being unable to rectify in their minds how Annwfn fits into their theological belief system. It is a realm that is separate to ours, yet it is not Nef, or "heaven." Therefore, it must be hell to them. As we will come to discover later in this chapter, Annwfn often moves between being viewed as a place all of its own, the Christian hell, or even a middle ground or purgatorial place between heaven and hell. Perhaps the origins of Annwfn as a concept predate Christianity, and this could be telling of a culture fighting to make sense of something that does not make sense within their personal theological philosophy.

The Otherworld of Welsh mythology is a complex and intriguing place. It is a world of opulence, grandeur, and beauty. Magic flourishes in this place, and the people are fair, often draped in brocaded silks of gold and living in shining castles that are full of the most wonderful jewels and treasures. Yet, this world is also one of mischief and trickery. Gleaming white animals can lead you into perilous and terrifying situations, places can vanish within the blink of an eye, and the denizens of this Otherworld are just as diverse in their morals as humans are. War,

30.   Ifans, *Y Mabinogion*, 110.
31.   Rüdiger, *Y Tylwyth Teg*, 49–50.

death, and territorial disputes are still very much present in this world, meaning it is not quite a paradise.

Interaction with this realm can often send one on an initiatory journey, launching you from one stage of life onto another. This can be seen in how Pwyll transformed from Pwyll Pendefig Dyfed to Pwyll Pen Annwfn in the first branch, establishing relations between his kingdom and the magical, almost divine kingdom of Annwfn. Owain in "The Lady of the Fountain" also goes through a similar journey of self-development and nobility; he is transformed from one of Arthur's men to a fierce guardian of a magical fountain.

The Otherworld of mythology, while diverse and mysterious, is also rather consistent. Though it is a place of enchantment and richness, it is also a place that is not too far away from our own world. It is a place that is accessible to humans and also not too unfamiliar.

The Otherworld of the Bards

The Welsh bardic tradition is at the very heart of Welsh culture. The bardic arts native to our land have grown and flourished since not long after the departure of the Romans from the shores of Britain. This bardic tradition is one that is in many ways stylistically distinct from the poetic traditions of the rest of Europe.[32] One of the most compelling attributes of the bardic tradition is the way in which it preserved much of our culture. If it were not for the bards of the sixth century all the way through to the modern day, Wales may very well have lost much of its cultural identity to colonialism and homogenisation.[33] The very poetic expression of our culture is echoed in our national anthem where we sing with passion: "Mae hen wlad fy nhadau yn annwyl i mi, Gwlad beirdd a chantorion enwogion o fri. The land of my fathers is dear to me, a land of bards and singers worthy of great praise."

As a child growing up in Wales, the word barddoniaeth, meaning "poetry," often left me feeling rather deflated and tired. Days upon days I sat in a stuffy classroom studying the works of poets, analysing their words, trying to understand what it was they were expressing with their often bewildering poems. However, as I grew older, I began to appreciate the fact we still to this day keep our bardic traditions alive and pass them on to new generations.

. . . .

32.   Conran, *Welsh Verse*, 17.

33.   Thomas, *Y Traddodiad Barddol*.

Woven into the poems of old is a power that vibrates from the words written upon paper. The bards of the past were influential, they had the ear of royalty, and they sang praises to the lords of the land. There was a supernatural quality to the work of the bards; their mastery over words was viewed as inherently divine and spiritual in nature.[34] One reason for this may be poetry's connection to the Otherworld.

Welsh poetry seems to reference the concept of the Otherworld fairly frequently, and it was important to the very foundational teachings of the bards. Throughout history, from the early poets of the sixth century right through to the poets of today, we see poetry conjuring visions of the Otherworld. This is what we will be exploring in this section of the book: how the bards perceived the Otherworld and what exactly the Otherworld meant to them.

To the bards, the Otherworld was the place where inspiration was created and distributed from. Poetic inspiration emanates from this unseen realm and makes its way into our lived reality, where poets and artists shape it and bring it to life. There is a word in the Welsh language to describe inspiration as a flowing, ethereal force. This word is Awen.

Awen can be described as the very source of poetic gift. It is the genius of inspiration, the muse that moves bards, a word that is derived from the same etymological root as words that mean "breath" or "blow." We breathe the Awen, and it moves through us.

It is this divine and enchanted force that allows the bards to construct and recite powerful, evocative poetry. Interestingly, the Awen seems to emanate from Annwfn, the Otherworld. As we see referenced in poems such as "Angar Kyfundawt" in the Book of Taliesin:

> *Yn Annwfn y diwyth,*
> *Yn Annwfn y gorwyth,*
> *Yn Annwfn is eluyd.*[35]

In this part of this very long fourteenth-century poem, the bard is speaking about how Awen ultimately originates in God, but that it is formed in Annwfn. A rough translation of the above is "In Annwfn, He (God) ranges it, it is in Annwfn

....

34. Hughes, *Cerridwen*, 32–34.

35. Haycock, *Legendary Poems from the Book of Taliesin*.

he makes it, in Annwfn the world below." This gives us an insight into the Otherworld of the bards as the very place where divine inspiration, or Awen, comes from God yet is formed and made in Annwfn.

Later in this same poem, it is mentioned that Awen is also formed in the air. This makes sense as Awen possibly shares an etymological root with another Welsh word: Awel, which means "breeze" or "wind."

Occasionally, we see Annwfn being viewed as synonymous with hell among the bards, such as in the works of a twelfth-century poet Meilyr Brydydd.[36] However, it would seem that for the most part Annwfn was viewed by the bards as a chthonic otherworldly domain where Awen was forged. Awen flows through the very air we breathe, and the bards bring it to life by singing its praises and reciting their poetry.

There are also, however, poems that refer to Annwfn as an island that requires a nautical journey across the sea to reach. The best example of this is "Preiddeu Annwfn," or "The Spoils of Annwfn," a poem found in the fourteenth-century Book of Taliesin recounting a tale where Arthur and his men venture to Annwfn on a great expedition.[37] This poem provides us with various names of Caerau or forts of Annwfn. Some of these names allude to other folkloric or mythical ideas surrounding the Otherworld, such as Caer Siddi, which is likely related to the Irish Sidhe, drawing upon the concept of the fairy mounds of Irish fairy lore. The fact that Arthur and his men travel to Annwfn via boats alludes to the idea of Annwfn being accessible via travel over the ocean. We have already seen an island Otherworld in the form of Gwales in the second branch of the Mabinogi and will explore more island Otherworlds in a later section on folklore.

In the works of later poets, such as the fourteenth-century poet Dafydd ap Gwilym, Annwfn and its denizens became a source of inspiration. One denizen in particular, Gwyn ap Nudd, caught the attention of poets. They sang of Gwyn and the Otherworld as guardians of the beauty of the natural landscape. We will discuss that further in the next chapter.

The Otherworld of the bards was one of formation, a place where inspiration was born and flowed from before breathing its way into us. Once we had breathed in the inspiration the Otherworld had to offer, we birthed it into creation via poetry and art. In the

....
36.   Conran, *Welsh Verse*, 137.
37.   Haycock, *Legendary Poems from the Book of Taliesin*, 433–451.

case of "Preiddeu Annwfn," the Otherworld is accessible via the sea and was a place of expedition and heroic journeys. Either way, contact with the Otherworld changed you in some capacity, whether by shaping you into a great knight or into an inspired poet.

A Call to the Essence of Awen

Cerridwen was a witch who lived near Llyn Tegid in Bala, North Wales. She had a son who was overlooked and hated due to his ugliness. Cerridwen, being a passionate and loving mother, wanted nothing more than for her son to be accepted. If she could not change his appearance, she decided she would ensure he was wiser and more intelligent than any other person in the world. She found a sacred book containing instructions to brew a potion that would distil the very essence of Awen. Upon drinking this potion, her son would know of all things that have been, that are, and that will be. He would see the world differently to anyone else and be admired for his incredible mind.

Though the story becomes convoluted from there, one thing is certain: Cerridwen succeeded in making this potion. She brewed a potion of pure Awen in a great big cauldron. Thus, she is now identified within Welsh streams of Paganism and witchcraft as the goddess of inspiration, the keeper of the cauldron of Awen.[38]

The bards strove to drink from the cauldron of Cerridwen. To be imbued with the very essence of Awen, and to breathe the Awen to life via their words. As a writer and an artist myself, I often find myself visualising drinking from Cerridwen's cauldron when I am embarking upon a new creative project. Over the years I have developed this practice as a method of drawing down the wonderful might of Awen, in hopes of imbuing my work with enchantment. If you are a creative person, or you wish to feel the stream of Awen pulsating through you, then I invite you to attempt this practice.

Exercise
Constructing a Shrine to Cerridwen

First and foremost, I constructed a shrine to the goddess of inspiration herself, Cerridwen. My personal shrine includes a votive statue of

. . . .

38.   To read more about Cerridwen, I recommend my previous book, *Welsh Witchcraft*, and Kristoffer Hughes's book *Cerridwen: Celtic Goddess of Inspiration*.

the goddess, a small brass cauldron, a vial of water gathered from Llyn Tegid, a wooden disc with the symbol representing Awen carved onto it, and a small tealight holder.

This shrine will act as a focal space for whenever you wish to leave offerings to Cerridwen, pray to her, call upon her wisdom and guidance, or conduct the following exercise. Your shrine need not be elaborate, large, or filled with expensive things. All that matters is that it is a space you dedicate to Cerridwen and to the Awen, a place of devotion and contemplation. If you are unable to have a shrine or altar in your home, perhaps a small box with a few pebbles upon which you have painted symbols associated with Cerridwen and Awen may be a good idea.

Spend time at this place; commune with Cerridwen. You might consider starting a conversation with Cerridwen by simply uttering the words "O Cerridwen, Cyfarchaf i ti, Duwies ysbrydoliaeth, ceidwad y pair hudolus, mam yr Awen. O Cerridwen, I call to thee, goddess of inspiration, keeper of the magical cauldron, mother of Awen."

Now simply speak to her. Sing a song that inspires you; recite a poem you wrote yourself. It may seem strange to do this at first, but by doing this you are establishing this shrine as a space of communion between you and her, a liminal space in your home that acts as a meeting point between you and Cerridwen.

Exercise
Creating a Maen Awenyddol–Inspired Stone

Find yourself a hagstone (a stone with a natural hole going through it). These can be found upon the banks of fast-flowing rivers or on rocky beaches. In many cultures, especially those of the Celtic nations, the hagstone is closely associated with the fair folk and the Otherworld. They have long been used in folk magic as protective tools and tools to peek into the realm of fairy.

Once you have chosen the perfect hagstone, place it on your shrine and leave it there for a while. Find yourself a piece of string. It does not need to be fancy or pretty, unless you want it to be. Take this string and sit with it. While holding the string, do something that inspires you. Read aloud a few lines of your favourite book or poem, sing songs that energise you. Whatever it is that lights your soul on fire, do just that while holding the string in your hands. Tie three knots in the string. The goal here is to be able to carry the hagstone around with you by the string.

Charging and Utilising the Stone

Take the stone on the string to your altar and call to Cerridwen. Then, recite these words while visualising the airy energy of Awen flowing from the depths of this world and into your breath.

Yr Awen a ganaf,

O'r dwfn y dygaf,

O Annwfn a ddaw,

I'n hanadl a eith,

Awena, Awena, Awena.

The Awen I sing,

From the deep I conjure it,

From Annwfn it will come,

Into my breath it shall go,

Awena, Awena, Awena.[39]

Sit before your shrine and continue to recite these words until you feel you have done enough. Leave an offering for Cerridwen. An offering could be a lit candle, incense, a small glass of good drink, or even a poem or song you have written.

Now this stone is imbued with Cerridwen's power and the ever-flowing force of Awen. Whenever you feel the need to, hold the stone up to your brow. Taliesin was the most inspired bard in all of Welsh folklore and history. His name means "radiant brow," for Awen shines upon his brow. Hold the stone up to your own Tal, or brow, and feel the source of all inspiration breathing life into your creative faculties. I find it incredibly useful to hold the stone up to my brow when a creative project feels

....

39.   Awena means "inspire." It is the verb of Awen. Awen is inspiration, and Awena is asking something to inspire.

stuck, or I am struggling with the dreaded writer's block. Recharge the stone frequently using this method.

The Otherworld of Folklore

As we traverse over to the fantastical realm of folklore, we shall begin to see an Otherworld taking shape that more closely resembles what most people picture when they envision a fairy realm. It is within folklore that the Otherworld becomes a diverse and enchanted place where fairies dance, where islands vanish, and where all manner of beautiful and wonderful things will attempt to entice us to leave our mortal cares behind and dive headfirst into a world teeming with magic.

Earlier, I explained how I define Welsh mythology as being the stories that are predominately preserved within medieval manuscripts. Therefore, the Otherworld we explored earlier in this chapter is the Otherworld of the four branches of the Mabinogi and other old stories.

However, there is more to the difference between mythology and folklore than simply whether the story was recorded in a manuscript or how old the story tends to be.

You will find many debates as to the difference between mythology and folklore. However, my personal definition is that mythology comprises the stories that are culturally relevant to an entire nation, whereas folklore comprises stories that are more specifically relevant to smaller communities within that culture.

A folktale can become a myth when it transcends its square mile and begins to influence broader culture. For example, the story of Cerridwen brewing a potion of Awen has long been defined as a folktale. And yet, this story is such an integral aspect of Welsh culture that it could be argued it has become a nationally revered myth.

Folklore, as the name suggests, are the stories of the common folk. These stories are rooted in the landscape where the communities who tell the stories are from. They are the stories you will hear being told down at the tavern, or by grandmothers to young children before bed. Elements of the stories, such as the settings and the characters, will be deeply familiar to those who hear them, because they are places and people they know from day-to-day life.

Folklore is fluid and constantly adapting. Certain motifs will be picked up from one place and transported into a new locale so that the story remains relevant to new listeners. We see this with numerous fairy stories: as we will explore later, the fairy bride motif is told in numerous regions across Wales, the idea of a fairy maiden marrying a mortal man. However, certain locales will colour this basic idea with elements that are specific to the region where the story is being told.

Folklore is inherently the stories of the people and the stories of place. The Otherworld we will explore in the following pages is the Otherworld of these regional tales told by the everyday common person. We will see how specific areas across Wales have perceived fairies and the Otherworld, and how many common motifs can be found across our lore.

Elidorus and the Land of Fairies

One of the most notable legends concerning the Otherworld that has potentially influenced later folklore is the legend of Elidyr and his time in a magical subterranean country. In *The Welsh Fairy Book*, a compilation of fairy stories collected by a Welsh schoolmaster in the late nineteenth and early twentieth centuries, this story is known as "Elidyr's Sojourn in Fairyland." This is likely one of the most popular books on Welsh fairy tales and is probably where most would know this story from. However, it has been retold numerous times. In fact, in my personal library I can count at least five or six books just in my current eyeline that have a version of the tale.

The original tale, however, was written in Latin and can be found in Gerald of Wales's *Itinerarium Cambriae*. The twelfth-century manuscript details a story about the life of a priest known as Elidorus who, as a child, spent some time living among a group of small human-like beings who dwelled in a chthonic or subterranean world.[40]

The story takes place near Swansea, where the young Elidorus runs away from home because he believes his parents to be too strict. After two days of hiding near the banks of a river, two very short men come to him and invite him to follow them into their world. He accepts this invitation and follows these fairy men through an entrance near the river into an underground world unlike anything he has ever seen before.

This is one of the earliest recorded fairy stories from Wales, and many motifs found in this tale seem to be echoed throughout Welsh folklore concerning the

. . . .
40.   Goodrich, "The Trifles of Monastic Writers."

Otherworld and fairies in general.[41] The world Elidorus encounters in this tale is a place of delights and wonder. Some of the grandeur and richness found in the Otherworld of mythology is echoed here, as the fair folk of this land play sports with balls made of gold. The people of this land are pure and elegant. But the land itself is unearthly and strange. Every day is as though it is twilight, an ethereal mist blankets the land, and there are no stars in the sky for the sky is actually the very crust of the earth, due to them being underground.

Eventually Elidorus longs to visit his mother, and with permission from the fairies he is allowed to see her. However, he is not permitted to take anything from their realm to the mortal realm. When Elidorus's mother discovers where he has been, she convinces him to steal one of the golden balls from the land of fairy. Upon doing this Elidorus loses all ability to travel between the mortal and fairy world, and he lives out the rest of his life in our world, where he later becomes a priest.

In this vision of the land of fairy, the Otherworld is described as a place of beauty. Meadows, rivers, and glorious woodlands dot the landscape: a world of rich courts, glorious views, and beauty held within a constant state of misty twilight.[42] The nights in this world are said to be pitch dark, and it is clearly a world that exists beneath our own in a cavernous, chthonic realm.

The Subterranean Abodes of the Fairies

In the story of Elidorus, the world of the fairies is under the earth. This motif is not limited to this tale, for this seems to have been a common belief in many streams of folklore across Wales. T. Gwynn Jones mentions in his work on folklore that the Welsh Otherworld can be accessed via liminal, chthonic places. Caves and holes in the ground, lakes and underground passages, can all sometimes be gateways into the Otherworld.[43]

This idea is echoed in various stories, one example being a tale dubbed "Owen Goes A-wooing," where a Welsh man, Owen, falls into a lake while on his way to meet a girl and finds himself in the world of fairies.[44] The tale describes how he falls into a lake, and as he sinks to the bottom he realises after a while that he has stopped sinking and is now falling through the air. He floats down to the ground,

. . . .

41.   Hartland, *Robberies from Fairyland*.

42.   Owen, *Welsh Folk-Lore*, 35.

43.   Jones, *Welsh Folklore and Folk Custom*, 52.

44.   This tale can be found in W. Jenkyn Thomas's *The Welsh Fairy Book*.

where he finds himself in a subterranean kingdom surrounded by strange yet joyful people. Wirt Sikes also recorded in *British Goblins* that certain caves and crags in the hill of Glamorganshire were the homes of various fairies, specifically a crag called Craig y Ddinas.[45]

Lakes as Gateways to the Otherworld

Across Wales the many deep and beautiful glacial lakes that dot the landscape have given birth to countless legends, from the infamous Llyn Tegid linked to the story of Taliesin's birth, to the eerie Llyn Barfog, one of many lakes that lays claim to being where a terrifying creature known as the Afanc once dwelled. It is no surprise, then, that lakes would also have a connection to fairies and the Otherworld.

The most well-known lake story pertaining to fairies is likely the story attached to Llyn y Fan Fach. We will explore this story in more depth in a later chapter; however, it is worth noting here that the fairy maiden in the story seems to use the lake as a doorway between her world and our own. At one point in the story the fairy maiden's family comes through the lake, as do a great number of cattle. At the end of the story the fairy maiden and the cattle return to their own world via the lake once again.

As famous and beloved as this lake fairy story is, it is certainly not the only one of its kind. According to one story, the lakes above Aberdyfi in Gwynedd, North Wales, were said to be a regular haunt for the fair folk. In particular the locals would often see the glorious white cattle of the fairies walking around the lakes. One farmer in particular caught one of these cows and made a lot of money from its cheese and milk. However, when the cow began to age, the farmer decided to kill it for its meat, and just as they were about to slaughter it, a fairy came out from one of the lakes and called the cow home. The cow and the fairy vanished into the waters.[46]

The most intriguing of lake-related Otherworld stories, however, is likely that of the island in the centre of Llyn Cwm Llwch in Bannau Brycheiniog. Every May Day, a magical door would appear on a rock near the edge of the lake, and upon walking through it, you would be transported to an invisible island in the centre of the lake. Upon the island were glorious gardens with the most beautiful aromatic flowers and enticing fruits. When mortals visited, the fair folk of the

. . . .

45.   Sikes, *British Goblins*, 6.

46.   A version of this story can be found in Hugh Evans's *Y Tylwyth Teg*.

island would enchant their guests with sweet music, good food, and intriguing tales. There was a taboo to the island, however: nothing from the island could be carried back to the mortal world. Unfortunately, someone did indeed steal something from the island, and from that day on the doorway never appeared again.[47]

Perhaps it is the liminal nature of water that makes lakes the seemingly natural gateway to the realm of fairy.

Islands of Enchantment

In the centre of Llyn Cwm Llwch, the Otherworld is presented as an island with glorious gardens and magical inhabitants. This is not the only reference to the Otherworld as an island found in folklore. It was once said that the people of Pembrokeshire often sighted magical islands in the sea.[48] Mysterious islands that appeared in the sea as if by magic were said to be called the Gwerddonau Llion, meaning "the green islands," or sometimes referred to in English as the Green Islands of Enchantment. However, it would seem that the term Gwerddonau Llion in relation to this mystical island phenomena originates in the works of Iolo Morgannwg.[49] Sir John Rhŷs noted the similarity between the word Gwerddonau and the Welsh word for Ireland, Iwerddon.[50] It is possible that Ireland itself may have been viewed as a sort of Otherworld to the Welsh at one point, and this is why the term Gwerddonau became associated with mystical otherworldly islands.

The islands in the sea were said to move and vanish occasionally. The stories about them were usually associated with coastal market towns, where it was said that the fairy inhabitants of the islands would visit the markets and purchase goods with fairy money.[51] They were described as being covered in green fields, and the occasional house dotted the landscape.

One core element of these otherworldly islands was the notion that time operated differently upon them. A few moments on these islands could equate to very many years in the mortal world. This is reminiscent of the island of Gwales from the second branch of the Mabinogi.

· · · · · · · · · · · · · · · ·

47.   Rhŷs, *Celtic Folklore: Welsh and Manx*, 21.

48.   Jones, *Welsh Folklore and Folk-Custom*, 53.

49.   Rüduiger, *Y Tylwyth Teg*, 83.

50.   Rhŷs, *Celtic Folklore: Welsh and Manx*.

51.   Thomas, *The Welsh Fairy Book*, 91–92.

As we can gather by looking at all these elements that make up the lore surrounding the Otherworld within the Welsh cultural continuum, the Otherworld is diverse and varied in nature. It would be more accurate to suggest that there is no one cohesive, homogenous Otherworld, and instead a vast network of Otherworlds. Whether we are looking at the Annwfn of mythology and the bardic tradition—a place of richness, magic, and beauty where all inspiration is born—or perhaps delving into the various subterranean and island-based Otherworlds of folklore, these places are linked and connected yet also diverse and unique in their own right. Just as our own world has many countries, islands, and territories, it would seem the Otherworld of Welsh belief is very much the same in this nature.

King of Fairy

At the edges of our world, in those liminal and secretive places where many dare not go, stands a figure who is enigmatic, powerful, and mysterious. It is this figure who guards the entryways into the realm of the Other, he who rides upon the mists with spectral hounds, leading the spirits of those who have fallen in mighty battles. He is a noble warrior, a gatherer of souls, a regent of the entities who reside within the periphery of our known world. He is Gwyn ap Nudd.

Within witching circles today, and in communities of Pagans, polytheists, and lovers of the folkloric tales of Wales, Gwyn ap Nudd is known as the king of fairy, a god of liminality, gatekeeper of the entryways from our world into the Otherworld. Gwyn is often depicted as an antlered man surrounded by the hounds of the Otherworld, the Cŵn Annwfn, walking out of the mist in a wild, untamed landscape. He has come to represent the animalistic and rustic elements of ourselves that we have lost much of. It is Gwyn who extends his arm out and invites us to reconnect to the wild within us. His very presence evokes a feeling of distress and fear, for he is as foreboding and mysterious as the dark paths into the untamed forests.

Gwyn ap Nudd has captivated folklorists, witches, Pagans, and academics studying Celtic literature for many years now. Robert

Graves drew upon Gwyn's mythos in his iconic, albeit nowadays controversial, work *The White Goddess*. This would in turn inspire people such as Gerald Gardner, Doreen Valiente, and Robert Cochrane, pioneers in the rise of modern Pagan witchcraft in the twentieth century. In the works of folklorists who focused on Welsh lore such as John Rhŷs, Wirt Sikes, and Elias Owen, Gwyn is bolstered as the noble ruler of the Welsh Otherworld. He leads his spectral hounds through the night sky in a version of the Wild Hunt, gathering souls and evoking fear in those who hear the howls of the hounds.

His role and appearance in Welsh legend and lore is varied as he appears in medieval Welsh poetry and prose, in the romantic early Arthurian legends, in folktales, and in the works of prominent bards stretching from the medieval period to the tail end of the early modern period. Sometimes he is described as a hardy, proud, and problematic warrior, riding upon a magical horse that can gallop over the waves of the sea and partaking in an annual battle. In other sources he is a seemingly bourgeois king sitting upon a golden throne, and yet he's incredibly deceptive and mischievous. Gwyn ap Nudd has even been utilised in poetry to evoke a sense of national pride in the glorious beauty of the rural Welsh landscape. He is multifaceted, complex, contradictory, and mysterious—qualities one would expect to find in a king of fairy.

However, is he truly the king of fairy? Where does this title originate? Gwyn wears many masks in the sources he is drawn from: a warrior, a king, a demon or devil, a fairy, a personification of the wild, untouched, beautiful landscape. Gwyn is all of these things and more.

We could not explore fairies within a Welsh context without touching upon him. In this chapter we will explore the enticing and enigmatic figure that is Gwyn ap Nudd. Together we will explore his appearances in Welsh mythology and poetry and delve into his role as king of fairy and the Otherworld, how he has influenced modern witchcraft and Paganism, and his divine nature.

Gwyn has, over time, become essentially the chief fairy of Welsh lore, the very force that stands between our world and the Other. He is the bridge between mortals and fairies and, to many, he is also a divine being, a god. In writing this book, I wanted you to gain a clear understanding of Gwyn and his domain before we discuss the denizens under his rule. This chapter acts as your introduction to the king of fairies, but also as a devotional offering to Gwyn himself.

Gwyn ap Nudd in Welsh Mythology

The earliest mention of Gwyn ap Nudd we have is found within a medieval manuscript known as the *Llyfr Du Caerfyrddin*.[52] This manuscript dates to approximately the mid-thirteenth century and is chiefly a collection of poetry preserved from possibly, based on the language utilised in the poems, as early as the ninth through the twelfth centuries.[53] Within this manuscript, amidst a variety of triads dedicated to the horses of notable Welsh heroes, is a poem known today as "The Dialogue Between Gwyn ap Nudd and Gwyddno Garanhir." The poem is exactly as titled: it is a dialogue between two figures, Gwyn ap Nudd and another named Gwyddno Garanhir.

Gwyddno Garanhir is a heroic Welsh character. He appears either in person or by name in a variety of Welsh texts and is often associated with Yr Hen Ogledd (the old north) as well as the legendary kingdom of Cantre'r Gwaelod, which sank into the sea.[54] Here, however, he is introduced as a warrior who comes face-to-face with Gwyn ap Nudd on the battlefield after a horrific battle has concluded between the Celts and the Anglo-Saxons.

Gwyn appears riding a white stallion, a dog following beside him. Gwyn and Gwyddno, once they have deduced that they are safe in each other's company, introduce themselves to one another. During the poem, Gwyddno requests protection from Gwyn, and in response Gwyn states that his horse, which he is unable to control, is hurrying him away and so he cannot stay.

The poem is made up of englynion, fourteen to be exact. An englyn is a traditional Welsh form of short poem. The majority of the dialogue between Gwyn ap Nudd and Gwyddno Garanhir involves Gwyn lamenting the loss of various princes, warriors, and heroes who died during the aforementioned battle. It is an incredibly interesting and captivating poem, which provides us with an image

. . . .

52. Peniarth Manuscript 1, designated *Llyfr Du Caerfyrddin* (*Black Book of Carmarthen*), National Library of Wales.

53. Huws, *Medieval Welsh Manuscripts*, 36–56.

54. Yr Hen Ogledd (the old north) refers to a region in the north of what is now England and the south of Scotland, which was once inhabited by Brittonic people. It is a place associated with mighty kings and noble heroes in Welsh poetry and mythology. Cantre'r Gwaelod is a legendary kingdom said to have once been located on a piece of land in Cardigan Bay, West Wales. It sank beneath the sea and is often referred to today as the Welsh Atlantis.

of Gwyn ap Nudd as a noble, brave, and well-regarded warrior. However, it also hints toward Gwyn's supernatural qualities. He is no mere mortal warrior.

Gwyn describes how he has been present at many battles and has witnessed many deaths. Some writers and folklorists, such as John Rhŷs, have stated that this poem gives us an insight into Gwyn as a psychopomp and a god associated with battles.[55] This view of Gwyn as a god-like entity who gathers the souls of fallen warriors and walks with them to the afterlife continues to this day among modern Pagans.

This medieval poem paints a picture of Gwyn as a glorious warrior, a brave fighter who laments the loss of many of his fellow men, and alludes to his other-worldly qualities and his role as a psychopomp. Beyond simply being present at the deaths of numerous legendary figures beyond the lifetime of a mere mortal, Gwyn is also able to offer a safe place amidst the conflict for him and Gwyddno to talk, a liminal space where the battle is continuing to rage and yet has been silenced or paused. Perhaps as an indication that Gwyddno is already dead by the time they are communing with one another, the poem associates Gwyn with ravens, birds often used as symbols of death within broader Celtic lore.

In one instance, Gwyn mentions being present at a battle that took place in Caer Fanddwy. This is of note because this location is also mentioned in "Pre-iddeu Annwfn" ("The Spoils of Annwfn"), a poem from the Book of Taliesin. Caer Fanddwy is a fortress located in the Otherworld. This provides us with yet another hint that Gwyn ap Nudd is otherworldly.

A noble man, a fierce warrior who rides upon a white steed and is present at a variety of battles, possibly a psychopomp who leads the spirits of fallen warriors to the afterlife. These are the characteristics that this poem gives to us of Gwyn ap Nudd. Let us now explore how these compare in other Welsh prose tales, legends, and myths.

Culhwch and Olwen

Gwyn also appears in an early Arthurian prose tale known as "Culhwch ac Olwen."[56] This tale is preserved in two medieval Welsh manuscripts, *Red Book of Hergest* and *White Book of Rhydderch*. It is a complex and long piece of prose dealing

· · · · · · · · · · · · · · · ·

55. Rhŷs, *Studies in the Arthurian Legend*, 155–158.

56. "Culhwch and Olwen," also known as "How Culhwch Won Olwen." This tale is usually included in English translations of the Mabinogion, such as the translation by Sioned Davies.

primarily with the legend of Culhwch, a cousin to the infamous King Arthur who longs to marry a maiden named Olwen. Culhwch is told that he will only be able to find Olwen with the aid of Arthur. He visits Arthur and invokes the names of Arthur's men in order to request Arthur's aid. One of the men mentioned in the list of Arthur's men is Gwyn, son of Nudd. Arthur agrees to help Culhwch track down Olwen, and eventually he sends Culhwch in the direction of Olwen's father.

Culhwch approaches Olwen's father, who happens to be a giant named Ysbaddaden, to ask for permission to marry her. Ysbaddaden says that Culhwch can marry Olwen if he can accomplish a variety of seemingly impossible tasks. One of these tasks is to hunt down the legendary Twrch Trwyth, a magical wild boar. However, the Twrch Trwyth can only be hunted with the help of a variety of warriors, hunters, notable figures, and special tools.

One such warrior that is required to aid Culhwch to hunt down the Twrch Trwyth is Gwyn, son of Nudd. Here he is, mentioned once again, but here we learn more about Gwyn. Ysbaddaden states that the Twrch Trwyth will not be hunted without the aid of Gwyn, son of Nudd, and that Culhwch must find him. He then goes on to describe Gwyn and says, "God has put the spirit of the demons of Annwn in him, lest the world be destroyed."[57]

Here we have a clear mention of Gwyn being connected to Annwn or Annwfn, the Otherworld. This reference to the idea that Gwyn has within him the spirit of all the "demons" of the Otherworld, and that he seemingly keeps our world safe from said demons, is incredibly interesting. This may be one of our first hints that Gwyn has a profound connection with the Otherworld. It implies that he is a gatekeeper between our world and Annwfn, and that he has mastery over the denizens of Annwfn, like a regent. Could this be an early reference to his role as ruler of the Otherworld? It certainly seems so.

What is interesting about Gwyn's role in this legend, however, is that not only is he needed to aid Culhwch in hunting down the Twrch Trwyth, but Ysbaddaden also makes clear that Gwyn will be of no use in the Hunt unless he rides upon the steed of another hero named Moro Oerfeddog. This steed is named Du, which means "black." Du is a legendary horse known in other texts from the Book of Taliesin as Du y Moroedd (the black of the seas).[58] Du is a magical horse that

· · · · · · · · · · · · · · · ·

57.   Davies, *The Mabinogion*, 199.

58.   Haycock, *Legendary Poems from the Book of Taliesin*, 392.

can run over the waves of the sea and has a clear connection to water.[59] Keep in mind that Gwyn is referenced here with a horse who is associated with the seas and with water, for Gwyn's connection to the element of water and to the sea will be discussed in further detail later in this chapter.

The next mention of Gwyn we have in the legend of Culhwch and Olwen is the tale of the abduction of Creiddylad. There is an early reference to the abduction of Creiddylad when Culhwch is invoking names of various characters near the beginning of this prose. Culhwch invokes the name Creiddylad and states that she is the most majestic maiden in all of the three islands of Britain. He then says, "For her Gwythyr son of Greidol and Gwyn son of Nudd fight each May Day forever until the day of judgement."[60]

This statement by Culhwch references an annual battle fought by Gwyn versus a foe named Gwythyr for the hand of Creiddylad, a fair and beautiful maiden. However, the story of how this annual battle came to be does not appear until later in the prose. This is likely an error of the scribe who copied the prose into the medieval manuscripts, or perhaps an error in translation. After all, this incredibly complex tale is found in full and in fragment across two medieval manuscripts, and the story itself is merely copied into these manuscripts from older sources. What is important to focus on here, however, is the tale of the abduction of Creiddylad, which acts as the instigator of an important element of Gwyn's lore.

Gwythyr, son of Greidol, is one of Arthur's men and is involved in some romantic manner with Creiddylad, daughter of Lludd Llaw Eraint, a beautiful maiden. During the escapades of the story of Culhwch and Olwen, Creiddylad visits Gwythyr, but before Gwythyr and Creiddylad can sleep together, Creiddylad is abducted by Gwyn ap Nudd. This leads to a slew of dramatic events. Gwythyr gathers an army to fight against Gwyn, but Gwyn defeats this army, which leads Gwyn to abduct many of the men Gwythyr had amassed to fight him. This all culminates in Gwyn killing a character named Nwython and cutting out his heart, and then forcing Nwython's son, Cyledyr, to eat his deceased father's heart. This sends Cyledyr into madness, and he is from then on known as Cyledyr Wyllt.[61]

. . . .

59.   Rüdiger, Y Tylwyth Teg, 91.

60.   Davies, The Mabinogion, 189.

61.   Wyllt meaning "wild." Cyledyr Wyllt translates to "Wild Cyledyr."

Eventually, King Arthur is made aware of all these events and travels to visit Gwyn and Gwythyr to intervene. After releasing the men Gwyn has captured, Arthur manages to reconcile the two men by coming to an agreement. It is decreed that Creiddylad will remain in her father's home, away from both Gwyn and Gwythyr; neither shall touch her. Every May Day from that year forth, Gwyn and Gwythyr shall battle one another. This battle will repeat annually until judgment day, or the end of time. Upon judgment day, he who wins the battle shall be granted Creiddylad's hand.

A complicated tale indeed. Beyond this, Gwyn's only other roles in the overarching story of Culhwch and Olwen are brief. Arthur asks Gwyn later if he knows anything about the Twrch Trwyth, which he does not. He then accompanies Arthur on a quest to obtain the blood of a witch.

The Gwyn of Welsh mythology is hardened, often violent, noted as a respected warrior by many, including the legendary Arthur. And yet, he also has a supernatural aspect to his identity. He holds within him the spirits of all the demons of Annwfn, and the notion that he will fight a constant, cyclical, annual battle with Gwythyr until the end of time indicates that he is no mere mortal. When paired with what we learned of Gwyn from the dialogue between him and Gwyddno Garanhir, it paints a picture of a rugged and fearsome supernatural entity: a psychopomp, warrior, hunter, lord of hosts imbued with demonic powers from the Otherworld.

Buchedd Collen

Perhaps the most relevant legend allocating Gwyn ap Nudd in his role as king of fairies and of Annwfn is part of the biography of a monk and saint called Collen. St. Collen lived and died between the sixth and the seventh century and was known throughout Wales, Brittany, and Cornwall during his life.[62] His life story was preserved in two Welsh manuscripts dating to the sixteenth century, though it must be taken into consideration that these manuscripts date to long after Collen's death and read more as legends or folktales concerning the saint, rather than as an actual biography.

The Welsh town of Llangollen takes its name from St. Collen. Collen spent many years abroad in France and elsewhere before eventually returning to Britain and becoming the abbot of Glastonbury monastery. The legends surrounding his

. . . .

62. Stephens, ed., *The Oxford Companion to the Literature of Wales*, 95.

life include an encounter with the king of the fairies and his court. The tale of Collen and Gwyn ap Nudd has become an iconic addition to texts on Welsh folklore. Here, I shall present my own retelling and translation of the legend.[63]

St. Collen's Audience with the King of Fairies

Collen was born in the sixth century and was a son of Ethni Wyddeles, a daughter of the ancient and legendary Irish chieftain Matholwch. He spent his early life studying biblical texts and travelling to foreign shores where he became a well-known and distinguished man of faith. Collen would eventually return to Britain, where he spent time in various locations, including Cornwall. His life led him to Glastonbury, where he decided to commit his life entirely to his faith and became a monk.

It would not take long before Collen's piety was acknowledged, and within three months he became the abbot of the monastery. However, Collen was not satisfied. He longed for a life of poverty, of austerity, and of sacrifice to display his devotion to living a life oriented toward God. His life as an abbot was indeed rewarding, but it was a life of high office, a life that involved some luxuries and great status. This fact did not sit well with Collen, and so he decided to take his leave from the monastery and his role as abbot. He would travel and preach the teachings of Christ. Unfortunately, things did not go to plan. Collen preached for many years, and while doing so he became utterly appalled at the impiety and lack of faith he witnessed around him. In order to rekindle his faith, Collen made the decision to retreat from society and live the life of a hermit.

Collen took himself away to Glastonbury Tor, where he found a stony nook and built himself a shelter to live within, far away from people, away from the well-trodden paths.

One day, Collen overheard two men walking and talking to each other near his shelter. They were speaking rather loudly, and Collen could not help but eavesdrop on the conversation. They spoke of a king named Gwyn ap Nudd, who was ruler of a realm known as Annwfn. Collen was not ignorant to local beliefs and superstitions; he knew well enough that Gwyn ap Nudd was a legendary otherworldly king. However, Collen, being a pious and dedicated man of faith, knew Gwyn ap Nudd was merely a demonic spectre. Gwyn and his tribe were not of

---

63. This retelling is my own translation and interpretation drawing upon the text found in *Rhyddiaith Gymraeg: Y Gyfrol Gyntaf, Llawysgrifiau 1488–1609*, 36–41.

the kingdom of God, they were diabolical forces from hell. The more Collen heard these two men speak about Gwyn and his kingdom, the angrier Collen became. Eventually he swung open the makeshift door to his humble shelter and shouted at the men, "Be quiet, the pair of you! Do not speak of such things! This supposed king of Annwfn and his host are nothing but demons!"

The two men were taken aback by this rude and angry hermit before them, and they became justifiably angry in response. They yelled back at this strange man, "You be quiet! Do not speak ill of Gwyn, lord of Annwfn! He shall rebuke your foul and harsh lies!"

Collen shook his head and muttered under his breath about these ignorant, vulgar men. He closed his door and retreated into his little nook.

Later in the day, long after the two men had left, Collen was startled by a sudden knock on the door and a voice shouting, "Hello? Is there anybody here?"

"Yes," replied Collen, "I am here! Who is it that is intruding upon my space and peace?"

"I am a messenger of the lord of Annwfn," said the voice from outside. "Gwyn ap Nudd has sent me to ask that you meet with him at the top of the hill at midday tomorrow."

With that, the messenger took his leave. Collen heard the footsteps trailing away from his shelter. Had he really been given an audience with the king of fairies? Collen was perplexed. What would he do?

When the time finally came the next day, Collen decided not to go and meet with Gwyn ap Nudd. He did not wish to tempt fate and mingle with diabolical forces. When midday had been and gone, once again there was a knock at Collen's door. This time Collen opened the door. Before him stood a handsome and well-groomed man clad in exquisite clothing. Collen noticed that this messenger's clothing was dual toned: one half of his clothes was a vivid and bold red, the other an equally bright blue.

"Good day once again sir," said the messenger. "I come once again to let you know that Gwyn ap Nudd has requested your presence. Please be at the top of the hill at midday tomorrow."

Before Collen had an opportunity to respond, the man had turned and walked away. The exasperated man of faith shook his head and slammed his door. He decided he would not go once again.

The messenger returned the next day for a third time. He repeated his message that Gwyn ap Nudd requested Collen's presence at the top of the hill at noon the next day. As Collen was closing the door, the messenger placed his foot before it and uttered a warning.

"Ensure that you do make an appearance tomorrow. If you do not, you will sorely regret it."

With that eerie threat, the messenger flashed a warm smile and walked away.

Collen would not admit it, but he was terrified. What could these hellish forces do to him if he did not comply for a third time? He hastily gathered some of his items and went away to make some holy water. He poured the holy water in a flask. The next day, Collen made the decision that he would wander to the top of the hill at midday to meet with the king of fairies. He grabbed his flask of holy water and fastened it on his leg, hidden underneath his robes. When the hour arrived, Collen looked to the sun stationed at its height in the midday sky, and he hastily made his way to the top of the hill.

Upon arriving at the top of the hill, Collen could not believe his eyes. Before him was not a stretch of grassy terrain, but instead a glorious castle he had never seen there before. It was the most exquisite and beautiful castle the monk had ever laid eyes on. Surrounding the castle were beautiful people, people clad in the same red and blue clothing, but oh goodness did they all look divine! They rode upon glorious white horses, and their hair seemed to dance in the breeze atop the hill. This was like a haven of beauty and majesty. Collen could not help but feel as though he had been transported into another realm of existence.

As Collen approached the castle gates, he was met by the same messenger who had knocked on his door the past few days.

"Welcome!" said the messenger. "The lord of the castle is awaiting you inside. You are scheduled to dine together."

Collen was led into the castle, down flamboyantly decorated hallways, past walls that were encrusted with precious gems. Such treasures were on display in this fortress. Eventually, the messenger led Collen into a grand hall. There in that elegant room were long tables adorned with beautiful flowers and covered in dishes of the most delicious-looking foods. Glorious tapestries hung on the wall, and there were courtiers at the periphery of the room chatting with one another, just as beautiful as the folks outside the castle.

And there, at the back of the room, sat upon a golden throne, was the man himself. The lord of this castle of riches. The king of all of this finery. Gwyn ap Nudd, monarch of Annwfn, king of fairy. Gwyn ap Nudd rose from his throne and welcomed Collen enthusiastically and kindly.

"Come," said Gwyn ap Nudd, gesturing to the food. "Dine with me!"

Collen, as if awaking from a trance, shifted his eyes from Gwyn, to the food, and back to Gwyn again before uttering with a tone of disapproval, "I shall not eat the leaves of the trees."

Collen knew that all this finery was but an illusion. This, in his eyes, was nothing more than the temptations conjured by devils. Gwyn looked at Collen, unamused, before grinning widely and gesturing to his courtiers at the edges of the room.

"Behold my court!" boasted Gwyn. "Have you ever witnessed finer individuals of such exquisite dress?"

Collen eyed the courtiers and replied, "Their clothing is fine enough, for what it is."

"And what might it be?" asked Gwyn.

"The red half of their clothing," answered Collen, "is symbolic of burning. The blue, symbolic of coldness. This clothing is but a metaphor for hell."

With that, Collen reached to his flask of holy water and flung it around the room, drenching everything around him. Suddenly, everything vanished—the courtiers, the castle, the food, even Gwyn ap Nudd himself. It all dematerialized out of reality. Where once stood a grand castle, now merely green mounds remained. Collen smiled proudly to himself, smug at the notion that he had vanquished Gwyn ap Nudd, a chief demon, and his unholy host.

This folk legend associated with the life of St. Collen gives us a different picture of Gwyn to that of Welsh mythology, medieval literature, and poetry. If anything, Gwyn's role in this tale is reminiscent of an enticing devilish character. He promises grandeur, wealth, and good food to Collen, who is a pious religious man dedicated to living a life of austerity or poverty, rejecting material possessions, and preaching as a righteous man of God. The tale is somewhat reminiscent of biblical legends such as that of Job, or of the temptation of Christ. Not quite as dramatic as these texts, of course, but in keeping with themes of temptation away from the way of God. Except in this instance, the devil enticing this pious and righteous man is an entity that is rather pagan in nature. A king of fairy, flamboyantly sat upon a golden throne.

On one hand, this legend could be interpreted as Collen vanquishing the infernal king of fairy and his host, rejecting his temptations as mere illusions and tricks. The grand feast the king of fairy offers is but leaves and mulch, the fanciful and glamorous clothing of his courtiers symbolic of the tortures of hell. Collen, as an intelligent and perceptive Christian man, can see through these deceptions and manages to escape the temptations of these entities that are surely conjurations of hell.

On the other hand, I have never read this tale out to a modern-day Pagan without them commenting on how unlikable and pompous of a character Collen is. He rejects kind hospitality and shows no gratitude for the invitation to dine with the king. Rather than a vanquishing of an illusion from hell, many modern Pagans I speak to interpret this legend to instead showcase how rude and self-important this Christian man is. It is certainly an interesting interpretation.

This story could easily be interpreted as an allegory for the transition within Wales from the pre-Christian pagan beliefs of the past to the newer, shinier religion of Christianity gripping the people, with Gwyn ap Nudd representing the old religion—a religion Christianity seeks to prove is illusory and will lead those who are tricked by it to a terrible place—and Collen representing the true religion, the true way to salvation.

In that interpretation, Collen would quite clearly be somewhat of a villain to any modern-day Pagan, the very counter and enemy to the old faith, though it is important to acknowledge that Collen's life in general is also very much shrouded in a veil of Celtic mythos. Within his Buchedd (life story) and the folklore that has built around him, we see mention of elements of his life that give him a legendary status equal to any deity loved by Pagans today. He arrives at Llangollen via water in a coracle, echoing Taliesin being sent out in a coracle by Cerridwen. He is the descendant of a knight of Arthur's court. He has connections to seemingly magical animals. I implore anyone with a desire to learn more of this tale to explore the life of Collen in greater depth than this book will cover.

One thing this legend clearly demonstrates is that the clerical opinion regarding both Gwyn ap Nudd and fairies in general, at least at the time this legend was recorded, was that they were demonic entities, shades and conjurations of hell. Perhaps this even alludes to the notion that the fairy faith, or a belief in such entities, would lead good Christian people into temptation and they would stray from the path of goodness and righteousness in the process. The church seemingly disapproved of fairies and their supposed monarch, whom they portrayed as Gwyn ap Nudd.

Gwyn Invoked and Petitioned by Soothsayers and Magical Practitioners

In the fourteenth century, we see the appearance of a Latin treatise that, among other instructions for clerics, condemns soothsaying. This manuscript is titled *Speculum Christiani*, and within its pages we find a rather fascinating reference to Gwyn ap Nudd.

The text includes reference to the notion that some people in Wales would invoke to Gwyn ap Nudd. Some sources claim this was carried out by soothsayers or early folk magical specialists prior to entering forests or woodland areas, which were considered his domain.[64] Angelika Rüdiger, however, states that this invocation was carried out when someone was believed to have taken ill at the hands of someone else.[65] This is a possible reference to Gwyn ap Nudd being called upon to avert the effects of a folk curse or "the evil eye," the notion that someone could cause ill fortune or even ill health upon you via harsh words, gestures, or even a glare.

The treatise claims that those who would recite this invocation would be carrying fire and iron. This is strange in my eyes, considering both fire and iron are commonly seen as things that protect mortals from the mischief, malevolence, and trickery of fairies. We will discuss more on that in a later chapter. One could argue that those reciting the incantation would carry the fire and iron as a safeguarding method to ensure that Gwyn ap Nudd did not smite them in the process of supplicating him and asking for his aid.

In this treatise, Gwyn ap Nudd is clearly identified as a king of fairies, referred to in Latin as eumenides, meaning "gracious ones."

. . . .

64. Lindahl, McNamara, and Lindow, eds., *Medieval Folklore*, 190.

65. Rüdiger, *Y Tylwyth Teg*, 39–40.

.   I am quite fond of the idea that this may have been a petitionary prayer carried out by soothsayers or folk magical specialists prior to entering forests or places that were considered his dwelling. Regardless of whether this invocation was originally intended to avert the effects of illness caused by others or to enter into Gwyn's dwelling, it is proof that clerics truly believed common folk still called to and invoked the name of Gwyn ap Nudd. If the invocation recorded in this treatise is to be believed, then that means that as far back as the fourteenth century, Gwyn has been associated with forests and wild places, was identified as the king of fairies, and was part of folk magical traditions and beliefs.

The Latin invocation is as follows:

> Gwyn ap Nudd
> Qui es ultra in silvis
> Pro amore concubine
> Tue permitte en venire domum.[66]

This invocation has been translated in various ways—for example, Rüdiger translates it as:

> Gwyn ap Nudd,
> You who are beyond in the forests,
> For the love of your lover,
> Allow us to come into the house.[67]

However, the Oxford encyclopaedia *Medieval Folklore*, which portrays this invocation as a call to Gwyn ap Nudd to permit soothsayers and magical specialists safe entry into forests, translates the last line as such:

> Permit us to enter your dwelling.[68]

. . . .
66. Roberts, *Gwyn ap Nudd*, 283–289.
67. Rüdiger, *Y Tylwyth Teg*, 40.
68. Lindahl, McNamara, and Lindow, *Medieval Folklore*, 190.

The "mate" or "lover" mentioned in the incantation is Gwyn's queen, who is not named in the Latin treatise. We could assume this is referencing Creiddylad, the lady he is besotted by in "Culhwch and Olwen" and in medieval poetry. However, the way this queen is mentioned here makes her out to be a fairy queen who is to be found in the forests and wild places with Gwyn. It is interesting that she is not named, as this is reminiscent of the fact that the king of Annwfn in the first branch of the Mabinogi, Arawn, also has a bride who is unnamed. The queen of the Otherworld, and the queen of fairies in Welsh lore, seems to be elusive.

Whether this is an invocation to Gwyn ap Nudd asking for safe entry into territories that are associated with him—the wild and untamed forests—or it is a petitionary incantation asking Gwyn to help those afflicted in some manner, it is a fascinating insight into Welsh fairy beliefs.

Exercise
A Call to Gwyn ap Nudd

Drawing upon the invocation to Gwyn ap Nudd from the fourteenth century, here I will outline a practice I have incorporated into my magical and ritual workings. The first time I ever heard of the invocation to Gwyn ap Nudd found in the *Speculum Christiani*, it was presented to me as a prayer to Gwyn carried out by folks who wished to petition him for safe passage through woodlands and forests. These places were considered his domain. I went about translating and altering the Latin invocation into the Welsh language to better suit my personal practice. My own version of this incantation goes as follows:

> *Gwyn ap Nudd,*
> *Ti sy'n bodoli yn y llwyn,*
> *Yn enw dy frenhines bonheddig,*
> *Rho caniatad i mi gael bod ar dy dir.*

It is important to note that my version is not a direct translation of the Latin, but rather an adapted incantation that specifically calls to Gwyn prior to entering a space where I will conduct my rites or practice my magic. A loosely translated English version of this incantation would be:

Gwyn ap Nudd,
You who dwells in the groves,
With your regal queen,
Grant me permission to walk within your domain.

I carry out this invocation prior to entering a place where I intend to hold a ritual or rite or perform a magical working. Specifically, I only do this if the place I am entering is associated in my view with a place that Gwyn and his tribe would reside: the wild places, liminal spaces, groves, forests, caves, burial mounds, or places that feel inherently numinous in nature.

I hereby present this intimate part of my practice and my devotional relationship with Gwyn to you, and you are free to also incorporate this into your practice or alter it so that it might suit you. Allow me to explain how it works.

Once you have chosen the location within which you will weave your magic or perform your rite, consider where you might believe the "entrance" to this place is. If you are heading to a forest or park, then the edge of these spaces before you enter into the blanket of trees would likely be a good place to perceive as an entrance. A cave or burial mound is also simple, as it has a mouth or doorway you can perceive as an entryway. Wherever your location, choose a point that you would consider your entryway into this place.

If you are carrying any tools, once you reach the entryway, put your tools aside for the moment. Stand with your feet apart, firmly rooted onto the ground. Position your arms so that your palms are facing the soil of the earth, the ground beneath you. Close your eyes.

Take a moment to breathe with the space, feeling the breeze upon your skin, hearing the sounds of the space surrounding you. Take three deep breaths, and then when you are ready, recite the incantation. You can choose to recite it in Welsh, English, or even Latin.

Feel the words reverberating through the space. Visualise the words dancing upon the wind and reaching the ears of Gwyn and his court. Know that once you have called his name, he is listening.

Once you have finished reciting the incantation, stand for a while. Sense the energy of the space you are about to enter. Do you feel as though something has changed? Do you feel as though Gwyn and his host have heard you? Take a few moments to simply be; you are in no rush.

If you are inclined to do so, you may choose to leave an offering at this place for Gwyn and his tribe. Ensure this offering is something that will not harm the local environment in any way. An offering can be anything from a tipple of good drink to a baked good, a handmade item that has been crafted with natural components, or even something as simple as a poem or a song.

You will know when it is time to move forward. Something in the environment around you will shift, and you will instinctually pick up your tools and head to your chosen location.

Gwyn ap Nudd as Leader of the Wild Hunt

When exploring the lore of Gwyn ap Nudd, you will often find a title placed upon him that is rarely ever delved into with much depth. This is Gwyn's role as leader of the Wild Hunt. Here I will outline some of Gwyn's roles in folklore, his association with the dogs of the Otherworld, and how he became known as leader of the Wild Hunt. Before exploring how Gwyn is involved with the Wild Hunt, we must first ask: What exactly *is* the Wild Hunt?

Morgan Daimler classifies the Wild Hunt as being a procession of spirits who "travel through the air in storms led by a Huntsman."[69] The spirits that take part in these tempestuous aerial gatherings can be referred to as fairies, ghosts and spectres, phantoms, or any form of spectral entity. The general idea is that it is a hoard of spectral beings flowing through a stormy night sky. The term Wild Hunt was originally coined by Jacob Grimm in the early nineteenth century and has now become an umbrella term to categorise this intriguing folkloric and legendary phenomena found in a variety of cultures.[70]

The motif of the Wild Hunt has at its core the notion of phantom armies or troops that surge through the night sky. However, there is usually also a leader at the head of this troop. Due to the wide-reaching nature of this folkloric motif,

. . . .

69.   Daimler, *A New Dictionary of Fairies*, 369–373.
70.   Hutton, *The Wild Hunt in the Modern British Imagination*.

who exactly leads the Wild Hunt depends on region, as local folklore adds flavour and colouring to the concept of the Hunt.[71] Psychopomp, demon, deity, legendary figure, witch, or Huntsman: the leader of the Hunt could be any one of these, or more than one. In Wales, however, it is said that the leader of the Wild Hunt was none other than Gwyn ap Nudd.

One of the most common aesthetic motifs related to Gwyn ap Nudd and the Wild Hunt is that of Gwyn leading a pack of his otherworldly hounds, the Cŵn Annwfn. Interestingly, we do not really find mention of Gwyn in relation to the Cŵn Annwfn outside of lore related to the Wild Hunt. The Cŵn Annwfn appear in the Mabinogion alongside Arawn, a king of the Otherworld, in the first branch. As we have already explored, the major pieces of legend and lore concerning Gwyn—whether from medieval poetry, legends such as "How Culhwch Won Olwen," or even folktales such as the mythologised accounts of the life of St. Collen—do not feature the Cŵn Annwfn alongside Gwyn.

He is, however, referred to as a Huntsman in "Culhwch ac Olwen." The fact that the hounds of the Otherworld are associated with Arawn, the king of Annwfn, and therefore associated with all things fairy and otherworldly, means that there is fair reason why Gwyn would later become associated with them.

The history of the Wild Hunt motif in Wales, however, is complicated. In Wirt Sikes's British Goblins, first published in the late nineteenth century, he claims that the belief in a Wild Huntsman figure leading his pack of spectral hunting hounds is not found in what was then contemporary Welsh folk belief.[72] In fact, when he later goes on to discuss "British" beliefs in the wild Huntsman, he claims that the leader of the Hunt, he who led the airborne hunting hounds of the Otherworld, was King Arthur, not Gwyn ap Nudd.

Among circles of folklore enthusiasts, I have noted a disdain toward Sikes's work due to the fact he was an American born in Watertown, New York, and not a native voice collecting folklore—not just from native Welsh folk, but from a variety of people who identify as Welsh folklore enthusiasts, Celtic Pagans, and witches. Some would say that perhaps the fact Sikes was an incomer into Wales meant he did not have as firm a grasp on Welsh folklore as a native person would. Personally, I am very thankful for Sikes's work, especially on the topic of fairy

. . . .

71.   Lecouteux, *Phantom Armies of the Night*.

72.   Sikes, *British Goblins*, 235.

beliefs, and would like to note that at the time he wrote books such as *British Goblins*, he was living in Wales and did so up until his death in 1883. The reason I bring this up is because when I have mentioned the fact Sikes claims the belief in the Wild Huntsman was not found in Wales at the time he wrote his book, many a folklore enthusiast has been quick to tell me that they would trust the opinion of a native voice instead.

John Rhŷs was a native voice in Welsh folklore, and he did indeed state that Gwyn is seen as a Wild Huntsman. Of course, Rhŷs also views Gwyn ap Nudd as a preservation of a pagan god of death and personification of winter.[73] However, many scholars now criticise Rhŷs's work for his theories regarding Britain's prehistory, Druids, Welsh medieval characters representing pre-Christian gods, and euhemerization theories regarding fairies.[74]

Therefore, we now have contradictory claims regarding the belief surrounding the idea of the Wild Huntsman and the Wild Hunt in general. Sikes states that the motif of the Wild Huntsman had no part of Welsh folk belief for a while, whereas Rhŷs is clear that this role goes to Gwyn ap Nudd in Welsh culture.

Another native voice to add into the mix was Elias Owen, a reverend from Montgomeryshire who in 1887 wrote an essay on Welsh folklore that won a prize at the National Eisteddfod and later in 1893 was published as a book.[75] In this work from the late nineteenth century, Owen references the concept of the Wild Hunt, as he claims that the Cŵn Annwfn—which are also known in various texts on Welsh lore as Cŵn Wybir, meaning "dogs of the sky"—could be heard howling on wild, stormy nights as they pursued the souls of those who were sinful or unbaptised.[76] Owen describes the Cŵn Annwfn as portents of death, awful creatures who travel in packs. Evan Isaac, another native Welsh voice writing on folklore in his book *Coelion Cymru*, published in 1938, also portrays the Cŵn Annwfn as portents of death, but intriguingly Isaac claims that these hounds were led by a horned entity.[77] He does not detail who exactly this horned entity is, just that the dogs are his to lead and that they are released from the Otherworld to claim the dead. We will explore the Cŵn Annwfn in more depth, alongside other animals

· · · · · · · · · · · · · · · ·

73. Rhŷs, *Studies in the Arthurian Legend*.

74. For more on this, read Rüdiger, *Y Tylwyth Teg*, 203–228.

75. The National Eisteddfod is a Welsh cultural festival that awards prizes to poets, writers, singers, and so on.

76. Owen, *Welsh Folk-Lore*, 126.

77. Isaac, *Coelion Cymru*, 83.

related to fairies, in a later chapter, but for the purpose of this chapter, it is important to note their role as omens of death who run through stormy skies, howling
in the night. They certainly match the motif of the Wild Hunt, but what of their
leader? Is Gwyn present? In Owen's *Welsh Folk-Lore* and in Isaac's *Coelion Cymru*,
Gwyn ap Nudd is not mentioned. Instead, Isaac states they belong to an unnamed
horned entity, whereas Owen specifically states they belong to Arawn.

This leads us to ask what exactly Gwyn's relationship is to Arawn. I have
mentioned Arawn a few times in this section, and I am sure to those who are not
intimately familiar with Welsh folklore and mythology, it may seem strange that
I have referenced Arawn as a king of Annwfn while simultaneously discussing
Gwyn ap Nudd, who is also deemed the ruler of Annwfn. Are these characters
connected? Are they the same person? If not, how could they both be a king of
Annwfn? These were all questions I also had when I first began exploring Welsh
mythology and folklore. If I am being honest, they are questions I continue to
ponder to this day.

Arawn

We have already briefly touched upon Arawn, alongside the other chiefs, kings,
and leaders of the Otherworld, in the previous chapter. However, Arawn is
important to bring up here not only because of his apparent folkloric connection
to the Wild Hunt, but because of his status as the mythic king of Annwfn. The
first branch of the Mabinogi clearly identifies Arawn as being Pen Annwfn, the
head or chief of the Otherworld.

In attempting to decipher whether Gwyn and Arawn are one and the same
entity but under different names, or two distinct entities in their own right with
their own distinct personalities, I'm afraid we must move away from the realms of
literary sources and into the realms of personal gnosis. I do not personally believe
that Gwyn and Arawn are necessarily the exact same figure, or two manifestations
of the same core entity. Regardless, it is clear that many motifs surrounding the
two entities are extremely similar and there may be overlap in the way in which
they were perceived. I have heard it said that the Mabinogion were tales written about and for nobility, whereas folklore, of course, is the lore of the common
folk.[78] It is interesting to note that Gwyn ap Nudd appears more frequently as an

....

78. Davies, *Pedeir Keinc y Mabinogi*, 5–12.

otherworldly king in folk belief as opposed to in the medieval literature that, for a long period, would have been restricted to nobility and religious clerics.

Perhaps the identity of the king of the Otherworld to the Welsh depends on who it is you are asking. To those who were learned in the myths recorded in medieval manuscripts, it is clearly Arawn. However, to the common folk, it may more likely be Gwyn ap Nudd.

In the Mabinogion it is clear that Arawn is the king of Annwfn and also the leader of the Cŵn Annwfn. Therefore, it is easy to understand why authors such as Trevelyan learned in their folkloric studies that the leader of the Wild Hunt, which involved these otherworldly hunting hounds, was indeed Arawn. Let us move on from Arawn now and circle back to the Wild Hunt.

Marie Trevelyan was a folklorist in the late nineteenth and early twentieth century. She was born in Llantwit Major, and her books on folklore, myths, and legends are still adored today by many. Trevelyan spoke of the Cŵn Annwfn as airborne spirit hounds and death portents. She mentions that who exactly leads the hounds varies depending on region, though it is usually a tall or large dark and mysterious man, often clad in grey.[79]

When we compare the work of all of these folklorists, it seems apparent that the belief in some form of Wild Hunt was present, and that the common element among most accounts was the inclusion of the Cŵn Annwfn or Cŵn Wybir: hunting hounds that run through the air, through stormy clouds in thunder and rain, their howls being heard by those who would soon either die or have death's shadow upon their life. However, who exactly led these hunting hounds is a complicated matter—a nameless horned entity, King Arthur, or Arawn. To further complicate matters, we have another contender for leader of the Wild Hunt to add into the mix.

Marie Trevelyan also names a female leader of the Wild Hunt in Wales, Mallt y Nôs. Trevelyan translates this entity's name to mean "Matilda of the Night," though I find it interesting that the word Mallt is rather similar to the Welsh word Mellt, meaning "lightning" or "thunderbolts." That may seem unrelated, however, considering Mallt y Nôs is associated with these processions of supernatural hunts, which are often conflated with wild stormy nights. I believed it important to make note of this.

. . . .

79.   Trevelyan, *Folk-Lore and Folk Stories of Wales*, 47–58.

According to Trevelyan, Mallt y Nôs hunts through the night sky alongside Arawn. It is Mallt y Nôs who drives the dogs forward as she cries loudly. Trevelyan's version of the Mallt y Nôs legend states that she was once a mortal woman who was Norman in origin and had connections to Gloucester and South Wales. She was said to be very fond of hunting, and once proclaimed, "If there is no hunting in heaven, then I shall never go there!"

This statement doomed her, and upon her death her soul was collected by Arawn who ordered her to join him and his hounds in their hunt for all eternity. Mallt y Nôs is depicted as a wailing spirit dressed in a long cloak, often in colours such as pale green or dark shades of blue or red.

Beyond Trevelyan's account of Mallt y Nôs, another reference to her is in *The History of Early English Literature* (1892). In a small passage, Mallt y Nôs is referenced as being "a she-demon associated with the cold malarious fogs on marshy lands at night."[80] Trevelyan also connects the hounds of the Otherworld and the nighttime processions or hunts to a figure known as the Brenin Llwyd (the grey king), whom she identifies as also being the Monarch of the Mist.

It seems that if a Wild Hunt does exist in Wales, who exactly leads it is up for debate. It is important to note, however, that regardless of who exactly leads the Hunt, the motifs surrounding it remain the same. It is an air-bound hunt featuring fearsome hounds of the Otherworld, led by a hunter who is associated with mist or fog. It seems clear to me that the idea of this leader being specifically Gwyn is either extremely regional dependant, or a more modern interpretation of the lore surrounding the Hunt.

Gwyn ap Nudd in Modern Paganism and Witchcraft

What we have learned up to this point is that Gwyn ap Nudd is a figure who is multifaceted, enigmatic in nature, with many traits to his overall legendary persona. His role in myth and legend of old is varied and complex, and yet we can paint a picture of a cohesive Gwyn by looking at the various ways he is portrayed. Now, I wish to pull us to a more modern understanding of Gwyn, and his role in modern Paganism and witchcraft.

· · · · · · · · · · · · · · · ·
80. Brooke, *The History of Early English Literature*, 84.

Gwyn plays a prominent role in modern Pagan culture. There are temples dedicated to him, altar statues adorning the altars of modern practitioners depicting an interpretation of him, books dedicated to him written specifically for Pagans and witches. Gwyn is very much present in modern Paganism and witchcraft today. It is interesting to note, however, that Gwyn seems to have always been a prominent figure in the emergence of modern Pagan witchcraft.

Notable witches and Pagans of the late twentieth-century revival of modern witchcraft and Paganism, such as Gerald Gardner, Stewart and Janet Farrar, and Evan John Jones, all mention Gwyn in their influential writings on Wicca and Traditional Witchcraft. The inclusion of Gwyn would continue right through to the turn of the century, and now Gwyn is more popular than ever and is adored across the world by many practitioners as a god of liminality, transition, death, and the Otherworld. On a personal level, I am acquainted with folks who revere Gwyn from England, the United States, Canada, Germany, and Australia, and even once met an individual from Thailand who was just beginning to incorporate Gwyn into their practice.

How did this happen? How did a mythical figure from Wales gain such popularity? And how do modern Pagans and witches perceive Gwyn? In order to come to some semblance of an answer to these questions, we must first examine where the forerunners of the witchcraft revival drew their inspiration from.

Gerald Gardner was rather obviously inspired, in part, by the work of English poet, writer, and novelist Robert Graves. We know this because there were extracts of Graves's writings found amidst other magical information within manuscripts written by Gardner himself, such as one manuscript titled *Ye Bok of Ye Art Magical*.[81] Likely the most influential of Graves's work on modern Paganism and witchcraft is *The White Goddess* (1948). While the primary focus of *The White Goddess* is to establish a theory concerning a European goddess of birth, life, and death, Graves does indeed touch upon numerous mythical figures from across Britain, Ireland, and Europe as a whole. One such figure he touches upon is none other than Gwyn ap Nudd.

In *The White Goddess*, Graves emphasises Gwyn as one of the expressions of the consort of the White Goddess, a supreme goddess to whom ancient cultures devoted themselves and gave many names. It is in this text we begin to see Gwyn's

· · · · · · · · · · · · · · · ·

81.   Heselton, *Gerald Gardner and the Cauldron of Inspiration*, 286.

legend of battling with Gwythyr once a year at May Day influencing the concept of what would become a highly popular modern myth in modern Paganism, the Battle of the Holly and the Oak Kings.

In chapter 10 of *The White Goddess*, Graves mentions a ballad titled *Sir Gawain's Marriage*, which references a lady seated between oak and green holly. Graves goes on to state that this lady is none other than Creiddylad, whom "in Welsh myth, the Oak Knight and Holly Knight fought every first of May until Doomsday."[82] It is clear with the reference to Creiddylad, the battle on the first of May, and the fact this battle rages until doomsday that the Oak and Holly knight, in Graves's eyes, are Gwyn and Gwythyr. Gwyn is represented by the oak tree, as Graves also claims that Gwyn was buried in an oak coffin. This may be confusing; however, it is important to note here that Graves followed a belief that essentially goddesses and gods often had various names and identities across cultures. The idea that Gwyn was buried in an oak coffin seems to derive from the fact that Graves associates Gwyn ap Nudd and King Arthur as being two expressions of the same entity. King Arthur, according to some streams of Arthurian lore, was buried in an oak coffin at the Isle of Avalon. Graves saw both Arthur and Gwyn as expressions of the Sacred King, and due to the fact that they both had connections to a mythical isle—namely the Welsh Otherworld of Annwfn and the Isle of Avalon—they were quite obviously both an expression of the solar consort-god to Graves's white lunar goddess.

Graves's *The White Goddess* has endured strong criticism in the last few decades. It is clear that it is a highly poetic and influential piece of work, and we cannot deny how much it has helped shape modern witchcraft and Paganism—especially in regard to the concept of the triple moon goddess and her consort, a god of the wild woods with solar connotations. However, many view Graves's scholarship as flawed and it continually adds confusion to the already murky and difficult subject of Celtic studies.[83] It is interesting to read the book not only to appreciate Graves's poetic insight, but also to see the jigsaw pieces of elements that make up much of modern-day Paganism. So many ideas found in modern Paganism and witchcraft originate here.

. . . .

82.   Graves, *The White Goddess*, 175.

83.   Hutton, *The Pagan Religions of the Ancient British Isles*, 145.

Graves's inclusion of Gwyn ap Nudd in this work led figures in the rise of modern Pagan witchcraft to view Gwyn as an aspect of the Horned God of the witches. Gerald Gardner stated that Gwyn ap Nudd was an epithet of the god of the witches; specifically, Gwyn was seen as a god associated with hunting and death.[84] Gwyn's role as leader of the Wild Hunt in folklore made its way into the ritualistic Wild Hunt lore in Gardnerian witchcraft.

Evan John Jones, a member and later magister of the original Clan of Tubal Cain, the coven or working group founded by Robert Cochrane, whom many call the father of what we now refer to as Traditional Witchcraft, also wrote on Gwyn ap Nudd. He wrote that Gwyn was a guardian of the old mounds, the ancient prehistoric burial chambers long associated with fairies and folklore. Gwyn was also considered a gatekeeper to the underworld, and it was believed that the hounds of hell were his to control.[85] Within Cochrane Craft and in later streams of Traditional Witchcraft, Gwyn became a god associated with death, the underworld or Otherworld, liminal spaces, and the Wild Hunt.

This is how Gwyn's identity seems to persevere in modern-day witchcraft and Paganism. He is the gatekeeper or ruler of the Otherworld, a liminal god who is associated with death, transition, liminality, and otherworldly forces. While his identity in this modern age may seem simplified and somewhat divorced from his old mythical context, I believe it is still in keeping with who Gwyn has always been: a figure of contradiction and mystery, simultaneously a fanciful, flamboyant, folkloric king of fairy, yet also a rugged, cruel, and hardened warrior and hunter.

Today Gwyn is often depicted as an antlered wild man residing in the dark woods. His antlered appearance seems to be a wholly modern invention, likely fusing him with other popular entities in modern Paganism and witchcraft such as Cernunnos and Herne the Hunter. The sprouting of antlers may also be partly to do with Gwyn's role as an epithet of the Horned God of the witches in modern witching traditions.

It may seem difficult to marry all of Gwyn's multifaceted identities together. Often, I have found it is hard for many to accept that the Gwyn of folklore, the Gwyn of mythology and medieval literature, and the Gwyn of modern Paganism and witchcraft are the same entity. Yet, it is his very fluid and liminal nature that

. . . .

84.   Gardner, *The Meaning of Witchcraft*, 158.

85.   Jones, *Witchcraft, a Tradition Renewed*.

makes him the perfect king of fairy. Fairies have long been associated with otherness, and because of this their lore seems full of the most delicious contradiction.

From a personal perspective as a modern-day devotee of his, I view Gwyn as not only a complex and enigmatic entity, but also as a very nurturing ruler of all that falls into his domain. As I said, otherness has always been associated with all things fairy, and therefore it is no surprise to me that many Gwyn devotees I have met over the years have been marginalised individuals or those who feel they do not fit in this world. Neurodivergent people, women, and queer people have been the majority of those who revere this otherworldly god today, in my experience. It is almost as though he has opened his arms and said, "So long as the world makes you feel othered, you are under my domain."

Gwyn is revered today because he is needed. He is the shadowy and enchanting ruler of the Otherworld who rides upon the mist and can be found in the darkest hollows of the forest. Listen to the way the wind rushes through the branches of the trees in a woodland on an autumnal night as the sun sets, and you may hear the music and revelry of his host and his voice travel upon the air.

Exercise
Dedicating a Shrine to the King of Fairy

In building relationships within a magical, spiritual, or devotional context with fairies, one simple method is to construct a shrine to the deity associated with them. By constructing and dedicating a shrine to Gwyn, you can create a focal point to aid in strengthening and deepening relationship with him.

While the study of entities like Gwyn is important, to gain a clear understanding of who Gwyn has been within the Welsh cultural context, contradictions and all, it is also incredibly important, if approaching these topics from a spiritual or magical perspective, to also gain real lived experience in interacting with these entities.

Luckily, constructing a shrine in honour of Gwyn is a fairly easy task, as his lore is full of symbolism. First, by looking at Gwyn's lore in both mythology and folklore, we can glean that there are specific colours associated with him, namely white, red, and blue. White because of his name and because of white's association with the Otherworld. I also like to personally associate Gwyn with grey tones. Then we have blue and red, the colours that Gwyn's courtiers don in the story of St. Collen's audience with the king of the fairies.

I personally do not like to mix all these colours equally, as the colours red, white, and blue tend to remind me too much of the Union Jack, and an altar or shrine covered in these colours will seem more like a tribute to that than Gwyn in my eyes. My preference is usually to use these colours in a subtle manner to denote the various facets of Gwyn. You could also argue that green and earthly tones might be associated with Gwyn due to his associations, both modern and in lore, with burial mounds, woodlands, and the wild.

With this as a base, your shrine could include an altar cloth of one or more of these colours. Then take into account other symbols associated with Gwyn and find items that remind you of him to place on the shrine.

Other symbols within lore associated with Gwyn include fairies, horses, hunting hounds, hunting horns, weapons, the colour gold, screech owls, water, and mist.

Take these things into account, but also allow your intuition to lead you to build a shrine that not only expresses who Gwyn is, but specifically how you perceive him. Something need not be upheld by textual lore in order to take pride of place on a shrine you are personally dedicating to Gwyn. Allow space for this shrine to be an intimate, personal place of connection between you and him.

You may also look to the later chapters at trees, animals, plants, and other things associated with fairies in Welsh lore that may inspire the way in which you construct your shrine.

Once your shrine is ready, dedicate it to Gwyn by leaving offerings upon the shrine and reciting a dedication such as the one below.

Gwyn ap Nudd,
Pen Annwfn. Brenin y Tylwyth Teg.
Mae'r allor hon wedi'i hadeiladu gyda pharch i ti.
Gad i'r lle hwn fod yn le porthol,
Lle i ni gydnabod ein gilydd.

Fel fydd hi yn y deyrnas uwchlaw,
Felly fydd hi yn y deyrnas islaw.

Gwyn ap Nudd,
Chief of Annwfn, king of fairy,
I dedicate this shrine in your name,
May it be a place of connection,
A bridge between your world and ours.
As it shall be in the realms above,
So it shall be in the realms below.

Leave offerings here, come here to pray, and look to Gwyn whenever possible. Keep him in your mind and heart and allow this shrine to be a liminal space where you and the king of fairy join as one.

The Denizens
of the Otherworld

We have now explored the Otherworld of Welsh lore, the realm from which the fair folk are said to originate, and we have explored the king, or kings, of this enchanting realm. Now, let us approach the folk who dwell in this place.

In this chapter we will be exploring the fair folk in more detail. First, however, allow me to define who exactly I mean when referring to the fair folk. This chapter will not explore the ethereal, goblin-esque entities such as the ellyll and the coblynnau who are very deeply connected to the natural landscape and specific features in the landscape. Instead, this chapter will focus more so on the humanoid entities who are said, or alluded to be, of the Otherworld. The goblin-esque entities that dwell in the hollows, the mines, and the household will be explored in the next chapter.

In many ways, the fair folk explored in this chapter are not too dissimilar to humans in their appearance and nature. What makes them different are certain "othering" qualities, magical abilities, and the fact they are said to have come to our world from the Otherworld.

These humanoid otherworldly entities feature prominently in the mythology and folklore of Wales. Mortals often interact with them, marry them, and fear them. They are the denizens of the Otherworld, and as such play a significant role in not only shaping fairy belief, but in the very legendary landscape of Wales.

Throughout this chapter, we will explore the many names they have been given by humans for many centuries. As we explore these names, we will also explore how they are described within myth and lore in appearance, nature, and temperament.

Welsh Names for the Fair Folk

Before we explore names given to describe the inhabitants of the Otherworld, I believe it is important to first note how the fair folk featured quite prominently in Welsh mythology long before the terms we now associate with such entities in the Welsh language came into use.

What do I mean by this? Well, the most common name given to otherworldly or fairy entities within the Welsh language today is likely Y Tylwyth Teg. And yet, this name does not appear in any Welsh texts prior to the fifteenth century.[86] However, characters that are denizens of the Otherworld, or who have certain qualities associated with fairy traditions, long predate that.

The best example of Welsh texts that describe fairy-like entities without explicitly using any descriptive terms denoting their fairy nature is, of course, the corpus of medieval literature. The myths preserved in medieval manuscripts provide us with otherworldly characters that are never referred to by terms such as Tylwyth Teg, and yet, as we will see later in this chapter, they still fit within the general description of such beings rather perfectly.

Characters such as Arawn and Rhiannon from the Mabinogion are quite clearly otherworldly or fairy in their nature, and stories such as that of Elidorus's adventure into the Otherworld clearly portray beings that we would today describe as fairies. However, in these texts, generally accepted terms to describe fairies within the Welsh language are never used. In the case of Elidorus and the small men he comes into contact with that lead him to the subterranean Otherworld, this original text is actually in Latin.[87] Regardless of the lack of Welsh terminology in these texts to describe such entities or beings, it is rather clear that these texts had influence on the development of fairy traditions and beliefs within a Welsh context, and as such cannot be ignored.

· · · · · · · · · · · · · · · ·

86. Rüdiger, Y Tylwyth Teg, 12.

87. Cambrensis, The Itenarary through Wales, 68–70.

Throughout various texts and folkloric traditions, the fair folk have been given many names that vary based on time period and region. To make things all the more confusing, many folklorists and translators have for many centuries attempted to define types of fairies from Welsh folk belief using non-Welsh terms—for example, defining the ellyll as elves. This has muddied the water quite a bit and made it difficult to neatly classify and contextualise fairies. However, it is my belief that any attempts to definitively understand fairies will always be redundant. They are entities of complexity, contradiction, and are by their very nature incredibly mystifying.

Instead of offering a definitive guide to fair folk, what I will attempt to do here is lay out as much information as possible so as to try and offer an accessible and comfortable context for these elusive beings. To make things slightly easier, I will focus predominately on the more common terms for fairies or fair folk within the Welsh language, such as Tylwyth Teg and Bendith y Mamau. We will also touch upon names such as Plant Rhys Dwfn and the variations of that name. The reason I am examining these names is purely because I believe that much can be discerned regarding how the people of the past once perceived these beings by examining what they chose to call them, and why.

Y Tylwyth Teg

Let us begin with this common term for fairies. Today, most Welsh speakers will recognise this term as being the word we use to describe fairies. It has, within a modern context, become a catchall term for all things fairy. It is used to describe the ethereal, supernatural entities found within our myths, legends, and folktales, and yet it has also evolved to describe fairies within a more modern context. Tinker Bell from J. M. Barrie's *Peter Pan* would be described as a Tylwyth Teg in Welsh translations today, as would the flower fairies of Cicely Mary Barker's illustrations, or the fairy that brings children money in exchange for their teeth.

Yes, Tylwyth Teg has become a rather diverse term, and variations have begun to spring up from it as well. I have encountered modern Welsh-language fantasy books, television series, and media dropping the Teg and simply describing fairies as Tylwyth, or describing a singular fairy as Tylwythen. I vividly remember the Welsh dub of the Italian cartoon *Winx Club*, known in Welsh as *Clwb Winx*, using Tylwyth and Tylwythen in this manner. However, this is rather comical when one considers what it is that Tylwyth Teg actually means.

Tylwyth comes from the word Teulu, which describes a family. Y Teulu, meaning "the family," was another euphemism used to describe fairies in some regions. However, Tylwyth is a little more complex than that, as it can also be used to describe a tribe, host, war band, or troop. It is essentially a word that describes a related group of people or beings. It could also mean "genus," meaning a grouping of things that share common traits or characteristics.

Teg means "fair," "beautiful," "pure," or "amiable." Within a modern context, we would use the word Teg in conversation to denote fairness, for example in phrases such as digon teg (fair enough) or Chwarae teg (fair play). Within the context of Tylwyth Teg, however, it is a descriptor. This is a beautiful, or fair, family, host, or tribe.

This means that the term Y Tylwyth Teg is describing a family or grouping of beings that are considered fair, beautiful, or pure in nature. The reason I consider the modern shortening of the term to simply Tylwyth comical is because it is essentially then just referring to fairies as "family" or "grouping." However, it does work, as the only time the term Tylwyth would ever come up in a modern Welsh conversation is within the context of fairies. It is not a common word, whereas Teg, meaning "fair," is.

Where does this term come from? And when did it become associated with otherworldly entities and beings? In order to understand that, we must familiarise ourselves, at least somewhat, with a Welsh poet called Dafydd ap Gwilym.

Dafydd ap Gwilym was a fourteenth-century poet, regarded today as one of the great poets of Wales. Many of his poems denote a reverence for the natural world and the Welsh landscape, and as such he occasionally makes references to themes associated with fairies. Gwyn ap Nudd, the ellyll, and the supernatural are evoked in a handful of his very many poems. While the term Tylwyth Teg does not appear in the poetry of Dafydd ap Gwilym, he does utilise the word Tylwyth in relation to fairies. In the poem "Y Niwl" ("The Mist"), he refers to the fairies as Tylwyth Gwyn, which translates to mean "the family, tribe, or host of Gwyn," a reference to the king of fairy, Gwyn ap Nudd.[88] In another line of this same poem Dafydd ap Gwilym uses the phrase "Gwyn a'i Dylwyth," which translates to mean "Gwyn and his tribe" or "Gwyn and his host."

· · · · · · · · · · · · · · · ·

88.   Parry, *Gwaith Dafydd ap Gwilym*, 185.

This is particularly interesting, as not only do we have the word Tylwyth being used in relation to fairies, but we also here see the fairies being clearly identified with Gwyn ap Nudd. This, along with the Latin incantation mentioned in the previous chapter focusing on Gwyn ap Nudd, is clear evidence in my opinion that Gwyn was decidedly associated with fairies within folk tradition in the fourteenth century. It is likely that Dafydd ap Gwilym was drawing not only upon his knowledge of Welsh literature, but also common folk belief of his time when referring to fairies in the manner he did.

Still, this does not answer the question of where Tylwyth Teg comes from. The first literary evidence of this term is found in a fifteenth-century apocryphal Dafydd ap Gwilym poem.[89] This poem is titled "Y Niwl Hudolus" ("The Magical Mist"), and while it shares a similar stylistic expression to Dafydd ap Gwilym's work, especially "Y Niwl," the poem's true author is unknown.

Of course, this is merely the earliest literary mention we have of the term Tylwyth Teg. Perhaps the author of the apocryphal Dafydd ap Gwilym poem drew inspiration from terms such as Tylwyth Gwyn and crafted the term themselves. Interestingly, the Welsh words Gwyn and Teg can be used synonymously to denote purity, or fairness, and so perhaps the author was simply using an alternate term to Gwyn. Alternatively, perhaps Tylwyth Teg was already established within contemporary folk vernacular by the fifteenth century. We cannot know for certain. However, what we do know for certain is that the term would eventually become part of common language across the entirety of Wales.

The Nature of Fairies

Now that we have explored what the term Tylwyth Teg literally translates to mean, and where it may have originated, we can begin to explore *who* the Tylwyth Teg are and how they are presented within folk belief. What is their nature? How do they look? And what role do they play in folklore and folk belief? This is what we will explore here.

One might assume, based on the idea that Tylwyth Teg translates to mean "the fair family," that these entities were perceived to be beings that radiate a gentle, amiable, and light nature. This may not necessarily be the case. Tylwyth Teg may be a term that is less descriptive, and more so a positive euphemism utilised

. . . .

89. Rüdiger, *Y Tylwyth Teg*, 12–13.

by the common folk to avoid the wrath of these powerful, arcane entities that have influence over our world and our lives. In various cultures that hold a fairy tradition, there was a certain taboo about speaking ill of the fairies, or in using terms such as fairy and fae, and so euphemisms were utilised instead.[90] Morgan Daimler explains in *A New Dictionary of Fairies* that the use of euphemisms was due to a fear that the fair folk may overhear you, as they were known to travel invisibly.[91]

The notion that fairies travel invisibly and could inflict harm upon those who offend them is certainly found within Welsh folklore. The fair folk were said to frequent markets in Pembrokeshire, and though they were sometimes seen wandering the markets themselves, they were never seen arriving or departing.[92]

A tale recorded by the folklorist W. Jenkyn Thomas titled "Fairy Ointment" features numerous instances of fairy invisibility and an instance of fairies causing harm to someone who offends them.[93] In this tale, a nurse is approached by a mysterious man who asks her to aid in the birth of a child. The nurse agrees, rides upon his horse through the mist, and is eventually led to a great manor house. In this manor house she sees no one besides the man who collected her and the mother who is giving birth. Despite this, everything the mother might need to deliver safely, as well as food for those in attendance, is seemingly delivered by invisible hands into the bedchamber. Later in the tale, the nurse is asked to rub an ointment on the eyes of the newly born child, but to take care not to let the ointment touch her own eyes. The nurse accidentally rubs her left eye with the ointment, and she gains the power to see through the illusions conjured by the fairies. Suddenly, the room she is in is revealed to be a damp cave, and she sees small men and women preparing the items that previously seemed to appear by invisible hands. The nurse lives with this ability to see fairies and to see beyond any glamours cast by the fair folk for some time. Eventually, however, she acknowledges a person stealing from a market stall who happens to be one of the fair family. In retaliation for her peering into the unseen world, the fairy blinds the nurse in her left eye.

· · · · · · · · · · · · · · · · ·

90. Narvalez, *The Good People*, ix.

91. Daimler, *A New Dictionary of Fairies*, 121–122.

92. Jones, *Welsh Folklore and Folk Custom*, 65.

93. Thomas, *The Welsh Fairy Book*, 133–136.

Fairies were known within folk belief to be able to cause all manners of mischief and harm to mortals. Other stories tell of how men would sometimes fall asleep near where the fairies dance, and they would wake up to find that they had been bound with ropes made of gossamer that held the magical ability to render the victim invisible … unable to be helped by their peers.[94] They cause travellers to become lost while walking in rural areas, kidnap mortals—even babies—and trap mortals in their dances, which transport them to a new temporal reality where what feels like a few hours could actually be a few years. They are certainly not strangers to revenge and harm, qualities that are quite far from being perceived as "pure" or "fair."

This all provides us with context as to why a positive euphemism to refer to these beings might be required. Later in this book we will also explore the numerous charms and practices utilised by folk to protect themselves from the mischief and dangers of the fairies. It is quite clear that most ordinary folk did not want to mess with these chaotic supernatural forces.

Interestingly, the *Speculum Christiani*, the fourteenth-century text that includes an invocation to Gwyn ap Nudd as the king of fairy, describes Gwyn's subjects as eumenides.[95] The term eumenides comes from the Greek euphemism to describe the goddesses of vengeance, or the Furies.[96] Eumenides means "the kindly ones," and thus this gives us another clue into the idea that perhaps terms such as Tylwyth Teg and other respectable, positive terms to describe the fairies are euphemisms to avoid becoming targets of their wrath.

Therefore, I believe there is enough evidence to direct us to the idea that though they are referred to as the fair tribe, or fair family, this term is not a descriptor but instead a euphemism. As is evident from the previous examples of the fair folk causing chaos and harm to mortals, they do not always express a disposition that is fair and pure. However, I also do not believe it is fair to perceive them as purely evil or malicious either. They are entities that come from the Otherworld, and as such should not be labelled or judged by mortal moral standards. After all, a spider might be evil to a fly, but to the spider they are simply living their life and surviving. Similarly, perhaps to the many species we, as humans, view as food, pets, or resources, we would also be seen as malicious and evil. Yet,

. . . .

94.   Jones, *Welsh Folklore and Folk Custom*, 66–67.

95.   Rüdiger, *Y Tylwyth Teg*, 32.

96.   Seyffert, *The Dictionary of Classical Mythology, Religion, Literature, and Art*, 224–225.

most humans would never classify themselves as evil for enjoying a steak or keeping a fish in a tank.

We now know that Tylwyth Teg is likely more so a euphemism than a descriptor, but could it be a descriptor of their appearance? Perhaps they are not always fair and pure of temperament and nature, but could this perceived fairness and purity be a reference to how they look? Let us explore how the fair folk are described aesthetically.

In the twelfth-century writings of Gerald of Wales, when recounting the tale of Elidorus—who spent some of his childhood in the subterranean realm of the fairies—the writer describes the fair folk in quite a bit of detail:

> These men were of the smallest stature, but very well proportioned in their make; they were all of a fair complexion, with luxuriant hair falling over their shoulders like that of women.[97]

The majority of the fair folk with whom Elidorus comes into contact within this tale are said to be men, though they seem to have qualities that the author perceives as inherently feminine. In particular, the male fairies are said to have long, flowing hair. Their size is also interesting, as they are described as being small in stature but well proportioned. Their size is emphasised by the fact that they ride horses and own greyhounds that are in proportion to them. This subterranean world seems to be a mirror image of our own, but shrunk down. The people of this world look like us, albeit small and fair, and they present qualities that denote these beings as inherently "other" in nature.

The idea of fairies being small is rather consistent with modern depictions of fairies. Though, it must be noted that while fairies in media today are often the size of insects, or no taller than a few inches in height, even the smallest fairies of Welsh lore were usually said to be only as small as mortal children. However, it is important to note here that the size of fairies is yet another subject loaded with contradiction and diversity. Sometimes they are small enough to dance atop the heather, and other times they are the same height as human men.[98]

While most tales refer to the fairies as being incredibly beautiful and ethereal in appearance, some tales describe them as being as diverse in appearance

. . . .

97. Cambrensis, *The Itinerary Through Wales*, 69.

98. Jones, *Welsh Folklore and Folk Custom*, 62.

as humans. For example, one tale describes how a man falls into a lake while on his way to meet his sweetheart and is transported to the Otherworld. When he arrives in this Otherworld, the first denizen he comes across in this strange yet beautiful land is a man described as a "short, fat old man."[99] While tales concerning floaty, ethereal fairy brides are more common, the lore surrounding fairies tends to describe them as varied in appearance, just as humans are.

They often dress in bright, brocaded silks, perhaps a reference to the denizens of the Otherworld in the first branch of the Mabinogi. Colours associated with their garments are often red, blue, green, white, or gold. The fairies of Gwyn ap Nudd's court upon Glastonbury Tor, in Buchedd Collen, were said to be dressed in clothing that was half red, half blue, representing the coldness and heat of the Christian hell.[100] An account of a fairy dance witnessed by Dr. Edward Williams in 1757, as recorded by Elias Owen, describes how fairies dancing at a field called Cae Caled were dressed in garments of red.[101] These garments were said to resemble a military uniform, and they had red handkerchiefs with yellow dots tied around their heads.

But what of other terms? Tylwyth Teg, after all, is but one of many terms used to describe the fair folk within the Welsh language. Let us explore some of the other names given to the fairies.

Bendith y Mamau, Plant Rhys Dwfn, Plant Annwfn

It would be very easy for those new to exploring the fairy traditions of Wales to assume that the various terms associated with the fairies denote related yet different entities. This does not seem to be the case. All these terms seem to describe the same entities, and these differing terms seem to have sprung up due to regional vernacular.

Growing up in North Wales, I had only ever heard the term Tylwyth Teg to describe fairies within our cultural continuum. It was not until I began exploring fairy lore and general folklore in more depth that I became acquainted with terms such as Bendith y Mamau or Plant Rhys Dwfn.

While all of these varying terms seem to be regional euphemisms to describe denizens of the Otherworld, the terms themselves are incredibly interesting in

. . . .
99.   Thomas, *The Welsh Fairy Book*, 153.
100. *Rhyddiaith Gymraeg Y Gyfrol Gyntaf*, 36–41.
101. Owen, *Welsh Folk-Lore*, 98.

their own right and deserve further exploration. After all, exploring why folks call them by those names tells us quite a bit about the lore pertaining to them.

The term Bendith y Mamau, meaning "the mother's blessing"—or sometimes Bendith eu Mamau, "their mother's blessings"—is a regional-specific fairy euphemism found in Glamorgan, in the south of Wales.[102] It is used synonymously with Tylwyth Teg and describes the same otherworldly beings. However, what is interesting in this euphemism is the specific mention of mothers. The folklorist John Rhŷs equated this euphemism for the fairies with the concept of mother goddesses.[103]

In modern Pagan circles, I have heard some attempt to draw connections between the fairies and ancient goddesses, claims that the fair folk, especially those ethereal fairy brides attached to lakes, are the echoes of nature goddesses surviving in folk traditions, somewhat diminished. This belief is found in some Welsh sources too. John Owen Huws explains that the belief in goddesses associated with rivers, lakes, and bodies of water extends to the Iron Age, when great hoards of treasures were thrown as offerings into bodies of water.[104] Beyond this, many rivers also have names associated with goddesses such as the Hafren or Severn, associated with the goddess Hafren, or Sabrina.

As romantic of a notion as it is, and as much as I long for it to be true, I unfortunately am sceptical of the fairies-as-diminished-deities theory due to lack of evidence. Nevertheless, I felt it important to make note of this theory. Interestingly, there are other folktales that lead me to theorise a possible survival of belief in lake-specific deities or spirits, specifically the legend of Llyn Cwm Llwch. We touched upon the legend concerning the fairy door that appeared near this lake every May Day as a gateway to an invisible island at its centre in the previous chapter. There is another legend associated with this lake that takes place after the incident with the island.

Years after the incident where the fairies closed off the island to mortal visitors, the human inhabitants near the lake assumed the fairies had up and left. Wondering if perhaps the fairies had left behind some treasure beneath the lake, the people planned to drain it. The story tells how they dug a deep trench the water would flow down once they had dug into its banks, and this trench can still

102.   Rhŷs, Celtic Folklore: Welsh and Manx, 174.

103.   Rhŷs, Celtic Folklore: Welsh and Manx, 102.

104.   Huws, Y Tylwyth Teg, 12–13.

be seen today. However, as they were about to deliver the final blow that would send the water of the lake down the trench, draining it entirely, the atmosphere surrounding this place changed entirely. Dark clouds formed above, lightning streaked across the sky, thunderous roars echoed across the landscape. The water in the lake began to thrash about, as if there was a violent storm, and from this furious water emerged a gigantic figure. Looming over those who wished to drain the lake was a fierce-looking spirit. He had long hair and a beard, and he spoke with a booming voice. He warned the people that if they dared to disturb his peaceful lake, he would make certain that their town and the surrounding valley would drown in horrendous floods. And with that, he vanished beneath the waves. The atmosphere calmed, and the people decided it might be best if they did not drain the lake.[105]

This story clearly details an angry and vengeful spirit protecting its domain. Perhaps this spirit was a god, or perhaps he was the living embodiment of the lake. Nevertheless, it is clear he was a powerful and looming force. Perhaps, in the very spirit of tales like this one, there is some truth to the notion that fairy stories may have echoes of older gods and spirits long forgotten due to the rise in Christianity.

Speaking of lakes, another theory surrounding the use of the euphemism Bendith y Mamau concerns the motif of the fairy bride. Elias Owen theorises that perhaps the euphemism originates in the lore pertaining to the idea that some people descended from fairies on their mother's side.[106] After all, the idea of fairy women marrying mortal men and having children with them is not uncommon in folklore.

The Fairy Bride Motif

A version of the fairy bride or supernatural bride motif is found in folklore across the world. The general idea is that the tales that fall under this motif involve a union between a mortal man and a nonhuman woman. There are examples of nonhuman men marrying mortal women too, but for the purpose of this section we will be delving into the concept of the fairy bride as it pertains to the folklore of Wales.

. . . .

105.   Adapted from the tale recorded in Thomas, *The Welsh Fairy Book*, 71–75.

106.   Owen, *Welsh Folk-Lore*, 3.

Likely one of the most famous fairy bride stories from Wales is that of the fairy maiden of Llyn y Fan Fach, a lake in Carmarthenshire, South Wales. This legend can be found in almost every popular book on Welsh folklore.[107]

A farmer, while out watching his cattle, sees a fairy maiden bathing in a lake and instantly falls in love with her. In an attempt to woo her, he offers her some of his bread, to which she quickly responds that his bread is far too hard, and she vanishes beneath the water of the lake. The farm boy tells his mother of this encounter, and she suggests he take unbaked bread to offer her. The fairy maiden refuses this unbaked bread too, and so the next day he brings her half-baked bread. This she finally finds appealing, and she asks him what it is that he desires from her. He tells her that he wishes to marry her, and so she fetches her father to see if he agrees to this union. Her father agrees, so long as the farm boy can tell the difference between the fairy maiden and her identical twin sister.

The father asks the boy to gesture to the correct sister. The boy flounders and cannot, so the fairy maiden helps him by extending her foot forward as a hint. Thus, he chooses correctly, and is given permission to marry her. The father offers them great bounties in the form of fairy cattle that produce the best milk, which makes them rich. They live a life of comfort and have children together.

However, there is a taboo to this union, one that the farm boy knows of before he commits to the marriage. If he were to strike the fairy maiden three times, the union would be terminated, and the bounties would be taken from him. He agrees to this with ease, but the fairy maiden's perception of a "strike" differs greatly from his perception. One day, she agrees to fetch the horses from the field they are grazing in, but as she is preparing to fetch them, she complains that they are too far away. "Go!" the farmer says to her, and he gives her a light nudge on the shoulder. This is the first strike. Years later, at a christening, the fairy maiden bursts into tears at how weak and frail the baby being christened looks. The farmer nudges her on the shoulder as a hint to calm down as she is causing a scene. This is the second strike. The third strike comes when she is at a funeral, and she cannot contain her laughter. She laughs hysterically at the joy of a soul freed from the pains of its physical form. Her husband nudges her again, as he did at the christening. And so, that is the third strike. With that, she leaves, returning to the lake and taking all the fairy cattle with her.

. . . .

107.   It can be found in Thomas, *The Welsh Fairy Book*, 1–11; Jones, *Welsh Folklore and Folk Custom*, 68–72; and Sikes, *British Goblins*, 38–40 (to name a few).

The farmer "struck" the maiden predominately because she was subverting social norms. She cried at a christening, an event that is meant to be joyful, and she was joyous at a funeral, an event that should be solemn. Perhaps her lack of understanding of human social convention was due to her fairy nature.

The general equation of these fairy bride stories is that a mortal man marries a fairy woman; this leads to them becoming extremely comfortable, usually bathing in the glorious bounties the fairy can provide; a taboo is then broken and the fairy maiden leaves. Once she has left, the family loses the bounty.

The Llyn y Fan Fach legend first appeared in print form in 1861 and has gripped the folkloric culture of Wales since then.[108] While this legend is likely the most famous of its kind, it is certainly not the only one. The earliest literary mention of a fairy bride story is found in Walter Map's *De Nugis Curialium* from the twelfth century.[109] In one such legend found in Map's compilation, a man witnesses a group of fairy maidens emerge from Llyn Syfaddan in the southeast of Wales. As they dance underneath the moonlight, the man captures one of them and she agrees to stay with him under the condition that he not strike her with a bridle.[110] As with all fairy bride stories, this taboo is indeed broken and the maiden returns to the lake. Similarly, another fairy bride legend found in Walter Map's work takes place in the Welsh Marches. This legend features an eleventh-century Anglo-Saxon figure known as Wild Edric. An interesting figure in his own right, Wild Edric has become a legendary character within Salopian and Welsh Marches lore, and some sources even associate him with a myth akin to the Wild Hunt.[111] Wild Edric married a fairy maiden; the tale surrounding that union was very similar to the one from Llyn y Fan Fach, though there is no lake. He witnesses fairy maidens dancing and decides to capture one of them. The taboo in this tale, however, is that he must not judge or disapprove of the maiden for her sister's actions. Eventually, this taboo is also broken, and the maiden vanishes into thin air, leaving Wild Edric in grief for his loss.

108. Wood, *The Fairy Bride Legend in Wales.*
109. Wood, *The Fairy Bride Legend in Wales.*
110. A version of this tale can also be found in Rhŷs, *Celtic Folklore: Welsh and Manx.*
111. Burne, *Shropshire Folk-Lore,* 25–32.

While many of these fairy bride legends are associated with regions in the south of Wales, there is one tale I recall being told as a child that is based in the north. This tale takes place in Nant y Bettws, Caernarfonshire.

A man comes across the fairies dancing in the woods; falling in love with one of the fairy maidens, he snatches her away and takes her into his home. Due to his front door having an iron lock on it, the fairy maiden cannot leave, and the fairies in her company cannot enter to rescue her. While she is kept as his prisoner, he begs her to marry him. She refuses, but eventually she says to him that if he guesses her name correctly, she will at the very least stay with him and be his servant. He guesses every name he can think of, but every guess is incorrect.

One day, while returning home from market, he overhears the fairies in the same spot where he had kidnapped the maiden lamenting her loss. In the midst of this conversation, he overhears one of the fairies refer to her as Penelope. He runs home and tells the maiden he can guess her name: "Your name is Penelope!" he says, smugly. The maiden agrees there and then to be his servant. She warns him, however, that if he were to ever strike her with iron, she would be set free.

Years go by and they eventually grow to love one another, marry, and have children together. One night, however, while trying to settle an agitated mare during a storm, the husband throws a saddle to the fairy maiden and the iron bit strikes her. The moment the iron hits her skin, she vanishes into thin air.

Not wanting to leave her children with nothing to remember her by, she appears one night at her husband's bedroom window and whispers advice to him:

> Rhag bod anwyd ar fy mab,
> Yn rhodd rhowch arno gob ei dad;
> Rhag bod anwyd ar liw'r càn,
> Rhoddwch arni bais ei mam.[112]

This translates to:

> Should my son catch a cold,
> Place his father's coat upon him.
> Should my daughter catch a cold,
> Place her mother's coat upon her.[113]

. . . .

112.   Fardd, *Llen Gwerin Sir Gaernarfon*, 95.

113.   My translation. It must be noted here that bais in the final line of the Welsh could be referring to a petticoat, skirt, or coat worn by a woman.

It is said that this family, which now has fairy ancestry, is known by the surname Pelling. If you happen to be a Pelling and your family descends from the Caernarfonshire or North Wales region, you may indeed have a fairy ancestor, according to lore.

And there we have some examples of fairy bride stories, many of which feature the fairy maidens becoming mothers to children who carry fairy ancestry. Perhaps this is, indeed, where the euphemism Bendith y Mamau originates.

further Names Given to fairies

Tylwyth Teg and Bendith y Mamau are not the only native names used to describe the denizens of the Otherworld. Various regions across Wales have their own unique names for these ethereal beings. Let us wrap up this discussion of names and lore pertaining to the denizens of the Otherworld by looking at a brief overview of some other terms one might come across in Welsh folklore.

Plant Rhŷs Dwfn, Plant yr Is-Ddwfn, Plant Annwfn

Another interesting name given to the fairies is Plant Rhŷs Dwfn. This translates directly to "the children of Rhŷs the Deep" and is a term used to describe the fairies predominately in the southwest of Wales, such as in Pembrokeshire.[114] Many have theorised who Rhŷs Dwfn is and why the fair folk were considered his children in this territory. One theory is that he was a ruler of a lost country that sank beneath the sea, hence the emphasis on dwfn, meaning "deep."[115]

However, a more likely explanation behind this strange name for the fairies is that it is, in fact, a corruption of Plant yr Is-Ddwfn, meaning "the children of the lower worlds" or "of the very deep."[116] This would make more sense, as Plant Annwfn or Plant Annwn is another term that occasionally appears in collections of folklore relating to fairies.[117] This term simply means "the children of the Otherworld" but can also be translated to "the children of the very deep." As mentioned in the previous chapter, Annwfn, the name for the Otherworld, can be translated to imply depth.

. . . .

114. Jones, *Welsh Folklore and Folk Custom*, 61.

115. Rowland, *Straeon y Cymry*, 11–13.

116. Rüdiger, *Y Tylwyth Teg*, 32.

117. Owen, *Welsh Folk-Lore*, 3.

Once again, these are all but terms to describe otherworldly beings and have been used synonymously with Tylwyth Teg throughout history. Due to these terms being quite fixed to the southwest regions, however, these fairies were often associated with the otherworldly islands in the Irish Sea and the Celtic Sea. One such tale recalls that there was one such island off the coast of the old kingdom of Dyfed, and that it was only visible if you were to stand on a very specific patch of grass on the mainland. The herbs and plants grown on this otherworldly island were said to be imbued with magical virtues that provided the island with its power of invisibility.[118]

Due to these islands being quite small, the fair folk would sometimes move to live in Welsh cities along the southwest coast. As such, they were also said to frequent various markets, such as the ones in Cardigan, Millford, Haverfordwest, and Fishguard.[119] Usually the fair folk were no trouble when visiting mortal markets; they would simply buy their goods and get on with their day as any normal patrons would. However, occasionally they were said to exchange in fairy money—money that would transform into useless lumps of coal once the fairies had received their goods and were long gone.

Tylwyth Teg, Bendith y Mamau, Plant Rhys Dwfn, and Plant Annwn/Annwfn are likely the most common terms one might come across to describe the fair folk. They are synonymous terms and euphemisms with various connotations alluding to regional-specific lore surrounding these enigmatic entities. It is fair to say, with the information we have looked over thus far, that the fair folk have enchanted and intrigued people in every region of this land. Here is a chart outlining the terms and euphemisms explored on the previous pages, as well as a few other lesser-known entries and their translations. This is not an extensive list, as I am sure there are others I am unfamiliar with. I am also only including native Welsh terms in this list. I am aware that there are anglicised names for the fairies in certain regions of Wales, such as Verry Volk, but these will not be included here.[120]

. . . .

118.   Rowland, *Straeon y Cymry*, 11.

119.   Roberts, *Myths and Legends of Pembrokeshire*, 6–7.

120.   This is a term apparently from Gower, in the Southwest of Wales. As detailed in Evans-Wentz, *The Fairy Faith in Celtic Countries*, 158.

Name/Euphemism Given to Fairies	Translations and Additional Information
Y Tylwyth Teg	"the fair family"; "the fair tribe" Now the standard translation for "fairies" in the modern Welsh language. A euphemism found across Wales.
T Teulu	Literally, "the family" or "the tribe" A term used by poets such as Ieuan Fardd in the eighteenth century, and apparently used in various parts of South Wales.
Bendith y Mamau, Bendith eu Mamau	"the mother's blessings"; "blessings of the mother"; "their mother's blessings" A euphemism from the South of Wales, specifically linked to Glamorga.
Melltith y Mamau	"the mother's curse" It is theorised that Bendith y Mamau was a euphemism for Melltith y Mamau, which denotes the more dangerous nature of the fairies.
Plant Rhys Dwfn	"the children of Rhys the Deep" A euphemism from the southwest of Wales, especially coastal regions such as Pembrokeshire.
Plant yr Is-Ddwfn	"the children of the lower worlds" or "the very deep" Plant Rhys Dwfn is likely a corruption of this term.
Plant Annwn/ Annwfn	"the children of the Otherworld" Annwn and Annwfn are the same place; for more on that, refer to the chapter on the Otherworld.
Dynion Bach Teg	Literally, "fair little men" Yet another term from Pembrokeshire and the surrounding regions.

Name/Euphemism Given to Fairies	Translations and Additional Information
Gwragedd Annwn/ Annwfn	"the wives of the Otherworld" or "the women of the Otherworld" This term is usually used to describe the lake and fairy maidens from fairy bride stories.

Changelings

Changelings have become incredibly popular in the fantasy genre, yet they are also drastically misunderstood. If you were to read many modern fantasy novels or watch one of many fantasy series today, you might assume that changelings are fairy children that are left in the care of humans. These fairy children grow up unaware of their fairy nature, until something happens that reveals their true nature. The truth regarding changelings is somewhat more complex. While the lore concerning changelings can be found across a variety of cultures, I will be focusing on Welsh lore here.

Stories associated with changelings are found across all regions in Wales. In the native tongue, they are plentyn newid, which literally translates to "changed child," or, in some cases, they are crimbil, which is a term that, interestingly, means both "changeling" and "wizened person." This gives us our first clue as to the nature of changelings.

While modern interpretations of changelings interpret them as being no different to human babies, unaware of their fairy nature, this was certainly not the case in folklore. Changelings were usually very much aware that they were fairies, and they were said to be far wiser and more mature than human babies.[121]

This is evident from the fact that, in many tales associated with changelings, one method of determining whether a child truly is a changeling is for the mother to perform a strange task before them to see if they will react. Most of these tales involve the mothers being told by local cunning men or wisewomen to do something such as brew beer in an eggshell. Upon seeing this, the wizened changeling

. . . .
121.   Owen, Welsh Folk-Lore, 54–63.

would say something such as, "I have witnessed an acorn grow into an oak, I have witnessed a hazelnut grow into a hazel tree, but never have I witnessed someone attempt to brew in an eggshell!"[122]

This would be proof that the child was indeed a changeling who had lived for many, many years. Changelings were insinuated to have lived much longer than human babies and were probably not babies themselves. A key characteristic of changelings was that they would not grow. They would remain stumpy, small, and baby-like.

This, of course, was only if the changeling was indeed a fairy at all. On some occasions the changelings were enchanted pieces of dead wood made to look like a human baby.[123]

The Changeling Twins of Ysbyty Ifan

In a village in North Wales called Ysbyty Ifan, a woman once lived in a cottage near a fast-flowing river. She lived in this cottage with her husband and her two beautiful, golden-haired baby twins.

The woman's husband worked hard and was often away for days on end. And so, she was left to take care of the house and the land around the house while he worked. They collected fresh water from the river each morning and owned a cow that provided them with milk. Their life was a quiet, content one.

One morning, during a week when the husband was away working, the woman decided to go milk the cow. She considered taking the twins with her, but as she peered into the crib she noticed that, like little glorious angels, they were fast asleep, snuggled up next to one another. She smiled at them and decided she did not wish to disturb their slumber. And so, she locked the door and made her way down to the bottom of the field to milk the cow.

The fairies were known to loiter around this area. A local wisewoman had warned all the mothers of the area to place iron above or near the cribs of sleeping babes so as to protect them from the mischief and malice of the Tylwyth Teg. Usually, the woman who lived in this cottage would always leave an iron object near the crib. Today, however, it had completely slipped her mind.

. . . .

122.   My translation from Fardd, *Llen Gwerin Sir Gaernarfon*, 96–97.

123.   Huws, *Y Tylwyth Teg*, 20.

She returned to the cottage with a pail full of milk, humming a cheerful tune. It was such a beautiful day. She washed herself up and then went to check on the babies in the crib.

Her heart sank as she looked into the crib. Two little creatures smiled back at her eerily, silently. These were not her babies. These things lying in the crib had eyes that seemed as though they had witnessed all the terrors of this world. Their eyes were deeply sunken into their faces, and open so very wide. Their mouths grinned from ear to ear … a bigger grin than any human could possibly achieve. They had teeth. So many teeth. These babies did not have golden hair like her babies. No; these creatures had white hair, as white as snow.

They sat there. Smiling. Staring. The woman felt as though they were staring into her very soul.

She knew what had happened instantly. The fairies had come and swapped her beautiful babies with these foul things. She remembered a story a friend had told her, about a woman who'd sought the help of the local wisewoman after this very ordeal had happened to her. The wisewoman had suggested she throw the changeling into a nearby lake, and by doing this her own children would return.

And so she knew what to do. She grabbed these two foul beings under her arms and marched over to the lake. She stood atop a bridge that crossed the river Conwy, and she held the babies up before her. Without a second thought, she tossed the strange beings into the waters below, murdering them in hopes her own children would return.

Just before the two hideous creatures hit the water, two of the Tylwyth Teg appeared out of thin air and rescued them. Once the creatures that had replaced the human twins were taken to safety, the fair folk turned to look at the woman with a wicked and angry look upon their faces. They began running toward her.

She ran toward her cottage home. She could hear the fairies cackling and screeching behind her as they got closer and closer.

"Catch the wicked mortal hag who tried to harm our own!" the fairies shouted as the chase continued. Eventually the woman got to the door of her cottage, and she slammed the door closed with force. She bolted the door with iron, and she ran to the crib.

And there they were: her children, returned. She had no idea how this had worked, but clearly the local wisewoman knew how to deal with the fairies. From that day on, the woman never left her babies alone again. She nailed an iron horseshoe above their bed and made them always carry twigs from the rowan tree so that she knew they were safe. She never saw the fairies again.[124]

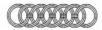

The fear of children being changed by the fairies gripped mothers, and so they would utilise protective charms to ward the fair folk away. The best form of protection was to get the child baptised, but before this was possible, they would hang pieces of iron in the shape of a cross above the crib. The presence of the mother was often enough to deter the fairies from stealing the human babies away.

The belief as to why the fairies stole human children was seemingly that fairy babies were considered weak stock. This corresponds with other tales, such as the tales concerning fairies needing human midwives present in order to deliver their babies successfully.

When a baby was suspected of being a changeling, beyond going to the local conjurer, wisewoman, or cunning man for advice, there were some rather unspeakable practices carried out to regain the original human babies. Some of these tests involved throwing babies into rivers or lakes and leaving them under oak trees overnight. The belief was that despite having swapped their babies, the fair folk still cared for their young and would not let any harm come to them. And thus, by rushing to protect the fairy babies from harm, the human babies would be returned to their rightful mothers.[125]

The lore pertaining to changelings is all rather bleak, and I cannot help but think these beliefs likely stemmed from ignorance toward sickly, disabled, neurodivergent, or simply fussy and difficult babies. By crafting a scapegoat, folks could easily find justification to harm, abuse, and even kill children considered "too much." Hence why I am uneasy with the obsession in modern fantasy with changelings. Besides being folklorically inaccurate, it is also entirely tasteless in my eyes. Changelings were never considered "special" or "chosen" children with magical gifts, as they are often portrayed in modern fantasy, but rather undesirable creatures worthy of abuse, or worse, extermination. This is a complex topic that I believe deserves unpacking.

. . . .

124.   My own reimagining of a folktale found in Evans, *Y Tylwyth Teg*, 58–59.

125.   Owen, *Welsh Folk-Lore*, 53.

Spectral or Corporeal?

Now that we have explored the euphemisms, names, and terms used to describe the fair folk, we must look to the question: What exactly are they?

In the broadest, vaguest of definitions, the fair folk are quite obviously not entirely of our world. They are deeply associated with the Otherworld in its many guises, and the oldest literary evidence of characters that fit within the fairy tradition are predominately denizens of Annwfn, or the Otherworld. However, one question continues to plague the minds of those who attempt to gain clarity as to the nature of the fair folk: Are they spirits?

Some entities that come under the "fairy" umbrella within Welsh tradition are quite clearly spectral, phantom-like beings who are often conflated with ghosts and bwganod.[126] However, when it comes to the Tylwyth Teg, the question of whether they can be defined as spirits is a little more complex.

As previously mentioned in this chapter, a twelfth-century pastoral manual known as the *Speculum Christiani* describes the subjects of Gwyn ap Nudd as eumenides and as evil spirits.[127] Yet, in contrast to this, the *Itinerarium Cambriae* by Gerald of Wales, another twelfth-century work, describes the fair folk a Welsh boy named Elidorus encounters as merely being a race of men not too dissimilar to humans, albeit smaller and living in a subterranean world.[128]

Many folklorists and writers have had mixed views as to whether the fair folk can be classified as spirits. T. Gwynn Jones described them simply as "non-ghostly apparitions," implying that while they may indeed be spiritual in nature, they are certainly not ghosts.[129] Yet, the eighteenth-century reverend Edmund Jones, who published a collection of testimonies on spirits, very clearly included the fair folk among tales of ghosts and phantoms.[130] Notable folklorists such as John Rhŷs and Elias Owen pushed the narrative that the stories of the fair folk were the echoes of a race of people that lived alongside humans, a race that preceded the Iron Age Celts. We will explore that theory in a little more detail later, but it is clear that they viewed the fair folk as being the memory of physical people as opposed to spirits.

. . . .

126.   A ghost, goblin, or bugbear. We will explore bwganod in more depth in the next chapter.

127.   Rüdiger, *Y Tylwyth Teg*, 40.

128.   Cambrensis, *The Itinerary Through Wales*, 68–70.

129.   Jones, *Welsh Folklore and Folk Custom*, 59.

130.   Jones, *A Relation of Apparitions of Spirits in the County of Monmouth and the Principality of Wales*.

Then we have Hugh Evans, who made his view on the subject very clear in his compilation of fairy stories titled Y Tylwyth Teg:

Nid wyf yn hoffi'r rhai sydd yn ysgrifennu am y Tylwyth Teg ac yn eu cymysgu ag ysbrydion. Nid ysbrydion oeddynt, ond pobl fychan.[131]

I do not care for those who write about the fair folk and mix them up with spirits. The fair folk were not spirits, but little people.[132]

The jury is still out on whether they can be considered spirits. Though, it seems very certain that they are predominately considered something rather different to the spirits of the dead. While the fair folk may hold certain qualities that would associate them with the realm of spirit, they are certainly not ghosts or phantoms. Despite this, however, the dead are often linked to fairies within various streams of folklore. The dead are sometimes seen travelling with the fairies, and of course let us not forget the fact that Gwyn ap Nudd, king of fairy within the Welsh context, is also considered a psychopomp and leader of the Wild Hunt. Beyond this, some streams of folklore also state that the souls of humans, once detached from their corporeal bodies, can travel to the land of the fairies.[133]

One thing that cannot be denied is the corporeality of the fair folk. Despite countless sources recounting their ability to travel invisibly, to vanish into thin air, to appear out of nowhere, or to transport themselves between our world and the Other, they are certainly not shadowy spectres that one's hand would penetrate as though they were mist or water. They have physical bodies that we can touch. They are, in many ways, just like us—flesh and bone. This is clear from stories that involve mortal men kidnapping fairies and mating with them.

This prompts the question, however: Does corporeality mean that they cannot be classed as spirits? Not necessarily. Spirits of various classifications have long been believed to be able to affect the physical world and display some semblance of corporeality.

. . . .

131.   Evans, *Y Tylwyth Teg*, xiii.

132.   My translation.

133.   Jones, *Welsh Folklore and Folk Custom*, 62.

The author Emma Wilby poses the idea that fairies exist in a liminal state between being pure spirit and being creatures of flesh and bone.[134] This betwixt-and-between quality fits well with the inherently liminal nature of all things fairy. Hence why, when asked these days if I consider fairies spirits, I usually answer with a vague "Yes and no." While spirits have not always been considered incorporeal, I do believe that there is a quality we in this modern age associate with the word spirit. We assume that spirits are very much merely apparitions and are not held to the same physical limitations as corporeal beings. Fairies lie somewhere in between, in my belief.

What is absolutely clear is that the fair folk have preternatural, and even supernatural, abilities beyond the human experience. They have certain magical powers and can seamlessly travel between our world and the Other. They seemingly have knowledge of things we do not, such as the location of hidden treasure and knowledge of the future, of prophesy, and of the virtues of the natural world. They seem to live far longer lives than we do, and often live in an entirely different temporal reality. The concept of time as we know it means nothing to them, as is evident from tales that recall how a few minutes in the Otherworld can be days, weeks, months, or years in our time.

The fair folk are inherently *other* and perhaps we will never definitively understand them. Hence why simply labelling them as "spirits" tends to not sit right with me.

Fairy Origin Theories

Beyond simply being the denizens of the Otherworld, numerous theories have sprung up as to who and what the fair folk are and where they originate. I believe that many of these theories have likely sprung up due to a culture that was predominately Christian attempting to make sense of the strange entities that were known to lurk the landscape. If these beings were not human, not the spirits of the dead, and not angels or demons, then what exactly were they? People have attempted to answer this question in a manner that fits their personal cosmology. The question of fairy origins has also been answered in a manner to fit within people's specific political or historical beliefs.

. . . .
134.   Wilby, *Cunning Folk and Familiar Spirits*, 19.

The latter seems to have been the case for writers such as Sir John Rhŷs in the late nineteenth and early twentieth centuries. Rhŷs believed that many of the motifs found within folk belief surrounding the fair folk were echoes of a race of Stone Age pygmy people who survived and lived alongside modern humans, albeit hidden.[135] Certain aspects of fairy lore, such as their dislike of iron, their liking of part-baked bread, and their connection to lakes, were said to be due to their Stone Age nature. Rhŷs was not the first to pose this theory of euhemerization. Elias Owen also presented the fair folk within a euhemerized model in *Welsh Folk-Lore* in 1887. In his eyes, the stories surrounding the fair folk were but the remnants of the history surrounding a conquered tribe who preceded the modern Welsh.[136]

Many of these euhemerization theories were developed in order to satiate personal political, historical, or academic ideals, or to make clear that fairy lore was not simply a topic too frivolous or juvenile to study. However, many of these theories are today either rejected or seen as merely fanciful.

Another theory as to the origin of the fair folk states that they are the spirits of Druids. The Druids existed in a time before Christianity reached these shores, and therefore they did not have the ability to be christened. Being too virtuous to be sent to hell, but unbaptised and too wicked to enter heaven, they became trapped in a liminal state, wandering the earth as spectral apparitions.[137]

Another intriguing origin theory I want to discuss is one that apparently comes from my home region, Ynys Môn, the Isle of Anglesey. This origin tale is wrapped up in a strange folkloric take on Christian cosmology, yet, despite being somewhat confusing, it is incredibly interesting. It tells of a mother named Cadi who gave birth to twelve children. She lived on the Isle of Anglesey, and one day she was surprised to hear that none other than Jesus Christ himself was set to visit her community. Feeling ashamed of having twelve children, she decided to hide them in the woods away from the eyes of the son of God. After Jesus had departed, she set out to find her children in the woods, but she could not find them anywhere. The children had become one with the forest, and they became the ancestors of what would become Tylwyth Teg yn y Coed, "the fair folk of the

. . . .

135.   To read about these theories in more detail, see Rüdiger, *Y Tylwyth Teg*, 207–230.

136.   Owen, *Welsh Folk-Lore*, 1–2.

137.   Evans-Wentz, *The Fairy Faith in Celtic Countries*, 147.

woods."[138] Some versions of this tale state that the mother was not an Anglesey woman named Cadi, but instead Efa, or Eve, from the story of Adam and Eve in the Bible.

There are countless stories that explore who the fairies might be and what their origin is. People clearly wanted to understand who and what these enigmatic neighbours who danced under the light of the moon were. In my personal belief, the fair folk are the inhabitants of the Otherworld; they originate in and are native to that strange, liminal place. The reason I personally believe they are seen so often within our world is due to the fact that our world and Annwfn are connected in intricate ways. It is clear, based on the lore we explored of the Otherworld in the first chapter, that our world and the Other are undoubtedly linked. It makes sense that these entities who reside in this deeper state of being would be able to traverse betwixt and between here and there.

Exercise
An Offering to the Tylwyth Teg

In a later chapter, we will discuss how and why magical practitioners would call upon, summon, and work with fairies. When we discuss the lore pertaining to fairies, it can seem rather confusing as to why anyone would want to interact with them within any capacity. As we have discussed in this chapter, though we refer to them with lyrical euphemisms that evoke a sense of lightness and twee, the fair folk can indeed be spiteful, harmful, and vengeful for seemingly no reason that makes sense to our mortal perceptions. However, as a magical practitioner, I do believe it is important to attempt to appease such beings. After all, our magic within a Welsh context is undeniably linked to the very Otherworld from which these beings are said to originate. Awen flows from the Otherworld, and the Otherworld often bleeds into our lived reality in ways we as magical practitioners should take note of.

Here I will include a simple offering ritual I conduct for the denizens of the Otherworld within my personal practice. Feel free to replicate this ritual as you see fit, or alter it to suit your own needs. At the core of this ritual is a desire to not only appease the Tylwyth Teg, but to also hopefully form a reciprocal relationship with them.

. . . .
138. Huws, Y Tylwyth Teg, 8–9.

This offering is best performed outdoors, especially at liminal places such as at the edge of forests or by riverbanks or on the shores of a lake. A core tenant of my personal practice is that I do not leave anything outdoors that will harm or clutter the natural environment in any way. "Leave nothing but footprints, take nothing but photographs" is a quote I often see on signs near footpaths or woodlands. It is something I have incorporated into my craft as a sign of respect for the spirits I work in tandem with. And so, this offering ritual requires you to return and collect the offerings from the same space after a period of around twenty-four hours. After all, it is the energetic virtue of the offering that you are gifting to them, and not the literal physical materials. Therefore, ensure you choose a location that is fitting for this task.

As an added form of protection from any mischief and malice, I recommend wearing or carrying a hagstone, a small piece of iron, or a charm made of rowan berries or wood while carrying out this ritual. Alternatively, wear a piece of clothing inside out.

Preparation

I carry out this ritual once per week, usually on a Tuesday or Thursday. In order to conduct the ritual correctly, I must first prepare what I wish to offer to the Tylwyth Teg. My choice of offering is usually a small bowl or bottle filled with saffron-infused milk, and I will sometimes also make them a craft from natural materials. If you do the latter, ensure the craft you make for them is not made from materials that they are known to have an aversion to, such as iron and rowan.

Saffron-Infused Milk

In the eleventh-century text that recounts the tale of Elidorus's sojourn in the land of the fair folk, it is said that the inhabitants of the Other-world like to drink milk infused with saffron. There are two methods of infusing the milk with saffron.

The first method is to warm the milk until it almost reaches boiling, and then to place a pinch of saffron into it. Stir the saffron well, and then allow the milk to cool. Once cooled, pour the mixture into a bowl or bottle and it is ready to use. This method is best when in a pinch and needing the infusion quickly.

I prefer the second method. Take a pinch of saffron and place it into a bottle or glass of milk. Stir well, then leave to sit overnight in a cool, dark place. In the morning, the milk should have turned a glorious golden colour. Once the colour is achieved, the mixture is ready to use.

The Ritual

If you wish to perform this offering near trees or woodland, first perform the call to Gwyn ap Nudd outlined in the second chapter of this book. Once this is done, you can move forward with this offering ritual.

Find a beautiful spot and take out your offerings. Place them somewhere they will be safe overnight, where they will not be disturbed by animals, humans, or the weather. Stand and face the offerings, and with arms extended, recite the following:

> *Oh, denizens of the Otherworld,*
> *The fair folk, the Tylwyth Teg, the children of the deep,*
> *Accept these as my offerings to you.*

I then recite the following poem, "Cân y Tylwyth Teg" ("The Song of the Fair Folk"). I often use this old Welsh poem as a call to them. Recite it in Welsh, English, or both.

> *O'r Glaswellt glan, a'r rhedyn man,*
> *Gyfeillion, dyddan, dewch!*
> *E ddarfu'r nawn, mae'r lloer yn llawn,*
> *Y nos yn gyflawn gewch.*
> *O'r chwarae sydd, ar dwyn y dydd,*
> *I'r dolydd awn ar daith,*
> *Nyni sydd lon, ni chaiff gerbron,*
> *Farwolion ran o'n Gwaith.*[139]

---

139. This poem can be found in various older Welsh texts such as Owen, *Welsh Folk-Lore*, and Isaac, *Coelion Cymru*. A reading of this poem can be found on my YouTube channel (*Mhara Starling*) so that you may learn the pronunciation, if needed.

From grasses bright, and bracken light,
Come, sweet companions, come,
The full moon shines, the sun declines,
We'll spend the night in fun;
With playful mirth, we'll trip the earth,
To meadows green let's go,
We're full of joy, without alloy,
Which mortals may not know.[140]

Once this is done, turn away from your offerings and walk home, ensuring not to look back at any point during the walk. Leave your offerings in their place for upward of twenty-four hours, then return and gather what is left of them and take them home. Dispose of what is left however you deem fit.

. . . .
140.   Translation of Welsh poem from Owen, *Welsh Folk-Lore,* 87–88.

Goblins, Ghouls, and Phantom Fairies

Some say that if you were to wander through the valleys, the hills, the cliffs, and the woodlands that dot our landscape by dark of night, or at twilight, you would come face-to-face with strange, enchanting, mysterious beings. Though these beings seem like whimsical, spritely little things, they are in fact truly terrifying.

Imagine, if you can, that you are walking home in a time before our modern transportation vehicles. A time before streetlamps, when the only way to return home to your little village from the bustling town was to cross through the deep valleys. As you wander home in the dark, you hear the strangest of sounds around you. The screeching of a fox, the hoot of an owl, the chirping of insects. The darkness seems to envelop you, closing in from every angle—when suddenly, a glimmer of hope. Ahead you see a shining light from a lantern! How marvellous, a neighbour of yours must also be heading home, and they were clever enough to bring a light with them.

You quicken your step and make your way toward them, thinking you could use the company, conversation, and most importantly the light! But no matter how quickly you try to catch up, they do not seem to get any nearer. You chase and chase after them and even occasionally call out in the hopes they'll stop, but they do not. You are entranced by the light of the lantern and cannot pull yourself away. Suddenly, a shock of adrenaline pulses through your body, as you realise you have strayed off the path. You stop and look around you, and you don't have a clue where you are. You look ahead again and notice the light is now higher up…but a realisation dawns upon you. You are on the edge of a cliff, looking out at another cliff ahead. Before you is a great drop; if you had taken one more step, you would have fallen to your death.

You glance over to the lantern light again, wondering how that person got over to the other side. They begin to cackle wildly, and the laughter echoes through the valley. They hold the lantern to their face, and you notice that the face staring back is no human face. A strange, impish beast looks at you. Grinning maliciously. Bursting out into fits of laughter. You turn around and run in the opposite direction … and all the while, the creature's laughter echoes around you!

These kinds of stories are common within our lore. Everyone knew to be careful when wandering across the rural paths at night, lest you run into a pwca or an ellyll.

In this chapter, we will explore these enigmatic entities that walk upon this landscape alongside us. Beings that are something between the otherworldly folk we learned about in previous chapters and hideous, terrifying ghouls and spectres. Beings that are linked deeply with the natural world.

Ellyllon

Lle'r ydoedd ym mhob gobant,
Ellyllon mimgeimion gant.

Where in every hollow resided,
A hundred sneering ellyllon.[141]

When one asks the ordinary person today to envision a fairy in their mind, they are likely to imagine something that looks akin to a tiny ballerina with gossamer wings dancing upon the flowers. If this is not the first image they conjure in their minds, it is usually something akin to a drawing by Brian Froud, a spritely and goblin-like being with pointed ears, sharp features, and animalistic qualities.

. . . .
141.   From the poem "Y Niwl Hudolus"; translation by author.

The former visual is a being that hides among the trees and bushes, giggling as they cause mischief and malice to unsuspecting mortals who dare cross their path. While we may not have the dancing tiny ballerinas with gossamer wings within our folklore, the more animalistic, mischievous, woodland-dwelling beings would not be too dissimilar to the beings we refer to as ellyllon. Or at least, that is what I always believed growing up.

As with all things fairy, the ellyllon are incredibly difficult to fully define. The stories of ellyllon I was raised with seemed to describe them as elf-like creatures who haunt the rural parts of the country.[142] I associated them in my mind with castle ruins, ancient monuments such as burial mounds and standing stones, and the dark hollows and groves across the country.

The earliest memory I have of a tale concerning the ellyllon was told to me when I was very, very young. The tale was read to me from a small red book titled *Chwedlau Gwerin Cymru* (*Welsh Folktales*). I loved this book as a child; I adored the cover illustration of a Celtic warrior stood before a mighty shadowed dragon. I also loved the beautiful illustration of a mermaid found on one of the first pages of the book and would spend hours staring at this illustration, wishing I could become a mermaid myself. I still have my childhood copy of this book, and in it there is a tale titled "Nant Yr Ellyllon" ("The Glen of the Ellyllon").

The story itself focuses on a glen or valley named after the ellyllon and a boy named Tudur ab Einion Gloff, who was a shepherd in the area. The valley itself is located on the side of a mountain between the town of Llangollen and the ruins of a medieval castle called Castell Dinas Brân in the northeast of Wales. Interestingly, the town of Llangollen is named after the same St. Collen who, according to folklore, had an interaction with Gwyn ap Nudd, as mentioned in a previous chapter.

In the tale, Tudur ab Einion Gloff was one day shepherding in the valley of the ellyllon, and he came face-to-face with what he perceived as a very little man. This man was sat upon a rock, with a fiddle no larger than a wooden spoon tucked beneath his arm.

Upon spotting Tudur, this strange little fairy man ran his fingers across the fiddle, and this produced the strangest, most ethereal music the boy had ever

. . . .
142. I am referring to the small, Christmas-style elves and not the tall ethereal types as seen in films such as *The Lord of the Rings*.

heard. So strange was the sound that it caused every single hair on the boy's body to stand on end, a shiver to shoot up his spine.

The boy and the little man conversed with one another for a while, and the little man told Tudur that if he stayed in the valley for a moment, he would witness the most amazing and enchanting dancers in all the land. The little man asked if he would stay and dance, but Tudur refused, saying that a Welsh man cannot dance unless a harp is present. The little man, sounding offended, stated that he could play better music than any harp with his fiddle.

At that moment, he began to play the fiddle, and hundreds upon hundreds of small spritely and elvish beings began scurrying and flying down the sides of the hills and mountains into this valley. They were diverse in appearance, dressed in the strangest of clothing. They seemed to float upon the landscape, as though their footsteps left no dent upon the soil they tread upon. And there they gathered in this glorious valley, formed circles, and began to dance.

They danced like the wind as the music picked up in speed and echoed through the hills. The sound of the music seemed to hypnotise the poor shepherd boy, and he could feel his body begin to move to the beat of the otherworldly fiddle. His fear, however, overpowered this strange ethereal trance, and though he began to sway and move to the music, he would not join the circles these beings had formed. The fiddler pushed and pushed Tudur to join the circles, to dance with them with unbridled joy. Eventually, after being pressured for a while, Tudur snapped at the fiddler and said to him, "Well now, you foul and wicked spirit, play your best, but I will never join those dancing rings!"

Upon hearing these words, the fiddler and the ethereal dancers in the valley all began to transform. The fiddler grew goat horns from his head, a tail sprouted from his lower back, his face grew longer and more frightening, and his legs and feet transformed into furry legs with cloven hooves. The other dancers in the valley began transforming into therianthropic beings. Some looked like goats, others like hounds or foxes, and others like cats.

The sight was indeed terrifying, and Tudur wanted nothing more than to leave this dreadful nightmare. However, the scene seemed to spin around him faster, and faster. He could barely control his own body as he danced within this frightful scene. The music grew louder and faster, and he could hear the strange beings he was among laughing and cackling as they continued their dance.

Then, Tudur heard a voice in the distance. The voice was calling his name. Tudur could just about hear that it was his master's voice, who had come searching for him. Though he could hear his master's voice, he could not see him. And so, with all his might, he mustered up the energy to shout, "Master! Help me! Stop this wicked dance!"

Upon hearing these words, Tudur's master shouted in response, "By the grace of God, stop!"

And as these words echoed through the hills, the ethereal dancers seemed to vanish like spectres on the wind. The entire scene came to a halt, and the valley became quiet and peaceful once more. It was nighttime, and the stars were sparkling in the sky above Tudur's head. The entire ordeal was so terrifying that Tudur immediately collapsed into his master's arms. It is said he was never quite the same after this event. He became a recluse, and those who lived locally knew him forevermore as a strange and wayward man who would not stop muttering about the wicked beings that live in the valley of the ellyllon.[143]

This tale made me believe, in my youth, that the ellyllon were strange spirits who resided in valleys, hollows, woods, and mountains, spirits who could change their shape, cause you to lose control of your own body and mind, and trick you into terrifying situations. They were dangerous, magical entities that one did not wish to come face-to-face with on a walk home. But is that truly who the ellyllon are?

Elves, Goblins, Fairies ... or Phantoms, Devils, Demons?

The first issue we come across when attempting to define ellyllon, especially outside of the confines of the Welsh language, is finding a translation for what exactly they are. The unfortunate truth for non-Welsh speakers, and for a writer like me who writes books on Wales but in English, is that there is no direct translation of ellyll into English.

Many folklorists, scholars, and writers have attempted to come to a suitable English equivalent for the ellyllon for centuries, and yet there is still no clear, commonly accepted translation.

. . . .
143.   My interpretation of the story "Nant Yr Ellyllon" as found in Rowlands, *Chwedlau Gwerin Cymru*,
         40–42.

T. Gwynn Jones describes the ellyllon as frightful and malevolent spectral apparitions.[144] Elias Owen translates ellyll as "goblin" or "hobgoblin."[145] In the glossary of William Rowlands's *Chwedlau Gwerin Cymru*, ellyll is translated to mean "elf."[146] The idea of ellyll being the Welsh equivalent to elf is corroborated by Wirt Sikes and was also the commonly accepted translation among the Welsh speakers I knew growing up.[147]

One need only look up the word ellyll in a Welsh dictionary today and the word will be translated into a multitude of English words such as elves, phantoms, goblins, wraith, demons, shades, fairies, familiar spirits, sprites, and so on.

Yes, the water truly is murky when it comes to translating the word into English. Perhaps it is a word that expresses something in the Welsh cultural continuum that cannot fully be translated. It is a complex word to describe complex beings loaded with contradiction and mystery.

The word has also been used by poets and folklorists to describe fairies in general, or specifically as a synonym for the Tylwyth Teg. For example, Elias Owen in *Welsh Folk-Lore* showcases a Welsh poem that uses the terms interchangeably; however, he then argues that poets likely did this for rhythmic purposes and with poetic liberties. Owen argues that there should be a distinction between ellyll and Tylwyth Teg, as they seem to describe somewhat related yet different beings. I am in agreement with Elias Owen that they are indeed distinct beings that may have occasional parallels but are, nonetheless, separate from one another.

The Celtic scholar Rachel Bromwich, however, leaned into the idea that ellyll is a word that is synonymous with the Tylwyth Teg in her explanatory notes in *Trioedd Ynys Prydein*.[148] The word ellyll appears occasionally in the triads, short texts that allude to aspects of myth and lore. It is believed that the word is mostly used in the triads to mean "spirit," "phantom," or "ghost." Triad 64, for example, focuses on the Tri G'wydd Ellyll Ynys Brydein. In this context, this title of sorts is translated to mean "Three Wild Spectres of the Island of Britain," with ellyll specifically translating to mean "spectres."

. . . .

144.   Jones, *Welsh Folklore and Folk Custom*, 59.

145.   Owen, *Welsh Folk-Lore*, 4, 111, 191.

146.   Rowlands, *Chwedlau Gwerin Cymru*, 70.

147.   Sikes, *British Goblins*, 12.

148.   Bromwich, *Trioedd Ynys Prydein*, 179.

Bromwich also explains that the word ellyll, as it is used in the triads, also seems to allude to the idea of an aspect of a person's spirit that can travel beyond the confines of the body. This idea is also found in the poetry of Dafydd ap Gwilym, such as in the poem titled "Dan Y Bargod" where he states, "Yna y mae f'enaid glân, A'm ellyll yma allan.[149] There is my pure soul, and here my spectre is outside."

This opens up further discussion as to whether the word ellyll was used to describe part of our own spirit or soul that could leave the body. Or perhaps that it is a similar concept to the fetch or supernatural double. That topic deserves far more attention, however, and we will not explore it in depth in this book because it is not entirely relevant here. Yet, the fact this question even arises from exploring the ellyll simply showcases just how complex this being is.[150]

The idea of the ellyllon being demons or devils is in keeping with the Christian idea that all fairies are essentially demonic entities associated with the Christian devil. The usage of ellyll to mean "devil" or "demon" is not very common among Welsh speakers today, at least not in my experience, and yet the underlying belief in this idea still seems to persist. This is apparent to me based on the way in which Welsh speakers have responded when I mention ellyllon to them.

Often, when I have asked friends to define what the ellyllon are without using English terminology, they define them as such: "Ysbrydion annifyr a chas, pethau bach direidus. Nasty spirits, mischievous little things." And yet, on the other hand, they often also describe them as the spirits of the natural world. On numerous occasions I have discussed with various people, both Pagan and non-Pagan, the nature of the ellyllon. Despite very many people stating they are not to be messed with, as they are nasty things, they also make it clear that they are deeply associated with the natural landscape.

Spirits of the Groves, Hollows, and Bogs

In the poem written by an anonymous poet, "Y Niwl Hudolus," it is made quite clear that the Tylwyth Teg reside in a remote location: an Otherworld, a place connected to yet separated from our world, whereas the ellyllon are associated with

. . . .

149.   Parry, ed, *Gwaith Dafydd ap Gwilym*, 244–245.

150.   To read more on the concept of ellyll representing either those who
        became "outside of themselves" or the spirit double, I recommend reading
        the explanatory notes of triad 63 in Bromwich, *Trioedd Ynys Prydein*, and
        also Angelika Rüdiger's literary analysis *Y Tylwyth Teg*.

hollows and earthly places.[151] As we discovered in the previous chapter, the Tyl-wyth Teg are essentially the denizens of the Otherworld, and usually they cross into our world from their own. This does not seem to be the case with the ellyllon, who throughout late medieval and early modern poetry are very much connected to earthly locations such as bogs, valleys, pools, and groves.

This likely echoes folk belief concerning the ellyll at the time, that though perhaps they were somewhat or somehow related to the Tylwyth Teg, they dif-fered in that they originate and dwell in our world.

This is the definition I tend to work with when speaking of the ellyllon. I define them as such: enchanting, mischievous entities that dwell in the natu-ral landscape. They haunt the old ruins of man-made structures that have been reclaimed by nature, as well as the remnants of structures built by our most ancient ancestors. They live in caves, hollows, mounds, and pools. Their shape is not restricted by corporeality, for they can take whatever form they so desire. Their nature mirrors the landscape itself, for while the hills and meadows may be beautiful and inspiring, if we are not careful, nature can be cruel and unforgiving. Just like nature, the ellyllon may entice us with their beauty and their enchanting music, but their mischief may be the end of us. We may never fully comprehend them, but it is important we note their existence and be wary of them.

Poetry and folklore tend to place them as living in burial mounds, hill forts, and other ancient monuments, as well as in valleys and bogs.

Ellyll Dân, the Fires of the Ellyll

The ellyllon are also known for their fire. In a folktale in a book titled *Llen Gwerin Sir Gaernarfon* (*The Folklore of Caernarfonshire*), there is a story that recounts how some of the people who lived in Llanaelhaearn once offended a giant who lived in a place called Tre'r Ceiri.

We know today that Tre'r Ceiri is the remains of an Iron Age fort that sits upon a mountain on the north coast of the Llŷn Peninsula, North Wales. How-ever, Tre'r Ceiri translates to mean "town of the giants." Ceiri shares an origin with the plural word for giants used in Welsh today: Cewri. It was once believed that giants dwelled here.

. . . .
151. Rüdiger, *Y Tylwyth Teg*, 17.

The offended giantess decided to fill her apron with rocks that she gathered as she walked up the mountain. Her intention was to warm these rocks with the sulphurous fires of the ellyll, and then she was to throw the flaming rocks down onto the village of Llanaelhaearn. However, as she was walking, a noble horseman came to speak to her, to dissuade her from causing harm to the village. She dropped the rocks from her apron and thus created one of many monuments to then be named Barclodiad y Gawres (the giantess's apronful).[152] It seems giantesses dropped rocks out of their aprons all over the place at one point in time, for I also grew up near a monument named Barclodiad y Gawres.

In this tale, the fires of the ellyll are described as sulphurous and very much physical and hot in their nature. The story alludes to the idea that the fires of the ellyll are perhaps physical fires warmed and stoked by these phantom-like beings that dwell in the landscape. However, the fires of the ellyll also play another role in our folklore.

Beyond this description of the fire of the ellyllon, the ellyll-dân (ellyll fire) is also described as being a spectral flame-like light that moves across bogs, mountain roads, and rural paths. In this context, we also see these strange lights called Tân Annwn (the fires of the Otherworld).

Wirt Sikes describes the ellyll-dân as "exactly corresponding to the English Will-o'-Wisp, the Scandinavian Lyktgubhe, and the Breton Sand Yan y Tad."[153] He goes on to explain that the ellyll-dân is essentially a type of alluring spectral light. The ellyll-dân lures unsuspecting travellers at night away from the well-beaten path and into the direction of danger. Those who fall victim to its hypnotic enticing glow will find themselves falling into bogs and swamps, where the light then vanishes, leaving them to perish in the darkness.

The ellyll-dân shares a somewhat aesthetic similarity to the Canwyll Corff (corpse candle), a type of spectre, so much so that many writers on the subject of ghost and fairy lore tend to group them as being one and the same.

Like the ellyll-dân, the very sight of the Canwyll Corff was often perceived as an omen of death. The ellyll-dân was a much more overt omen of death, literally leading travellers to their demise in terrain that was dark and difficult to navigate. The Canwyll Corff was more so sometimes a sign that the one who witnessed it

. . . .

152. Fardd, *Llen Gwerin Sir Gaernarfon*, 233.

153. Sikes, *British Goblins*, 18.

may die in the near future. The presence of the Canwyll Corff could also be an omen of a death in the family or in the parish.

The Canwyll Corff is described in a variety of ways across collections of folklore. It is sometimes described as being a "clear white flame, and when far off was as large as the flame of an ordinary lamp, but diminished as it grew nearer, until it was the size of the flame of a common candle."[154]

Other times it is described as small and having a bluish-grey glow. It will hover slowly over the path a person's coffin will take between where they died and the sight of their burial. According to some sources, the flame will come from the mouth of the dead, and the size of the flame depends on the age of the deceased from which the flame originated.[155]

While I acknowledge the similarities in their aesthetic appearance and their natures—a hovering, spectral, phantom light—I personally do not see them as one and the same. The ellyll-dân is described as a mischievous, fairy-like creature intent on playing fatal tricks on those who dare wander in the dead of night. The Canwyll Corff, on the other hand, is directly related to mortal souls. It can be an omen of death but is usually a light that wanders across the "corpse road."

Pwca and Bwbachod

I once had a teacher who was rather fond of folklore. When this teacher discovered I had a love for fairies, he would tell me the odd tale here and there. I remember once I had checked out a copy of *A Midsummer Night's Dream* by Shakespeare. This teacher I mentioned saw me carrying the book and said to me, "You know, Shakespeare learned all he knew about fairies from a Welshman!" He explained to me that there is a character in the play named Puck, whose name and character is based on a type of Welsh fairy, the pwca.

This teacher was known to, as we say in Welsh, malu cachu, which literally translated means to "break manure," but essentially means to make up stories and blabber on about absolutely nothing. And yet, as I grew older and began reading more books on folklore, I would come across this idea quite often. The notion was that William Shakespeare had a Welsh friend called Richard Price, and that he taught Shakespeare all about our fairy lore and folktales.

. . . .
154.   Jenkins, *Bedd Gelert: Its Facts, Fairies, & Folk-Lore*, 84.
155.   Isaac, *Coelion Cymru*, 70.

In the works of many notable Welsh folklorists, you will hear this idea being echoed: that Shakespeare drew upon Welsh legend and lore for quite a lot of his plays. Perhaps it is true, perhaps it is not. Nonetheless, the Scottish poet Thomas Campbell once wrote a letter where he declared that he discovered Shakespeare had visited a place in the south of Wales known as Cwm Pwca (valley of the pwca).[156] Campbell deduced that Puck's name and the events of *A Midsummer Night's Dream* must have happened in this magical valley.

The word pwca and its variations are likely not unfamiliar to you if you are knowledgeable of the folklore of Wales, Ireland, Cornwall, or even Iceland, to name a few! Quite a number of nations have a being in their legend and lore with a name that sounds similar. In Welsh texts you will see mention of pwca, pwci, or pooka. In Irish you may know of púca, in Cornish bucca, and even Icelandic demons are known as púki. All these beings, across diverse cultures, seem to predominately be devilish, mischievous, goblin-like creatures. I find it fascinating that a similar being, with such similar names, exists across so many cultures.

Within our Welsh tradition, the pwca is a fearful, spectral creature that haunts the landscape and can even infiltrate human abodes. Interestingly, Wirt Sikes states that pwca is but another term for the ellyll-dân.[157] This is likely due to the pwca showing up in folktales where they are carrying a lantern upon a path in the rural countryside at night and lure unsuspecting travellers to their doom.

The pwca tends to be a solitary creature, and they are often conflated with nasty, wicked spirits that haunt and hurt people. They are usually invisible, and you would only hear their voice echoing about you. They do not like to be seen and will rain terror upon anyone who catches a glimpse of them without their express permission. On the rare occasion they have been seen, they have been described as impish little creatures, or, contrastingly, as fair, dainty little things.

The Pwca as Familiar Spirit

The most famous folktale concerning a pwca is likely that of Pwca'r Trwyn, which recalls the tale of a pwca that haunted a house or farm in the parish of Mynyddis-lwyn, in what is today Caerphilly. This tale can be found in a number of collections of folklore, including *The Welsh Fairy Book* by W. Jenkyn Thomas. However, the likely earliest written version of this tale can be found in Edmund Jones's *A*

....
156. Sikes, *British Goblins*, 20.
157. Sikes, *British Goblins*, 20.

Relation of Apparitions of Spirits in the County of Monmouth and the Principality of Wales. This text is an eighteenth-century compilation of ghostly and supernatural sightings and experiences. Written by the preacher Edmund Jones, this book is a treasure trove of lore pertaining to ghosts, fairies, and other supernatural beliefs of the time.

Edmund Jones recalls the tale of the spirit that haunts the house of a man named Job John Harry. The word pwca is never used in this version of the story; the being is only referred to as a spirit, but it is clearly the same story, as it has similar events, names, and the same location as the later folkloric versions of the tale.

According to this account, the spirit was drawn to the household because Job John Harry's brother had dabbled in magical spells. Initially, the spirit was a frightful menace, lashing out at people, pelting them with rocks, scratching at them as they tried to sleep. Over time, however, the spirit became part of the household as a "familiar spirit."[158]

As a familiar spirit, the pwca would aid those in the household with certain tasks. He would also tell them secret things that mortals would usually have no ability to know. In this role, the pwca seems incredibly similar to the spirit familiars that magicians and witches are known to work with. We will explore the concept of fairies and fairy beings as familiar spirits in more depth in a later chapter.

The pwca's willingness to aid with certain tasks around the household also fits the role of a household fairy or spirit. In W. Jenkyn Thomas's retelling of the story, the pwca helps a farm maid with her chores, such as spinning wool, cleaning, and ironing. The farm maiden would leave offerings for him of fresh milk and slices of white bread. He would also speak to her as a disembodied voice, which seemed to come from the oven or hearth.[159]

The Bwbach

The pwca was not the only fairy creature within our lore that was said to be a household-dwelling spirit, which offerings were laid out for. Another household spirit was the bwbach. The word bwbach itself is interesting, as it can essentially be translated to mean "bugbear," and the word bwbachu can be used as a verb in the Welsh language meaning "to scare or frighten someone." This would imply that the bwbach was something rather frightening.

. . . .
158.   Jones, *A Relation of Apparitions of Spirits in the County of Monmouth and the Principality of Wales*, 30–33.
159.   Thomas, *The Welsh Fairy Book*, 248–252.

The idea of the bwbach being a frightening or terrifying spectre is one that T. Gwynn Jones echoes, as he categorises the bwbach as one of many ghostly terrifying apparitions.[160]

The primary text we can glean information regarding the bwbach from is Wirt Sikes's *British Goblins*. Sikes describes the bwbachod as good-natured goblins that reward those who keep the household tidy and warm.[161] One notable thing that Sikes also says about the bwbach is that it is very animalistic in appearance, being small and covered in brown fur or hair.[162]

The bwbach and the pwca share so many traits that it is very easy to wonder if they are indeed the same beings, perhaps the different names simply being a matter of location and time. They are both ghostly, fearsome beings who can be tricky and malevolent toward humans. The bwbach is not fond of preachers, religious people, and those who abstain from the joys and merriment of life in favour of a pious life. It also has the ability to change its shape, even sometimes transforming into a mirror image of the person it is haunting.

There are also tales of people leaving offerings out in their homes for both the pwca and the bwbach, the pwca being offered bread and milk and the bwbach being given fresh cream as well as the offering of a tidy and warm house. The pwca can become offended if the offering is not up to its standards, and once the pwca is offended, it goes back to causing mischief and pain for the household, regardless of how amicable it had been previously.

There are only two things I find that clearly differentiate these two fairy creatures in our lore, the first being appearance, with the bwbach being described as a furry little thing, and the pwca being a small imp or a fair and dainty, but mostly hairless, creature. Though, it is hinted that both beings can change their shape. The second is that we have accounts of the pwca moving from household to household, as well as stating that they originate in the natural world.

For example, in Edmund Jones's account of the haunting of Job John Harry's house, the spirit one day reveals to the household that it comes from a place called Pwll y Gaseg (the pit or pool of the mare).[163] Pwll y Gaseg is a place in the mountains above the house. In Thomas's telling of the tale of Pwca'r Trwyn, it is

. . . .

160. Jones, *Welsh Folklore and Folk Custom*, 59.

161. Sikes, *British Goblins*, 30.

162. Sikes, *British Goblins*, 133.

163. Jones, *A Relation of Apparitions of Spirits in the County of Monmouth and the Principality of Wales*, 33.

said that the pwca has the ability to enter physical objects, such as a ball of yarn or a jug of barm, and as such move from one place to another.[164] Once the pwca has left a place, it will never return.

Bwganod

The word bwgan is another worth mentioning here. Growing up, we were told stories of bwganod, which I had always interpreted as being ghouls, ghosts, or foul monsters. As a child, my parents would often take us to Caergybi (Holyhead), a town located on the small island of Holy Island, which is separated from the Isle of Anglesey by a narrow strait. After a day of shopping in town, we would usually go and get some fish and chips, and we would drive down to a beach called Porth Dafarch to eat. Along the winding little roads we would take toward the beach, there stood in a small, secluded spot a tall, looming, and glorious upright stone. This stone is called Carreg y Bwgan. Though, we always dropped the y (which means "the") and would simply call it Carreg Bwgan.

On dark winter nights, as we trundled down the bumpy road toward the beach, if there were no other cars in sight, my father would often stop the car directly next to the stone and he would tell us that if we sat there long enough, the stone would turn into a terrifying bwgan and chase after us. My younger brother and I would scream and beg from the back of the car for him to carry on driving so that the bwgan wouldn't get us.

A bwgan in my mind was always a frightful creature that might leap at you from the brambles and drag you into the dark abyss of the Otherworld. We also use the word to describe certain things, such as scarecrows. A scarecrow in Welsh is a bwgan brain, which translates to roughly mean "crow ghost" or "crow hobgoblin." We also referred to pumpkins at Calan Gaeaf (Halloween) as bwgan rwdan, which is likely an older term for the carved turnips or swedes people made at Halloween before pumpkins became common here, as rwdan means "turnip" or "swede."

The bwgan was a ghoulish and terrifying creature that haunted our nightmares as children. Our parents would warn us that if we stayed out too late, a bwgan would get us. But what does any of this have to do with the bwbach or the pwca?

. . . .
164. Thomas, *The Welsh Fairy Book*, 248.

The words bwbach and bwgan specifically serve a common purpose. They both describe a bugbear, hobgoblin, or nasty ghost. Further, though the bwgan in Welsh lore is predominately a frightening and dangerous monster, the word itself shares commonalities with words to describe a type of household fairy like the bwbach. A few common translations of bwgan and bwbach are often "bogie, bugbear, bug-a-boo, bogey-man, bogey-beast." In the Welsh Marches, specifically in Cheshire and Montgomeryshire, a household spirit is buggan.[165] The word buggan and the Welsh word bwgan are pronounced the same, and buggan may be an anglicisation of bwgan, or perhaps they share a common origin.

Perhaps bwgan is yet another word to describe a being within the same family as the pwca and the bwbachod, a frightening and mischievous ghoul that may occasionally attach themselves to a person, family, house, or piece of land.

Exercise
Dedicating a Space to Give Offerings to the Household Fairy

I would like to introduce you to the Welsh word aelwyd. This word means "hearth," the very beating heart of the home. Take a moment to just consider: Where is the heart of your home? Who is the heart of your home? What place, or what person, in your household is that central hub all inhabitants gravitate toward?

When we hear stories of the importance of the hearth, it's easy for us to think that the hearth of our homes must match that of our ancestors. A hearth to us is a fire or a stove where food is prepared. But the aelwyd is so much more than simply a fireplace or a cooker. In this modern day and age, where we have central heating and fidgety electric ovens tucked away in our kitchens … what is the equivalent of the hearth?

Perhaps it's a room where everyone gathers to watch television on a Saturday night. Perhaps it is the dining room, where every Sunday you gather to have a nice roast dinner. Really sit with the question: Where is the heart of your home? Perhaps the heart of your home is not a place, but a person. Maybe you live in a multigenerational home, and everyone gathers around a grandmother as she dispenses cookies or hard truths

- - - - - - - - - - - - - - - -
165.   Burne, *Shropshire Folk-Lore*, 45.

from her cosy armchair. Perhaps the heart of the home is that one room-mate who ensures all the bills are paid on time and everyone is keeping up with their chores for the week. Where, or who, is the heart?

As we have seen from these tales concerning the fairies of the house-hold, people once left offerings for the spirits or beings that resided within the home. They would usually leave these offerings by the hob, near the hearth, or next to the oven. They perceived that the spirit of the household resided in the warmest part of the home, both physically and emotionally. So where is that for your home?

Once you have determined where the heart of your home is, see if you can easily set up a space near the heart for a small, dedicated space to leave offerings. If the heart of your home is a person, and it is safe for you to do so, ask them where they think would be best to leave offerings for the household fairy.

Once you have found your space, make it look cosy and inviting. Perhaps find a small cloth or piece of fabric to lay down, or if you are someone who enjoys crafting, make one! A cute crochet doily would be perfect. Find a nice bowl, cup, or plate, an object that can house the offer-ings of your choice. It doesn't have to be anything expensive or fancy; the plates and cups I use for my offerings are quirky little things I found at an antique mall.

Now that you have your space set up, you can regularly come and leave offerings to the household fairy. Even if you do not believe you have a household fairy, there is nothing wrong with forging a loving relation-ship with the very essence of your home. And remember, according to the story of Pwca'r Trwyn, sometimes certain familiar spirits are drawn to you simply because you chose to dabble in magic.

Similar to the stories told in this chapter, you could offer the house-hold fairy bread, fresh milk, or cream. Alternatively, give something valu-able. I offer my household fairies baked goods, because I love a slice of cake or a homemade cookie, and giving away some of that which I con-sider a valuable treat feels more effective than giving something I do not particularly care about giving away. I have known folks in the past who offer coins, coffee, shiny rocks they find on their walks, tea, alcohol, and even poetry to their household fairy.

Trust me, you will know if you have offered the incorrect thing. As the stories tell, household fairies become rather nasty when offended. And so, if things begin to go awry at home, perhaps prepare better offerings!

Coblynnau

The word coblyn and its plural form coblynnau may seem somewhat familiar to those who know of the goblin. The Welsh word coblyn is more or less pronounced exactly like goblin, except with a hard K sound at the beginning instead of a G. It is clear these words share an etymological root.

One would be forgiven for assuming that the coblynnau, then, are essentially the same, or at least deeply similar to, the malicious, wicked little goblin fiends. However, you would be mistaken in thinking that, for the coblynnau are often described as benevolent, good-natured beings.

While coblynnau is the most common term you will find in books on folklore regarding these entities, they are also referred to as cnocars or "knockers." Similar beings can be found in Cornish lore as well.

The coblynnau are associated with rocky, earthly places such as caves, crevices, and, more specifically, mines. They are often described by folklorists as "mine spirits" due to the fact that they are mostly seen or heard deep in the mines.

Wales is a nation that has long been influenced by its mining culture. Upon this land we have mines that extracted coal, copper, gold, iron ore, lead, and silver, to name a few of the bounties rich within our ground. It is likely unsurprising to anyone with even the slightest knowledge of Welsh history that there would be bountiful superstitions and folk beliefs concerning our mines. On the island where I was raised, there is an ancient copper mine that has a history that extends back to the Bronze Age. Mining has been part of the very fabric of this nation for thousands of years.

However, we must ask ourselves: Are the coblynnau truly "mine spirits," or are they subterranean rock spirits we have come to associate with mining, due to mining being one activity that led us into contact with them?

The above question is one I have always pondered, though it is worth noting that the coblynnau seem to be described as miners themselves. They are rarely ever seen, only heard, and the noises they make mimic the noises made by miners. Mine workers often reported hearing the sounds of pickaxes, shovels, blasting, and holes being bored.

In a letter written by the eighteenth-century antiquarian and botanist William Morris, he describes the belief in the knockers, as he refers to them, in Cardiganshire. One of the most interesting aspects of the letter is the way he explains how the miners themselves feel about these fantastical beings:

> Our old miners are no more concerned at hearing them blasting, boring holes, landing leads, than if they were some of their own people and a single miner will stay in the work in the dead of night without any man near him and never think of any harm that they will do him, for they have a notion the knockers are of their own tribe and profession and are a harmless people who mean well.[166]

The letter recalls how older, seasoned miners are not in any way perturbed by the presence of the knockers or coblynnau, though it is made clear in one portion of the letter that younger, newer miners are often scared of them. They are most notably found in newer mines, where human activity is a novel thing, and once good ore has been struck in the mine, the phantom sounds of the coblynnau will come to an end. They are allies to miners, leading them to good ore.

So, though they may be earthly, rocky spirits, they are also miners themselves according to these aspects of the lore. The human miners see them as colleagues, as they bore into the depths of the earth.

In some Cornish accounts, offerings would be left to the spirits of the mines. In a tale recorded by the folklorist Katharine Briggs, a miner named Old Trenwith would leave a tenth of all the ore he had mined for the knockers.[167] A Cornish friend of mine also once told me that miners would often take pasties down into the mines for lunch, and they would eat the entire pasty except for the crust, which they would leave in the mine as an offering to the knockers.

. . . .
166.   Lloyd, ed., *A Book of Wales*, 291–292.

167.   Briggs, *Abbey Lubbers, Banshees & Boggarts*, 106–107.

Spirits of the Deeper Parts of Our World

Within my personal practice, I view the coblynnau as the spirits who reside in the subterranean parts of our world. They are the beings who reside within rock, dirt, and stone. They can be experienced in caves and upon rocky formations. When pondering over the classical element of earth, I believe that the ellyll rule over the pools, ponds, groves, and woodlands of our landscape, whereas the coblynnau are of the very depths of the apparent world.

Though, it is important to acknowledge that it is not as clear-cut as this. The ellyll are also said to reside in caves and craggy valleys. I personally perceive all of the entities spoken of thus far as beings that inhabit the very landscape upon which we walk. They are there, in every bramble bush, in every peat bog, in every cave and cliff. When I work my magic and call upon the powers of the land, sometimes they hear the call and may choose to aid me in my work.

While the denizens of the Otherworld—the Tylwyth Teg, Bendith y Mamau, Plant Annwfn, etc.—originate in a world beyond our own, beings such as the ellyll, pwca, and the coblynnau seem to be inextricably linked to our own world. They are of this plane of existence just like us, yet are strange, liminal beings. Though, despite this, they are often found in the company of the Tylwyth Teg and still hinted at being under the rulership of Gwyn ap Nudd in various tales and pieces of poetry.

Not quite spirit and yet very much spectral in nature, they are betwixt and between the very breadth of our perception. Perhaps we will never fully comprehend what exactly they are, and yet they coexist with us in this lived reality.

I believe a line from Shakespeare's *Macbeth*, uttered by the character Banquo as a description of the three witches, best explains how I would personally define these imperceivable wild and enchanting beings: "The Earth hath bubbles, as the water has, and these are of them."[168]

Gwrachod

Any Welsh speaker will likely read the title of this section and be somewhat confused. In modern Welsh, Gwrach and its plural form Gwrachod are the words we use to describe a witch or witches. I myself don the label of witch when speaking English, as I am sure many of you reading do too. So why am I including witches

. . . .
168.   Shakespeare, *Macbeth*, Act 1, Scene 3.

in this section of the book, where I am focusing on goblins, ghouls, and spirits of the land?

To understand that, we must first explore the word Gwrach. In my previous book, *Welsh Witchcraft*, I explained that I do not refer to myself as a Gwrach in my native language, despite this being the word I was taught from a very young age meant "witch." So why do I not embrace the word? Well, to put it simply, the main reason I do not use this word is that we have so many other, more suitable words to describe a practitioner of our native magical arts.

Some of these more suitable words include Swynwraig/Swynwr/Swynydd, Gwiddan/Gwiddon, Hudolwr/Hudoles, Dewin/Dewines, Dyn/Gwraig Hysbys, Dyn/Gwraig Cyfarwydd. This is but a taste of some of our native terms to describe those who are learned in the various expressions of magic found in our culture. I implore you to look to my previous book to learn more about them.[169] I refer to myself as a Swynwraig (charmer). Historically the charmers were magical practitioners who were predominately learned in a handful of magical charms that were passed down to them. Though, many Swynydd also practiced a variety of other magical arts beyond charming, especially divination. Swynwraig is a feminine term, with the masculine equivalent being Swynwr and a gender-neutral equivalent being Swynydd.

I have a fondness for the term Swynwraig because it is a word that makes my very soul sing. The word makes me think of Swyngyfaredd, a term that describes the very practice of magic and I often translate to mean "the art of enchantment." Swynwraig speaks to me on a much more visceral level than Gwrach ever did.

Gwrach is also a term that is much more complex. While today it has come to mean the traditional, stereotypical Halloween image of the cackling wicked witch, its history is multifaceted.

Originally the term was essentially used to describe anything grotesque or disgusting.[170] It sounds that way too! In my native language, when I want to exclaim that something is gross, I say, "Ach a fi!" and that "Ach" at the beginning has the

....

169. I speak of Welsh magical practitioner terminology in pages 24–27 of *Welsh Witchcraft*, and if you prefer to hear the words spoken aloud, I also have videos on both my YouTube channel and my Patreon. More info on where to find said videos will be in the back of this book.

170. Suggett, *A History of Magic and Witchcraft in Wales*, 42–43.

same feeling as the final part of Gwrach. It's difficult to say the word Gwrach without sounding absolutely repulsed. It later became a rather offensive word that targeted older women, similar to hag or beldam in English.

Interestingly, the term Gwrach was never used during the very few and rare witch trials that occurred in Wales. Instead, the courts often utilised a loan word, wits, which was essentially a cymricisation of the English word witch.

This is all very interesting, but what do Gwrachod have to do with fairy-like creatures such as the ellyllon, coblynnau, and bwbachod?

When I was growing up, I was rather obsessed with witches. Though, I noticed from a very young age that the Gwrachod of Welsh folklore tended to be quite different to the witches in other fairy tales and books and those who appeared on my television screen. While the witch was, in my mind, essentially a magical woman, sometimes wicked and cruel like the witches found in the tales collected by the Brothers Grimm or the Wicked Witch in *The Wizard of Oz*, the Gwrachod seemed to be something else entirely.

Gwrach y Rhibyn is one of the most well-known Gwrachod found within our lore. Though her title is often translated into English as the "witch" or "hag of the mist," the word rhibyn more so refers to a long strip of land or the edge of a cliff or quarry. She resides in a liminal place, at the very edge of something. She is likely referred to as the Witch of the Mist in English because she is said to inhabit and travel upon thick fog or mist.

Her very appearance was considered an omen of some evil that was to befall the people who saw her, and often this meant death. She is considered a death portent and is described as looking wild and haggard.

Her appearance is strange; she is said to not only be hideous—with blackened teeth, a body that looks undead, and unruly hair—but she also sometimes sprouts leathery, bat-like wings from her back.

Though a Gwrach in modern Welsh would be understood to be a witch or a hag, many folklorists have described Gwrach y Rhibyn instead with fairy-like terminology. Myrddin Fardd mentions that she is sometimes referred to as an ellyll hedegog (winged or flying ellyll).[171] Wirt Sikes refers to her as a goblin.[172]

. . . .
171. Fardd, *Llen Gwerin Sir Gaernarfon*, 104–105.
172. Sikes, *British Goblins*, 216.

Another folkloric Gwrach similar to Gwrach y Rhibyn is Hen Wrach Cors Fochno (the old witch/hag of Cors Fochno). This Gwrach lives in a peat bog in Ceredigion, in mid-Wales. She lurks around the misty bog in the dead of night and terrifies the locals of the nearby village of Borth. She is described as being incredibly tall, around seven feet in height, with jet-black hair that is so long it trails across the floor. She is thin and bony, as though close to death, and her skin is a sickly shade of yellow. When she bares her teeth, they are black as coal, and her head itself is absolutely gigantic.[173]

In one story, a woman saw the Gwrach one night while walking through the bog, and the Gwrach blew in her face. The poor woman was never the same after that incident. The Gwrach is said to be able to cause illnesses by simply blowing upon mortals. She would venture into the villages in the dead of night and breathe upon sleeping folk, which would render them feverish.

It almost sounds as though the Gwrach in this tale is the very personification of a terrible illness that may have swept communities in this area. Similarly, Gwrach y Rhibyn, as an omen of disaster, could easily be perceived as a personification of death and misery.

These are but two examples of the many Gwrachod within our folktales that are not simply mortal women who gained a notorious reputation for casting wicked spells, but are instead monstrous, goblin-like entities that are the very causes of death, disease, disaster, and misery.

In various cultures, the line between witch and fairy is often blurred, as there are many crossovers in lore pertaining to both.

In the Dafydd ap Gwilym poem "Y Niwl," he mentions Gwrachïod Annwn (the witches/hags of the Otherworld) who travel in the company of the Tylwyth Teg and the ellyllon.[174] This link between Gwrachod and the fair folk and ellyllon can be found in various streams of folk belief too. There is a cave in the Clwydian range known as Ogof Gwen Goch that was said to be the home of a Gwrach named Gwen Goch (Red Gwen). Gwen Goch lived in this cave in the company of the ellyllon, whom she was allied with. The ellyllon aided Gwen Goch in her mischief and magic.[175]

. . . .

173. Isaac, *Coelion Cymru*, 42–49.

174. Parry, ed., *Gwaith Dafydd ap Gwilym*, 184–185.

175. Isaac, *Coelion Cymru*, 111.

It seems there is a clear link between Gwrachod and the enchanting entities that dwell in the landscape around us. They travel in each other's company, live together, and share similar characteristics and abilities. Perhaps a Gwrach was never a witch in the first place, but instead the same ilk as the ellyllon, coblynnau, and pwca.

Gods and Spirits
of the Land

Many locations across Wales are tied to gods of old. Great lakes are said to be the homes of powerful, magical goddesses. Divine wizard-poets weave and utter their song spells, shaping the kingdoms and the people of the land. Otherworldly kings and queens slip through the mists into our world, galloping upon their mighty steeds, initiating adventure to unsuspecting mortals.

The mythical landscape these gods live within is teeming with magical life. Along the coast, mermaids swim alongside fishing boats. Sometimes they are tangled up in fishing nets or are beached along the shores of this land and interact with mortals. In the depths of the rural mountainous regions, giants walk, causing the very earth to shake as they take each step. Their bodies, upon their deaths, become the land itself, and the landscape is shaped by their choices to move stones that are nothing but tiny toys to them.

While the previous chapters of this book have focused intently on beings we would consider fairy, this chapter broadens its horizons to look at beings, entities, creatures, and characters that could have a fairy connection. Some of the gods, spirits, and beings mentioned here may indeed be obviously assigned as fairy to some, but their fairy nature is somewhat subjective.

First, we will explore gods who are associated with all things fairy, though perhaps not as overtly as, say, Gwyn ap Nudd or Arawn. Take, for example, Rhiannon, whose otherworldly nature is alluded to. From experience, I have found that referring to Rhiannon as a "fairy maiden" tends to evoke one of two reactions from people. They either raise their brow in confusion and argue that Rhiannon is not a fairy, or they wholeheartedly agree that she is certainly a denizen of the Otherworld.

To explore deities such as Rhiannon, we must also ask a few questions: *Who* and *what* are the gods of Wales? Are they *really* gods? And what associates them with fairies? Some of the deities explored will have clear fairy connections, while others are connected to that which we may consider fairy only via tenuous threads of lore, hints, and echoes.

We will then explore more of the beings that reside within the Welsh mythical and folkloric landscape that are fairy adjacent or who do not fit anywhere else within the confines of this book, beings such as giants and mermaids.

Overall, I hope that this chapter will provide two things for you, dear reader: First, for those who wish to develop a magical or spiritual practice connected to fairy beliefs, this will provide an insight into a somewhat devotional approach. Which gods, beyond the obvious king of fairies we have in our lore, can we devote ourselves to? And how? And second, this chapter will provide even further context toward the mythical landscape that influences beliefs in fairies and magic.

Who Are the "Gods" of Wales?

The purpose of this book is not, at its core, to aid you in building a devotional relationship with gods, per se. Perhaps another book of that nature will manifest soon. However, as a polytheist myself, I thought it beneficial for the broader context of this topic, as well as an act of devotion to the gods I venerate, to include some of the gods whose lore and identities are deeply entrenched in the realm of all things fairy.

However, before I begin simply listing some gods and their connection to the Otherworld or to fairy lore, there are a few things I must touch upon. First, who are the gods of Wales? Where do they come from?

This question is more difficult to approach than one might think. It may be enticing to believe that the gods of Wales venerated by modern-day Pagans and witches such as myself are to be found in the evidence of pre-Christian remains from the past, that perhaps the information we glean about our gods comes from ancient mythology or shrines we have found that our ancestors built in honour of the Divine. Unfortunately, this is not quite the case.

The gods we consider "Welsh gods" today primarily come from Welsh medieval literature and poetry. Rhiannon, Cerridwen, Brân, Lleu Llaw Gyffes, Arianrhod…these are all deities I have seen countless Pagans and witches from across the world revere. Every single one of them is found within medieval literature, poetry, and later folklore. The works that these gods are found within were scribed by Christians, during a Christian period, and not once in the literature are they referred to as gods.

This has led many who study these tales from a scholarly perspective to turn their nose up at modern Pagan practice and think us all a bit silly. Why are we worshipping literary figures from a Christianised culture?

Well, an argument could be made that these characters originate in possibly pre-Christian lore and belief. Or at least, they could be based on older figures that long predate the manuscripts they are preserved in.

We know with some level of certainty that the stories, as they are preserved, are far older than what we can date the manuscripts to.[176] It is believed that these stories have their origin in an oral tradition of storytelling. The big question, however, is whether that oral tradition the tales originated in extends back to the pre-Christian period at all.

Unfortunately, this is a question we may never truly have answered. Some scholars, such as Professor Ronald Hutton, believe that any preservation of pre-Christian belief found in the texts is tenuous and scattered at best, whereas earlier scholars, such as Rachel Bromwich, concluded that the stories preserved in medieval literature are the medieval expression of myths concerning Brythonic gods.[177] Bromwich explores, throughout the notes found in *Trioedd Ynys Prydein*, how certain characters found within the literature have names that are cognate with older deities. Beli Mawr, for example, the father of characters such as Gwydion and Arianrhod, is cognate with the Gaulish god Belenos. Mabon, the divine son of the divine mother, is cognate with Maponos.

Essentially, these characters' roles as "gods" is up for debate. Many who approach Welsh medieval texts from a scholarly angle may struggle to understand

. . . .

176.   Davies, *Pedeir Keinc y Mabinogi*, 6.

177.   Hutton, *Finding Lost Gods in Wales*; Bromwich, *Trioedd Ynys Prydein*, lxxii.

the need to view these characters as gods; however, scholarly study does not necessarily dictate devotional or theological needs.

Regardless of whether these characters were gods in an ancient past, they have become revered gods today via the process of apotheosis. While archaeologists may never find any shrines to Cerridwen from the ancient past, you can visit a temple dedicated to her in Bala today, as well as in other towns and cities across the world. While there may or may not have been a cult of Rhiannon long ago, there are certainly groups, orders, and covens dedicated to her today.

Something need not be ancient in order to be authentic and fulfilling as a spiritual practice.

And beyond all of this, as a woman who grew up in Wales, I've seen these characters become emblems of our national identity. For centuries bards have sung the songs of these gods. Perhaps they never called them gods, but writing poetry in their honour, preserving their stories and identities, is in my eyes a devotional act. The stories of our land have become the conduit for the culture, symbols of all it means to be Welsh.

The fact of the matter is, these gods speak to something deep within us at a cellular level. Their stories have been part of our culture and folk traditions for an incredibly long time. There is a reason we are so drawn to these stories and these entities; we feel a visceral need for them. I am not saying this purely from a Pagan perspective, but from a cultural one too.

These gods are alive and well and have been for an incredibly long time in regions such as where I grew up. I knew them long before I ever considered them gods, and yet I can say with some clarity that they resided within part of my being in a similar manner to gods, even without me realising it at the time. I feel many Welsh people may agree with that sentiment.

Gods Connected to fairies

The gods I have chosen to focus on here are those connected to fairies in some capacity. While it is not by any means an exhaustive list of all otherworldly entities, it is more so an exploration of deities venerated today who have ties to the fairy faith of Wales. Deities you will not see mentioned here are the likes of Gwyn ap Nudd or Arawn, who were explored in more depth in the first two chapters of this book.

While there may be more deities who belong here, these are the deities I call upon when working magic or wishing to undertake certain practices that may involve all things fairy and otherworldly.

Rhiannon

Rhiannon's name itself is our first clue of her being an otherworldly divine or great queen.[178] And that is certainly the essence she exudes throughout the stories that feature her. She is headstrong, independent, magical, and powerful.

Within many modern Pagan communities, Rhiannon is primarily regarded as a beautiful, regal goddess of sovereignty. People focus intently on her association with horses and her inherently divine and magical qualities. However, one aspect of Rhiannon I believe is often overlooked is her cunning and tricksy nature.

When the man she was initially betrothed to, Gwawl ap Clud, interrupts her wedding feast and tricks Pwyll into agreeing to give him Rhiannon back, it is Rhiannon herself who comes up with a cunning and mischievous plan to deal with him. She employs a magical bag that can never be filled. Gwawl, in trying to deceive Pwyll, ends up deceived and humiliated at the hands of Rhiannon's trickery. This is a quality not unlike the tricksy and mischievous fairies of our folklore.

Some might cringe at the mere thought of me referring to Rhiannon as a fairy; however, there is an abundance of evidence that Rhiannon is indeed a denizen of the Otherworld. From the moment we meet her, otherworldly motifs surround her. She is dressed in a golden brocaded silk gown, she rides a white horse, and she performs acts that cannot be described in any way other than magical.

When she appears upon her horse before Pwyll and his men, no earthly power is able to stop her. No horse is quick enough, no man powerful enough to stop her. The only thing that stops her is Pwyll asking her to stop by invoking the sake of the man she loves most.[179] The fact Pwyll invokes Rhiannon's love to beckon her to him reminds me greatly of the invocation to Gwyn ap Nudd mentioned in chapter 2 of this book. When people would invoke the power of Gwyn

178. Davies, *The Mabinogion*, 230.

179. Davies, *The Mabinogion*, 10.

ap Nudd, they would do so by invoking the name of his beloved: "For the love of your mate, permit us to enter your dwelling."[180]

Rhiannon makes clear that this is the correct way to garner her attention. This could teach us a lot about how to interact with otherworldly entities. There is a tendency among magical practitioners to assume that spirits, gods, and liminal otherworldly beings exist purely for us to work with and utilise. Some forget that they have agency and lives of their own. If we wish to call upon them within our magic, we must first get their attention, and if we wish to garner their attention, we should diligently determine the correct way of doing so, so as to begin the relationship on good footing.

Rhiannon's first appearance is also incredibly similar to the motifs found in fairy bride legends. In most fairy bride tales, the mortal man must complete a task of some kind to gain the fairy's attention and get her to agree to marry him. Rhiannon sends Pwyll and his men on quite the ordeal before they finally figure out that it might be best to simply ask her to stop. One could say that Rhiannon is essentially the blueprint for the fairy bride legend.

Rhiannon is the daughter of Hyfaidd Hen, a possible other king of the Otherworld. His court is described in the first branch of the Mabinogi as being quite opulent, and its courtiers dress in brocaded silks as those of Annwfn do.

Rhiannon is clearly otherworldly and magical in nature, though her otherworldly qualities seem to diminish as her story goes on. It seems that by marrying a mortal man, even one with the title Pen Annwfn (chief of Annwfn), and assimilating to mortal society, she becomes inherently mortal herself.

I have come across many devotees to Rhiannon who regard her as a queen of fairies, an otherworldly goddess whom they call to in order to part the mists and commune with the enchanting forces of Annwfn. Just remember, if you want her attention, you must first ask her to stop and take notice of you.

Exercise
Parting the Mists and Connecting to Rhiannon

There is a lot of talk in witchcraft spaces as of late of deities choosing us, as opposed to it being the other way around. In order to work with

---

180.   Lindahl, McNamara, and Lindow, eds., *Medieval Folklore*, 190.

or devote yourself to a specific deity, some claim, you must first hear "the call" from them. While I do not doubt that perhaps some people truly have heard a call or felt signs directing them toward specific deities, I am quite adamantly against the notion that this is the one true way to begin a relationship with deity. You can also simply make the choice to honour, work with, and call to a deity yourself.

You need not wait for permission to offer a prayer to a goddess, nor await some grand experience that pushes you in their direction. Perhaps the initiatory step in forging a devotional or magical relationship with a deity is simply reading about them or coming across imagery associated with them. We can look to countless cultures across the world, ancient and modern, and realise that the gods people choose to venerate and call to are often chosen because of need, desire, love, or regionality.

The notion of every single modern-day witch or Pagan having to wait for a deity to reach to us first baffles me, as it has no historical context upon which to draw, and I believe it often hinders newcomers who think they must have some transcendental oracular experience caused by divine intervention before they can begin a devotional relationship.

It is, however, part of my belief that it is never a bad idea to at least put feelers out while developing a devotional relationship. And that is exactly what this exercise is: a method of reaching out to a goddess to simply say hello. An initial step to developing what will potentially become a beautiful relationship.

This exercise outlines a method of initiating a devotional relationship with Rhiannon. It is an exercise I constructed many a moon ago for myself when first forging a relationship with this great queen and sovereignty goddess. Over the years I have returned to the rite, often around the beginning of the month of May when I personally feel Rhiannon's presence more strongly than at any other time of year.

Choose a Liminal Time

I recommend this rite be carried out at a liminal time of day, preferably sunrise or sunset. Within my personal practice, I associate Rhiannon with the sun. She has always appeared to me as a gleaming goddess riding upon a white horse. Within the first branch of the Mabinogi, she appears initially dressed in brocaded silks of gleaming gold and moves before Pwyll's men across the landscape in a manner that no human could ever catch up to. Like the sun moving across the sky through the day, only to vanish beyond the horizon.

Because of these solar associations, I prefer to work this rite as the sun is rising. I like to envision that the sun rising into view is like Rhiannon coming into Pwyll's vision as he stood atop Gorsedd Arberth. Because of this imagery, I also like to carry out this rite somewhere high, such as upon a hill or cliff that overlooks the landscape before me.

However, I believe this rite could be adapted to suit any liminal period of time, allowing the magic of a time between time to give a boost to the work being carried out. Choose a time that feels right to you and works with your current needs.

An Offering of Smoke and Words

Before setting off to perform your rite, first write a letter or poem to Rhiannon. Write it from the heart. Within the Welsh cultural continuum, words have immense power, and our bardic tradition is at the heart of our devotion to our land and our stories. I believe people often overlook the value of words as an offering to the gods or to the spirits of place.

One need not be a seasoned poet to offer divinely inspired words. A heartfelt letter, a touching song, a collection of words that spring to mind—these can all be truly powerful. Return to the Maen Awenyddol or inspired stone exercise found in the first chapter of this book, and use it to aid in writing out something dedicated to Rhiannon. I am leaving this instruction vague so that you might allow your creative self to produce something truly personal and of the heart. If the words do not flow, perhaps a painting or a piece of art would be more suitable.

While creating your offering and preparing for the rite, choose an incense blend that you believe represents Rhiannon. I usually choose a blend that is sweet, floral, and heady, or, alternatively, a blend that utilises local plants that grow in abundance.

Your words (or art) alongside the incense will act as your offerings during this rite.

The Call

Take yourself to your chosen location at your chosen liminal time with offerings at the ready. Once there, sit for a while and connect deeply to the space. Close your eyes and simply sense the very living quality of the space, the spirit present there. Perform whatever practices you have that will aid you in connecting deeper to this space and preparing yourself for magical work.

Take a moment to also consider Rhiannon's initial appearance in the first branch of the Mabinogi. Visualise Pwyll atop Gorsedd Arberth, looking at the landscape before him. See, with your mind's eye, Rhiannon emerging into his vision: a glorious figure dressed in gleaming golden silks, riding atop a white horse. See her vanish before his eyes into the distance, like the sun setting on a clear summer's night. And then remember how Pwyll called to her eventually, requesting she stop. And she stopped.

If it aids you in connecting to Rhiannon and to the story, take your preferred copy of the Mabinogion with you to the location and read that part of the story either to yourself or out loud.

When you are ready, look to the sky, raise your arms skyward, and call to her. If you so wish, you may utilise this invocation:

O Rhiannon,

Cariad mamwys y tir,

Duwies, arglwyddes,

Er mwyn y gŵr a geri fwyaf,

Aros amdanaf!

O Rhiannon,

Maternal spirit of this land,

Goddess, Great Queen,

For the sake of he you love the most,

Wait for me!

Light your incense at this moment and offer it to Rhiannon. I like to announce the offering by stating: "Offrymaf arogldarth yr wyf wedi paratoi, arogl dda, i ti, fy Nuwies. I offer this incense, sweet scent, to you, O Goddess."

Turn your attention to your creative offering. If it is a written piece of poetry or a letter, read it aloud to Rhiannon at this moment, with passion. If it is art, simply follow what you did with the incense and offer it to the goddess.

Sit for a while again, feel the presence of Rhiannon, and allow your offerings to rise into the air. Allow your words to echo throughout the location and for the intention behind this rite to be at the forefront of your mind.

At this point, I like to recite the following words three times.

Dreams that come to me tonight,
Brought forth by the Goddess bright,
Sing to me with birds of bliss,
Show me visions I can't miss.
Oh Goddess, I call to thee,
By the might of three times three,
I extend my hand to you,
Know that my intent is true.

When the rite is done and you have taken yourself home, begin to take note of all things that may make you think of Rhiannon. Take note of her presence in dreams or visions, appreciate when things in everyday life make you think of her. Simply allow her presence to flood various parts of your day-to-day life.

From here onward, continue to nurture a devotional relationship with Rhiannon. Construct a small shrine or altar space for her if you are able to in your home. Leave offerings to her. Acknowledge her presence in your life whenever you glance at the dedicated space. You have made first contact, have asked her to take notice of you, and now, as with any real-life relationship, you continue to water the seeds you have planted.

Gwydion

Gwydion, son of Dôn, is a magical character who tends to use his magic in order to cause mischief, or some would say wickedness. He is best known for the role he plays in the fourth branch of the Mabinogi. Via his magic, he tricks Pryderi, the son of Pwyll, into giving him pigs sent to him from Annwfn itself. He trades the pigs for twelve horses, twelve hounds, and twelve golden shields.

This deal may sound wonderful—some otherworldly pigs for all of this? Brilliant! Except that the horses, and the hounds, and the shields were all illusions. Gwydion had conjured them by magic.

He is a wizard full of trickery and deceit. And yet, it is not these qualities that have landed him on this list alongside gods associated with fairies. Though Gwydion is indeed a magical and mischievous character, there is nothing particularly otherworldly about him. He is earthly, albeit learned in the magical arts. However, it seems he may have become somewhat of a fairy character in later lore.

W. Y. Evans-Wentz collected a testimony in his book *The Fairy Faith in Celtic Countries* regarding a belief concerning Gwydion. A justice of peace named David Williams, from Carmarthen, said to Evans-Wentz that, according to his knowledge, the king of the Tylwyth Teg was Gwydion ab Don.[181]

According to the testimony, Gwydion, as king of fairies, resided in the stars in his fort, Caer Gwydion. The term Caer Gwydion is still used to this day in the Welsh language as a name for the Milky Way. Gwydion also has a queen, according to this testimony, named Gwenhidw, whom we will discuss in more detail in the section on mermaids.

Evans-Wentz's work is often seen today as the go-to manual for understanding fairies within a Celtic context. However, it is important to acknowledge that Evans-Wentz was a theosophist, and his work was likely influenced and filtered via that worldview. Further, his scholarship has been questioned as time goes by, meaning we should not take all that is written in his work as holy text.[182] I would hesitate to add this testimony to this book if it were not for the fact it is incredibly interesting and that there is further lore concerning Gwydion within a fairy context.

· · · · · · · · · · · · · · · ·

181.   Evans-Wentz, *The Fairy Faith in Celtic Countries*, 151–152.

182.   Rüdiger, *Y Tylwyth Teg*, 244–249.

In the 1990s, the Welsh television network had a series titled *Tu Hwnt i'r Deall* (*Beyond Belief*). The series dealt with the mysteries of our world. One episode captivates me above all others. This episode is mentioned in Professor Ronald Hutton's *Triumph of the Moon*, and Hutton himself is one of the interviewees on the episode. [183]

The episode focused on a secretive magical group operating on the Isle of Anglesey. I spoke in great detail about this group in my previous book, *Welsh Witchcraft*. [184] The group was named Cylch Cyfrin (secret or mystic circle), and they were followers of Gwydion. *Tu Hwnt i'r Deall* interviewed a member of this secretive magical group, and he explained that Gwydion was essentially their primary god.

The reason I am bringing this up is because, according to this tradition's lore, Gwydion had three sons: Eog Agor or Altor, Eog Ellyll, and Eog Gorach.

These names are incredibly intriguing. Eog means "salmon," and perhaps this has ties to the idea of the salmon of knowledge found in various Celtic traditions, and notably in Wales in the tale of Culhwch and Olwen. Agor or Altor seems to have been a conduit between the group's members and their god, Gwydion. Ellyll and gorach, on the other hand, are both words associated with fairies, ellyll of course being the phantom-like beings that dwell in the valleys and bogs. Gorach is a mutation of corach, used in modern Welsh to refer to Earth-dwelling fairies comparable to gnomes or dwarves in other cultures, from the Welsh word cor meaning "dwarf" or "pygmy." Interestingly, there is little to no older lore pertaining to beings known as corach in Welsh folklore, yet here we see the word being used to describe a child of Gwydion.

One interviewee also states that the fairies were essentially Gwydion's children. They exist either in a different dimension to our own, or under the ground and beneath the sea.

This magical group also worked most of their magic at liminal places, especially at lakes. Here we have, essentially, a magical group that devoted themselves to Gwydion and worked with the forces of the Otherworld, a group that claimed to have existed long before the start of the twentieth century, as the interviewee was said to have been initiated into it by his mother.

· · · · · · · · · · · · · · · ·

183. Hutton, *The Triumph of the Moon*, 303.

184. Starling, *Welsh Witchcraft*, 41–42.

Taking all of this into consideration, we could consider Gwydion as an alternate candidate for the king of fairies. There is quite clearly something within Welsh folk tradition that alludes to Gwydion's association with the fair folk. Perhaps it is his connection to the natural world that ties him to such things. After all, he conjured a woman out of flowers in the Mabinogion and summoned an army of trees in the *Kat Godeu*.

Merlin

The world-famous wizard Merlin may seem like a strange addition to this chapter. What does he have to do with Welsh deities? And in what way does he relate to fairies? The answers to these questions are complex.

Merlin as a legendary or mythic figure is incredibly complicated, and it would take far more words than I have allowed here to fully capture who he is and his origins. His very existence is multilayered and the sources that mention him are varied. We all know Merlin; he has become the archetypal wizard of the modern age, but the Merlin we know today is an amalgamation of various figures found in various legends and myths from numerous places.

The Merlin of the Welsh

Allow me to begin by briefly exploring how Merlin fits into the Welsh cultural continuum. Merlin as we know him today likely came to us, within a modern context, directly from the works of the twelfth-century writer Geoffrey of Monmouth. Whenever Merlin appears within modern fantasy, and media in general, most of the lore surrounding him can be traced to Geoffrey's work.

Likely best known for his *Historia Regum Britanniae*, or *The History of the Kings of Britain*, one of Geoffrey's earliest works featured the legendary Merlin. *Prophetiae Merlini* (*The Prophecies of Merlin*) is a series of prophecies apparently uttered by Merlin himself. Geoffrey would also go on to write *Vita Merlini*, a text that recorded the life and history of Merlin.

However, much of Geoffrey of Monmouth's work regarding Merlin was inspired by earlier Welsh texts. For example, Geoffrey's Merlinus was in part inspired by a boy named Ambrosius, or Emrys in Welsh, who appeared in a ninth-century text written in Gwynedd, North Wales.[185] The story of Emrys is known to many across Wales. It concerns King Vortigern, who, try as he might,

....
185. Williams, *The Celtic Myths That Shape the Way We Think*, 83.

cannot build a castle in Eryri. The castle walls continually fall down night after night, and so under the guidance of his wise men or wizards, he finds a local boy to sacrifice to the land. The boy ends up being a wise prophet who states the reason the walls continually fall is because of a battle happening beneath the ground between two dragons.[186]

The dragons beneath the castle are metaphors for the constant battles between the native Britons and the invading Saxons at the time of Vortigern's rule. The young boy utters a prophecy that states the red dragon, representing the Britons, ancestors of the Welsh, will vanquish the white dragon, representing the invading forces, eventually.

The imagery of this prophecy was upheld well into the future by kings who utilised the dragon upon their banners. Eventually it would become the national emblem of Wales, and it is why the red dragon still stands proudly upon our flag.

Emrys is but one piece of the complex puzzle that came together to create the Merlin we know today. Geoffrey also took inspiration from Myrddin Wyllt, a poetic prophet and wild man found in various medieval Welsh poems. Myrddin was present at a great battle that left him deeply traumatised, and so he went on to live the remainder of his wild existence in Coed Celyddon, or the Caledonian Forest, located in what is today the western lowlands of Scotland.

Yes, Merlin is a character deeply entrenched within Welsh lore. Many aspects of vernacular Welsh literature aided in inspiring the Merlin presented by Geoffrey of Monmouth. Merlin has now become a steady part of pop culture in general and has captivated the folk beliefs and traditions of Britain and certain parts of Europe for centuries.

Many corners of the modern-day United Kingdom lay claim to Merlin, and they all have valid reason to. Within traditional lore he is all over the place.

The boy-prophet Emrys is located in what is today Dinas Emrys, North Wales. Myrddin Wyllt is located in Yr Hen Ogledd (the old north) in the lowlands of Scotland and the northernmost parts of England. In later Welsh tradition he becomes associated with Ynys Enlli, Bardsey Island, where he resides with the thirteen treasures of Britain. Geoffrey of Monmouth pinpoints his origin as being Caerfyrddin in South Wales; Caerfyrddin, literally translated, means "the

. . . .
186.   A fuller version of this tale can be found in my previous book, *Welsh Witchcraft*, 120–122.

fort of Myrddin." And later lore would of course associate him with Tintagel in Cornwall and Glastonbury in England.

Merlin's Fairy Associations

The easiest way to connect Merlin to anything fairy in nature would be to look at Geoffrey of Monmouth's *The History of the Kings of Britain*. It is mentioned in this work that Merlin's father is a supernatural fairy-like being. Many modern translations use the word incubus to describe exactly what his father was.[187]

While this supernatural origin is certainly interesting and has been utilised in various modern adaptations of Merlin's story, I believe there is more that can link Merlin and the Welsh characters he is based on to the fairy tradition and, more specifically, the Otherworld.

While today Merlin is referred to as a wizard, older texts allude more so to him being a prophet and a bard. Bards, as we have already established, draw their creative inspiration from the Otherworld. In fact, there are links between Merlin, or more specifically his older counterpart Myrddin, and the most legendary bard in the Welsh cultural continuum, Taliesin.

In the sixteenth-century manuscript known as *Elis Gruffydd's Chronicles*, held in the National Library of Wales as NLW 5276D, we see a reference to Taliesin and Merlin potentially being the same entity. This manuscript includes the *Ystoria Taliesin*, the folktale of Taliesin's birth, but the text within this manuscript I am focusing on here is known as *The Death of Merlin*.

In this text, there is one particular passage of note regarding Merlin and Taliesin. The writer, Elis Gruffydd, explains how Merlin is essentially a spirit that takes human form and will sometimes vanish but be reborn in a later generation. And, specifically, he states that in the time of early sixth-century ruler Maelgwn Gwynedd, the spirit was known as Taliesin.[188]

This little snippet of information seems to allude to there being some form of prophetic, inspired spirit that takes human form from time to time. Merlin held this spirit, and so did Taliesin. Two faces of the same spirit.

· · · · · · · · · · · · · · · ·

187. Thorpe, *The History of the Kings of Britain*, 167–168.

188. Gruffydd, *Tales of Merlin, Arthur, and the Magic Arts*, 92.

Both Taliesin and Merlin are deeply embedded within the lore of the Otherworld, whether it be by their prophetic bardic natures or via very explicit references to magic and otherworldly motifs within their lore.

What Taliesin and Merlin can teach us is that a connection with the liminal otherworldly forces can bring forth an inspired, creative state. They teach us that the very wisdom of the Otherworld seeps into our world, awaiting vessels, which are poets, bards, and magical practitioners who will give voice to the moving, prophetic spirit and breathe it into the world.

Fairy-Adjacent Beings

Now let us turn our attention to more fairy, or fairy-adjacent, beings. Here I have focused primarily on mermaids and giants. One could argue mermaids are certainly an ocean-dwelling fairy, whereas giants are debatable. Nonetheless, giants are worth a mention for their importance in our traditional lore and their influence on the mythic landscape.

Môr-Forwynion, Mermaids

In 1603, in the village of Pendine in Carmarthenshire, a young yeoman named Thomas Raynold spotted something extraordinary in the sea: a creature that, from the waist up, resembled a beautiful woman. From the waist down, however, she was a monstrous fish creature. Thomas could not believe his eyes. He called others to come see this fantastical sight. There they stood, their eyes transfixed upon this glorious mystical creature before them.[189]

This story is recorded in a small seventeenth-century pamphlet in English. It is not the only mermaid sighting in Wales. In 1858, a mermaid was spotted between Fishguard and St. Davids.[190] Additionally, in 1910, a local Pembrokeshire newspaper printed a strange story concerning a woman whom people believed was a mermaid that had risen from the depths of Pwll Deri.[191]

With so many fishing communities and coastal villages, it would not be a shock if Wales boasted numerous sea-based lore. However, the nineteenth-century folklorist Wirt Sikes claimed that mermaids are notably absent from our folklore

. . . .

189.   P. G., *A most strange and true report of a monsterous fish.*

190.   Jones, *Welsh Folklore and Folk Custom*, 84–85.

191.   "Was it a Mermaid?" *The Pembrokeshire Herald and General Advertiser*, 1910.

in general.[192] While the idea that mermaids are completely absent is quite clearly untrue, considering the instances listed in the previous paragraph, they are somewhat rare compared to, say, beautiful fair maidens who seem to rise ethereally out of the lakes.

Growing up, the only mermaid story I had ever been told was the tale of the Conwy mermaid. The beautiful historic town of Conwy, with its dramatic castle overlooking the sea, was not too far to travel to when I lived on the Isle of Anglesey. If you choose to catch the train from the island into England, you have to pass through this place, and my, what an experience that is! As you enter the town, you are greeted by the medieval fortress with its lofty towers. As the train passes the castle, your breath is taken away once more as you cross the river Conwy and look out toward the harbour. This is truly a place where land, sea, and sky sing in complete harmony.

Whenever I pass through, and it is quite frequently now that I live along the border and must travel by train to go home and visit family, I cannot help but gaze at the water and think of the Conwy mermaid.

The version of the tale I grew up with went as follows.

Long ago, a mermaid got herself stuck on the shore as the tide went out at Conwy. She was gasping for the sea but could not muster up the strength to drag herself back to the water. Many people gathered, watching her as she suffered. They were mesmerised by the fact they were seeing a real mermaid.

She screamed to the people, begging them to help her, asking them to please carry her back to the water or else she would die. Eventually a group of local fishermen, giggling and whispering, went and picked her up. She was so glad they had decided to help!

Alas, her hopes were dashed as the men carried her toward the town, away from the water. They paraded her through the streets, singing and being merry as they showed off their prize they had caught down by the sea. During this entire ordeal, the mermaid continued to beg for them to take her back to her watery home.

No kindness would come from the men nor any of the people of Conwy. With her dying breath, she cursed the town. She cursed the place and the people, saying that nothing would come for them but poverty, disease, and disaster for the unkindness they showed her.

From what I've heard, various fires, floods, outbreaks of diseases, and bad times followed in the many years after the curse was cast. Many believe the curse has now run its course, though I have yet to ask someone who lives in Conwy if they agree with that statement.

The name for a mermaid in the Welsh language is môr-forwyn, which literally translates to "sea-maiden."

A quick note: I often hear folks from outside of Wales saying that a morgen is a Welsh mermaid. While morgens do indeed seem to be mermaid-like beings, they are part of Breton folklore, not Welsh, to the best of my knowledge. I have yet to come across a single piece of folklore from Wales that relates to mermaids as morgens or morgans, aside from in more modern works that usually have no sources attributed to them.

While I might be incorrect, even while researching this book, I could not find any reputable sources to substantiate the idea that the word morgen was ever used to describe a mermaid in Welsh. Further, I had never even heard this word in relation to mermaids until I was well into my late teens. The term we used growing up was always môr-forwyn. I only bring this up in case you are wondering why I am not mentioning morgens in this section.

In the late 1800s, the writer and poet Owen Wynne Jones, under the bardic name Glasynys, published a story called "Y Fôrforwyn," which tells the tale of a mermaid who marries a mortal man. This tale is told in the traditional fairy bride style, with the mortal man stealing a magical object belonging to the mermaid, without which she cannot return to the sea. Eventually she does find this object and heads back to her watery home, but in a twist to the usual tale, the story then follows as the man attempts to recapture her.[193]

Gwyn ap Nudd as Ruler of the Seas

 Glasynys was, in my opinion, divinely touched in the art of storytelling. He drew upon copious elements of traditional lore and crafted stories that evoked a sense of ancient knowledge while breathing new life into these ideas. His work

. . . .
193.   This tale can be found in the collection of folktales, stories, and histories *Cymru Fu*, 434–444.

would go on to even inspire later folklore beyond his time. Interestingly, Gwyn ap Nudd appears in "Y Fôrforwyn," where he is depicted as a ruler of the sea. Glasynys drew upon elements of Gwyn's lore and came to the conclusion that he was deeply associated with the sea.

While it may seem strange to consider Gwyn a ruler of the sea, when one considers it at any depth, things begin to click into place.

In "How Culhwch Won Olwen," Gwyn is said to ride upon a horse named Du, which belongs to a man named Moro Oerfeddog. There is another horse mentioned in Welsh poetry with the name of Du, and that is Du y Moroedd (black of the seas). Scholars seem to agree that Du, the steed of Gwyn ap Nudd in "How Culhwch Won Olwen," and Du y Moroedd (or in modern Welsh, Du'r Moroedd) are one and the same.[194]

Du'r Moroedd is a horse that can gallop across the waves of the ocean. Gwyn ap Nudd rides upon his back. Couple this with the notion that the Otherworld is often depicted as a place accessible via water, across water, or even under the sea, and the idea that the king of fairy is associated with the sea begins to make much more sense.

Treat the Merfolk with Kindness

Though they do not appear very much, when mermaids do make their appearance in Welsh lore, it is wise to be kind to them. Stories like that of the Conwy mermaid showcase that merfolk hold the powers of the raging seas. A storm brews within them and they will release that storm in an instant if you treat them badly.

Two contrasting stories showcase the importance of treating the merfolk well even more so. There are two tales featuring fishermen who capture a mermaid in their nets, and both stories have very different endings. A man from near Caernarfon in North Wales once caught a mermaid, and she begged him to release her. When he refused, the mermaid eventually died from not being in the water, and just like the Conwy mermaid, she cursed the man with her dying breath. From then on, he lived a life of poor health and miserable luck.[195]

Down in the south of Wales, in Pembrokeshire, another man also caught a mermaid. Upon being caught, she told him that if he were to release her, she

. . . .

194.   Rüdiger, *Y Tylwyth Teg*, 91.

195.   Owen, *Welsh Folk-Lore*, 142–143.

would ensure no bad would ever come to him nor his boat ever again. And so, he set her back into the sea. Not too long after this incident, he was out fishing when suddenly he heard a voice calling his name. He looked overboard and spotted the mermaid calling to him, "Pull up your nets, get back to shore! All the ships that remain here will soon be done for!" He followed her instructions and headed back to the shore. The moment he tied his boat up at the harbour, a huge storm could be seen out over the sea. Many fishermen died that day on the tempestuous waters, but he survived. The mermaid warned him of deadly storms two times after this.[196]

The etiquette of dealing with mermaids seems the same as the etiquette of dealing with any otherworldly entity. Treat them with compassion, respect, and most importantly, distance.

Gwenhudwy, Shepherd of the Waves

The poet and scholar T. Gwynn Jones noted in his book *Welsh Folklore and Folk Custom* a belief that he had heard of but could not find a source to verify, that there was a folk character named Gwenhudwy, who was a mermaid shepherd.[197] The waves of the sea were her flock, and every ninth wave was a ram.[198] The name Gwenhudwy is intriguing as it could be translated to mean "fair/blessed water spell/water magic." Essentially, it translates to "blessed sea spell." It is a name that evokes the idea of mystic, blessed waters.

Could she then be considered a sea deity or mermaid queen? A mermaid who is a shepherd to the waves of the sea, she who directs the waves as if they were her flock?

There is also a brief mention of Gwenhudwy in W. Jenkyn Thomas's *The Welsh Fairy Book*, in the story of Cantre'r Gwaelod (bottom hundred). Cantre'r Gwaelod is a legendary drowned region of Wales, a place that is now submerged beneath the waves. In Thomas's retelling of this classic tale, Elphin, the son of Gwyddno Garanhir, king of Cantre'r Gwaelod, is fishing under an ancient ash tree by the banks of a river. As he is peacefully enjoying the sound of the rushing

· · · · · · · · · · · · · · · · ·

196.   Jones, *Welsh Folklore and Folk Custom*, 84–85.

197.   This name has various spelling variations; you may find her name as either Gwenhudwy, or Gwenhidwy, or Genhudiw. I will use the variant Gwenhudwy for the remainder of this book, for it seems to be the oldest spelling of her name.

198.   Jones, *Welsh Folklore and Folk Custom*, 84–85.

water of the river and the gentle autumnal breeze, out of nowhere a strong gust of wind rushes through the trees. Upon the wind he hears a voice that whispers, "Beware the oppressions of Gwenhudwy!"[199]

We learn via this telling of the tale that Gwyddno Garanhir himself had also heard the portentous whisperings on the wind. Apparently, due to the fear these warnings caused in Gwyddno's heart, he had tried his best to avoid going anywhere near the sea since he'd first heard them.

The words act as a motif throughout the story as a spectral voice seems to warn of the drowning of this land. The fact that the warning is specifically a warning of the oppressions of this sea shepherd makes it all the clearer that she is a powerful and unforgiving mover of the waves of the sea.

The oldest mention of Gwenhudwy seems to come from a sixteenth-century poem by a bard called Rhys Llwyd ap Rhys ap Rhicert. In a poem where he describes a voyage to the beautiful Ynys Enlli, an island off the coast of the Llŷn Peninsula that is packed with legend and lore, he describes the waves of the sea as the sheep and rams of Gwenhudwy.[200] The fact that she appears in sixteenth-century poetry within this context implies she was already part of folk tradition by this point, and possibly is an earlier figure.

The only other reference to Gwenhudwy worth mentioning is found in *The Fairy Faith in Celtic Countries* by W. Y. Evans-Wentz. As mentioned earlier in the section on Gwydion, the mythical wizard Gwydion is described in a testimony recorded by Evans-Wentz as a king of the Tylwyth Teg. In this same account, Gwenhudwy (spelled as Gwenhidw) is said to be his queen.[201] The testimony also states that he who gave this information to Evans-Wentz said that his mother would call small fleece-like clouds the sheep of Gwenhidw. In this instance, she seems to have become more so a sky-based fairy figure as opposed to a mermaid shepherd. Still, the idea of her having some form of watery flock remained, this time clouds instead of waves.

Though she is as difficult to grasp as the clouds themselves, Gwenhudwy seems to be an entity intrinsically linked with the very movements of the sea. The waves that crash against our cliffs are her flock, she shepherds them, and as such

. . . .

199. Thomas, *The Welsh Fairy Book*, 27–41.

200. Jones, *Welsh Folklore and Folk Custom*, 84–85.

201. Evans-Wentz, *The Fairy Faith in Celtic Countries*, 151–152.

she can be frightening. Her power over the waves can bring down ships, drown those who enter her depths, and flood entire cities.

For many years now, within my personal practice, I have considered her the queen of the waves. She is the mermaid shepherd of the seas, and her power is to be found in those places where the foam of the sea froths upon the crashing waves and is thrown by the winds. In my tradition, Llŷr is god of the seas, but Gwenhudwy is the tempestuous and powerful voice of the waves.

Cewri, Giants

In the tale of *Iarlles y Ffynnon* (*The Lady of the Well*), often found in compilations of the Mabinogion, there appears a great and intriguing giant figure. This figure is described as having one eye in the middle of his forehead and one foot. The giant is considered incredibly ugly, and he carries a huge iron club that would take the strength of two men to carry. He is known as the Keeper of the Forest.

This foreboding figure sits atop a mound in a clearing amidst the trees of a dense forest. A regal stag stands beside him. When the heroes of the tale from which he originates ask him what power he holds, he declares, "I will show you," and he picks up his mighty club and strikes the deer beside him. The deer, upon being struck, lets out the most unearthly bellow that echoes throughout the forest, causing the heroes to jump in fright.

Then, as if by magic, in answer to the call of the stag, all the creatures of the forest in their great numbers gather like an assembly before the Keeper. They bow before him, and he commands them to return to their grazing. All the creatures, great and small, rush back into the depths of their woodland homes. With that, the giant turns to the heroes and says, "*That* is my power," with a prideful grin.

The Keeper of the Forest is an interesting character, and yet one that is often overlooked. To my Pagan sensibility, he gives off the imagery of a great and powerful forest god. The mere image of him sat upon a mound with one foot touching the ground, one arm holding his enormous club, and a stag beside him evokes an image similar to that of Cernunnos found on one of the plates of the infamous Gundestrup cauldron. This black-haired rugged creature is as tough, unbecoming, and wild as the woodlands and the animals he rules over.

The presence of a monstrous giant in a chivalrous tale such as this would make one think the noble heroes in the story who interact with him, Cynon and

Owain, would end up needing to battle him as a foe. Yet, this is not the Keeper's function in this tale. He acts instead as a guide, leading the heroes onto the correct path for them to complete their task. While he is rude and described as grotesque, he poses no real threat to the men. They leave him be, and he leaves them be, perhaps an allegory for how we should treat the natural world—with respect and courtesy.

While the notion that giants and fairies may have anything at all in common might seem a strange and novel idea at first glance, they share a common mythic landscape. Giants, like fairies, are beings that are very much associated with the natural world. Rural, quiet locations that are just beyond the domain of mortals are their stomping ground.

As we saw in the folktale concerning the Giantess of Tre'r Ceiri in the last chapter, giants sometimes interacted with entities such as the ellyll and their fires. Giants are certainly, in my eyes, fairy adjacent, inhabiting the liminal, otherworldly, and rustic parts of our world. I believe a knowledge of giants and their place in the mythic and folkloric landscape is incredibly helpful in building a good picture of all things fairy within the Welsh context.

The Foundations of the Land

Giants are often associated with the formation of the landscape, hills, cliffs, and mounds, or they literally make up parts of the landscape. Take, for example, the folkloric motif of the Giantess's Apronful. I grew up near a prehistoric burial chamber known as Barclodiad y Gawres. The name of this monument translates to mean the "giantess's apronful."

We know today that this impressive cruciform burial chamber, with its earthen mound and elaborately decorated stones, was likely a prehistoric tomb, due to archaeological work finding evidence of burial rites here.[202] However, long before these burial mounds and ancient monuments were truly studied or understood, people made sense of them in the only way they knew how. These structures were often attributed as being the work of giants, and that is obvious from their names.

The story of Barclodiad y Gawres states that a giantess was once wandering with a stack of large stones in her apron, when her apron strings snapped, and

. . . .
202. Lynch, *Prehistoric Anglesey*, 34–43.

she dropped the rocks at her feet. Out of frustration, the giantess simply left the stones where they landed, and there they remain to this day.

This particular type of story is a common folkloric motif found across Wales. Many ancient sites don the name Barclodiad y Gawres, or its potentially earlier variant Arffedogiad y Gawres, which means the same thing. We also see sites called Baich y Gawres (the giantess's burden), and Crud y Gawres (the giantess's cradle). And, of course, who could forget the fact that the remains of a vast Iron Age hill fort located atop a mountain in the Llŷn Peninsula, North Wales, is called Tre'r Ceiri, meaning "town of the giants."

Yes, giants feature prominently in the folklore concerning standing stones, burial chambers, and ancient monuments. It is hard to believe sometimes that the gargantuan upright stones we see today at ancient sites were put there by the people of the past and not by giants or by magic. The Welsh name for the world-famous Stonehenge is even Côr Y Cewri, meaning "the assembly, circle, or choir of the giants."

It is not simply that giants were used as a means of explaining these impressive stone monuments, however; giants were also very much considered instrumental in shaping the very landscape upon which we walk daily.

Take Yr Wyddfa, for example, the peak of the tallest mountain in Wales. Known today in English as Snowdon, because there is often snow sitting upon the peak, the native name has ties to legend and lore concerning King Arthur and a great giant monarch.

According to legend, there was once a great and ferocious giant named Rhitta Gawr who dwelled amidst the mountains of North Wales. Rhitta became tired of all the squabbling mortals who lived near him that referred to themselves as kings, and he decided to attack two warring kings, Nynio and Peibio.

Rhitta vanquished these two already weakened kingdoms and crowned himself king. As a further sign of disrespect, Rhitta shaved off the kings' beards, their very emblems of manliness and strength, and wove the beards into his cloak.

As time went on, the many kings of Britain came to fight Rhitta, but he defeated them one by one, every time adding a new beard to his cloak. Eventually he defeated nearly all the kings—all, that is, except the legendary King Arthur. Rhitta, in his arrogance, sent a messenger to Arthur, requesting he shave his beard and send it to Rhitta so that he may add it to his cloak and spare him the embarrassment of shaving it off himself.

Arthur was furious at the audacity of this giant, and so he rode out and met with Rhitta atop the tallest mountain in Eryri. There they had a tremendous battle, but it was Arthur, with a last swish of his sword, who dealt the last blow and won. Rhitta was so injured that he died on the spot. Arthur commanded his men to place stones atop Rhitta's body, and thus his stone-covered body became the peak of the tallest mountain. From then onward, the peak of the mountain was known as Gwyddfa Rhitta (Rhitta's grave). This name evolved to become what we call it today, Yr Wyddfa.[203]

There are many tales like this one that associate giants with certain natural landmarks, from another mountain named Cadair Idris, associated as being the chair of the giant Idris Gawr, to the giant named Gwendol Wrekin ap Shenkin ap Mynyddmawr, who formed a hill known as the Wrekin in the Shropshire area of the Welsh Marches.

With these many examples we see that giants often feature in onomastic tales to explain the very formation of the land and as an explanation for the strange ancient monuments that line the landscape. In this regard, we may consider giants as ancient, earthly beings connected to the very fabric of the soil upon which we walk, mighty beings whose bodies make up the hills and mounds, part of the rock and dirt itself.

Interestingly, giants, if they have names in tales, tend to have names associated with the natural world. Take, for example, Ysbaddaden Pencawr, the giant father of Olwen in the tale of "How Culhwch Won Olwen." This giant's name translates to essentially mean "Hawthorn, chief giant." Even Brân, or Bendigeidfran, from the second branch of the Mabinogi, has a name that translates to mean "crow" or "corvid." Their connection to the natural world seems apparent, even in myths where they are portrayed as noble kings.

An entire book could be made purely on the subject of giant lore, as there is so much more that is worth mentioning than this. I implore you to delve deeper into the lore concerning giants if you wish to glean an understanding of the mythic landscape of Wales. This is but a snapshot into these intriguing titans of our lore.

. . . .

203.   This tale is my own retelling based on those found in works such as Rhys, *Olion Cewri*, as found in
       Rhyddiaeth Gymraeg Y Gyfrol Gyntaf, 130–133, and Huws, *Straeon Gwerin Ardal Eryri Cyfrol 2*, 456–457.

fairy flora
and fauna

"From grasses bright, and bracken light, come, sweet companions, come!" So the poetic translation of a common old Welsh poem about the Tylwyth Teg goes. Though, a literal translation of the opening line of "Cân y Tylwyth Teg" would actually be "From grasses fair, and delicate ferns, sweet companions come!"

Fairies have long been associated with the natural world and its virtues. It's an element of fairy lore only further exaggerated in the Victorian era through to the early twentieth century, as images of Cicely Mary Barker and Margaret Tarrant's flower fairies were ever so popular. Despite the twee imagery playing down and sanitising the true nature of fairies, it would be a mistake to assume that the association between fairies and flowers or trees is purely a romanticised, modern idea.

Throughout our folklore, fairies dance beneath ancient trees, mix concoctions out of fragrant herbs, and are averse to certain prickly shrubs. In the first part of this chapter, we will be exploring trees, plants, herbs, and fungi associated with fairies. As we explore these associations, I will also include little insights of how to incorporate these plants and such into your own magical practice, if you so desire.

The second part of this chapter will focus on fairy animals. This will include a look at animals associated with fairies or the Otherworld, as well as animals that are of the Otherworld themselves.

Trees and Plants Associated with Fairies

Let us begin by exploring some of the trees and plants that are associated with fairies within Welsh lore. This will be but a brief overview of the extensive plant lore found in Wales.

Along with plants and trees, we will also touch briefly upon fungi, as Welsh lore seems to adore associating fungi, mushrooms, toadstools and such with the fair folk, an association not unbeknownst to us in the modern day, as mushrooms and fairies tend to go hand in hand on an aesthetic level.

When looking at plants, trees, and fungi, we must first establish that we can separate belief surrounding their associations with fairies into two categories. First, apotropaic. Apotropaic is a term used to denote a thing that holds the power to protect an individual, home, or community. Essentially, protective forms of magic or belief. Certain plants and trees were said to avert the mischief and malice of the fair folk. We will discuss apotropaic plants and trees first.

Second, there are plants, trees, and fungi that are believed to be beloved by the fair folk. These plants, trees, and fungi, rather than keeping the fair folk at bay, seem to draw them closer to us. They have a fondness for these, and many stories and pieces of folk belief express their connection to them. We will discuss the plants, trees, and fungi beloved by the fairies later in this section.

Apotropaic Plants and Trees

As we will explore in the next chapter, interactions with the fairies were not desirable to the everyday person throughout history. While magical practitioners were often in relationship with fairies, for the average non-magically inclined person, they were dangerous entities worthy of avoiding.

The fairies could cause malice upon your life, and if you were not learned in how to deal with them and commune with them, you would want to avoid any interaction with them at all costs. While there were obvious methods of keeping the fairies away, such as hanging iron above doorways, there were also plants and trees that were said to be imbued with a virtue that was undesirable to the fair folk.

Eithin—Gorse

Gorse shrubs are found in abundance across the width and breadth of Wales. From the rural coastal paths, to dotting the roadsides on the outskirts of towns, it is not too difficult to find this prickly, evergreen shrub. In fairy lore, it is said the fairies are particularly averse to this common plant.

Gorse shrubs are robust evergreen plants covered in rather terrifying large thorns. They have yellow flowers between January and June and are ubiquitous in my mind with country roads. Many country roads around the island upon which I grew up were lined with gorse, as were the coastal paths around the coves and beaches.

In Welsh they are called eithin, and you may come across cottages and farms called things such as Tŷ Eithin (gorse house) or Cwm Eithin (eithin valley) in rural villages.

Gorse has been used for centuries for an abundance of reasons, such as fuel for fires or as a colourant in dyes. In older folk tradition, however, the plant was specifically said to protect people or land from the fairies.

The folklorist Wirt Sikes stated that the gorse acted as a barrier for fairies, that they could not or would not go anywhere near a household or area where gorse was present.[204] A hedge or fence surrounding a property composed of gorse would keep them away, and a barrier of gorse in windows or doorways would ensure they would not bother you at night while you slept.

A particular story associated with this belief comes from Caergybi, or Holyhead, a town on Holy Island just off the coast of Anglesey. An elderly lady named Mrs. Stanley was so troubled by the fairies that she constructed a barricade of gorse around her bed.[205] A similar story of the gorse barricade can be found in *The Welsh Fairy Book*, but that story is set in Carmarthenshire.[206]

When dealing with the mischief and malice of the fairies, a branch of the gorse shrub laid across the window or hung above the bed may keep them at bay. Though it seems it is the branches and the thorns they are particularly averse to, as some stories feature the fairies wearing the flowers upon their clothes.

. . . .

204. Sikes, *British Goblins*, 115.

205. Sikes, *British Goblins*, 115–116.

206. Thomas, *The Welsh Fairy Book*, 262–265.

Cerddinen/Criafol—Rowan

The rowan is one of my favourite trees. On an aesthetic level, the trees are simply beautiful, with their feather-like leaves and their scarlet berries that gleam in the summer sun as they ripen. This tree is as common nowadays as the gorse we spoke of, as it has become the tree of choice to plant along roadsides and in modern developments. This glorious fruit-bearing tree, however, is absolutely packed with folklore.

Even the Woodland Trust on their official website reference the folkloric qualities of this tree. Though in other cultures and traditions this tree has become synonymous with deities and witches, in Welsh lore it is viewed as a tree that protects from the fairies.

Sticks of the rowan tree laid across a bed would protect the sleeper from being harassed by fairies.[207] Similarly, keeping a stick of the rowan tree above where a baby sleeps would protect the child from being stolen by the fairies. Rings and crosses fashioned of rowan wood, as well as the dried berries strung up in the household, kept all evil away from the household.[208] The trees planted outside the home would keep the ellyll and wicked spirits away, and the berries or wood, carried by a person under the spell or curse of a fairy, would render the fairy magic ineffective.[209]

As a modern-day Swynwraig, when people approach me claiming they believe some form of wicked entity is causing havoc for them in their home, I will often fashion rings of rowan wood or strings of the dried berries for them to place around the household.

Beyond the rowan tree's protective qualities, it is also associated with divination. In particular, the spirit of rowan was worked with at Nôs Galan Gaeaf (October 31) in divinatory practices known as Rhamanta, which were usually carried out by young women. Rhamanta is essentially a practice of romantic divination, wherein young maidens would divine about their future lovers or husbands. Some women would construct mattresses from rowan leaves and fern seeds, as well as pillows from maidenhair to sleep on the night before carrying

· · · · · · · · · · · · · · · · ·

207.   Thomas, *The Welsh Fairy Book*, 135.

208.   Owen, *Welsh Folk-Lore*, 246.

209.   Isaac, *Coelion Cymru*, 159.

out these divinatory practices.[210] This indicates the tree is also a powerful ally in magical workings of divination.

Exercise
Protective Rowan Rings

Find a local rowan tree and build a connection with the tree. Leave it offerings, speak to it, and use your intuition along with your perceptive skills to sense whether the tree is responding well to your presence. If the tree does respond well to you, and you will know if it does not, then you may collect some branches from it.

Cut off a few thin branches from the tree, long enough that they will bend into the shape of a ring. Ensure the branches are fresh and pliable and can easily be bent into a circular shape. Take the branches home and begin shaping them into the form of a ring or circle. As you bend them into shape, recite this incantation:

> *Pren criafol, llon chwedloniaeth hynafol,*
> *Dyro i mi dy fendithion amddiffynnol.*
>
> *Rowan wood, this ring now imbue,*
> *Your great qualities and protective virtue.*

When you have them in the shape you are happy with, bind the ends of the branches with twine. Add some extra twine to the rings to hang your creation up, and leave it to dry for a while. You may need to ensure the twine is incredibly tight so that the shape does not come undone.

These rings, once secure and ready, can be placed under doorposts, above doorways, near the front door, or above the bed as protective charms. Use them for yourself or give them to those who might be troubled by the fairies or wicked spirits.

. . . .
210.   Owen, *Welsh Folk-Lore*, 280.

Plants, Trees, and Fungi Beloved by the Fairies

Now that we have explored gorse and rowan, which are said to keep the fairies at bay, we will now take a look at some plants, herbs, and fungi that are beloved by the fairies. These plants and trees tend to be apparent in areas where the fairies are usually seen, or they are said to be particularly favoured by the fair folk.

Grug, Rhedyn, a Brwyn—Heather, Ferns, and Rushes

It may seem strange at first that I am grouping these plants together into one entry; however, within fairy lore, these plants appear usually side by side. In the Welsh language, the gossamer spiderwebs found strewn across marshy, rush-covered terrains were once referred to as Rhaffau'r Tylwyth Teg (ropes of the fair folk).[211] Marshes, or fern- and heather-covered landscapes, were said to be the haunts of the fairies throughout the summer months.

Folktales amass concerning mortal men falling asleep in these locations, and upon waking up, realising they have been bound in the fair folk's ropes. These ropes were said to be of the same material as a spider's web, silky and delicate to the eye. And yet they were incredibly strong. These gossamer ropes would bind a fully grown man, and he would not be able to escape their grip.

To make matters worse, the gossamer ropes acted as a cloak of invisibility. Not only were the men trapped and unable to move, but so long as the ropes were on them, they would be invisible to the human eye, and no one would be able to hear their cries. People would go searching for these men and would walk right by them. And they'd lay there, unable to move or scream for help, all the while hearing the giggling of the ellyllon or the fair folk who had placed them there.

Perhaps this is a warning about not spending too long in their domain, or not letting our guard down when spending time in locations where they are known to spend their days.

Regardless, what I have found is that these locations—marshy areas where heather, ferns, and rushes grow in abundance—are the perfect places to leave offerings to the fairies or call upon them and petition them for aid. If taken with care, and without overharvesting, you can also create an incense blend out of heather and fern to use in magic requiring their aid.

. . . .
211.   Owen, *Welsh Folk-Lore*, 112.

Exercise
Heather-and-Fern Fairy Incense

Find a location where heather and ferns grow side by side in abundance. Spend a little time getting to know the location, leaving offerings to the fair folk there and ensuring that it feels safe and respectful to work with this location and the entities that reside there.

In order to create the incense blend below, you will need to gather heather flowers near the end of their growing season, so likely in the autumn. This means you can begin working with the landscape and its spirits long before carrying out this task.

When the time is right, gather the flowering stems of heather. Remember not to overharvest. Gather enough to create a jar full of incense. Once the heather has been collected, gather some fern leaves as well. Make sure there are no insects on the leaves and collect leaves that are healthy and strong. Some species of fern die back in the autumn, so perhaps it would be best to gather fern leaves before the heather.

Take the bundles of heather and ferns home and bind them into small bundles. Hang these up in a dry, warm place and wait for them to completely dry out. Once dried, place into a mortar and pestle and crush down into a fine powder. Mix the dried fern powder and heather powder. You could stop here and burn this on charcoal as an incense. I like to add some personally gathered pine resin into the mixture to carry the incense and produce a wonderful smoke.

Place your mixture in a jar and store in a cool, dry place. Whenever you are practicing magic, you can burn this incense to draw upon the magic of the fair folk and invite their presence into your workings.

Caws Llyffant—Fairy Fungi

Fungi and fairies tend to go hand in hand in our modern culture. It is not difficult to find an image of a twee winged being sat upon a toadstool adorning the covers of children's books. Associations between fairies and fungi, however, seem to extend rather far back into history.

While today when we envision a fairy ring we tend to envision rings of mushrooms or perfect fairy-tale-esque toadstools, fairy rings within Welsh lore tended instead to be rings of discoloured grass. Interestingly, even these rings of discoloured grass tend to be caused by fungi whose fruit we cannot see above the surface.

The association between fairies and fungi in our lore can be seen clearly in the names we give to various mushrooms and fungi. For example, bwyd yr ellyllon is an umbrella term for all manners of toadstools, mushrooms, and fungi. It translates to mean "the food of the ellyllon." This provides us with a glimpse into the idea that people possibly believed fairies ate mushrooms and fungus.

Another similar example is Ymenyn y Tylwyth Teg or "fairy butter." Though traditionally used to describe a type of oily substance found on stones and cliffs, I have heard people refer to any gelatinous-looking fungus as Menyn y Tylwyth Teg. We tend to use menyn, not ymenyn, these days in my area, though it means the same: "butter."

Another term for fungi such as toadstools and mushrooms is caws llyffant, which translates literally to mean "the cheese of the frogs." While not associated with fairies, this term is used among Welsh speakers today, especially among those of the magical persuasion.

In some magical traditions and practices today, mushrooms are offered to fairies during magical workings. The magical group Cylch Cyfrin would weave baskets made of rushes and reeds and place mushrooms as well as bay leaves into them before throwing them into lakes as offerings to the fair folk. This is something I have adopted into my own personal practice, and I will occasionally leave woven baskets with mushrooms and picked flowers at locations I know to be the haunt of fairies. While leaving the basket, I recite a poem or song I have written for them.

Menyg Ellyllon—Foxglove

The foxglove is known in Welsh as menyg ellyllon or menyg Tylwyth Teg, "fairy" or "ellyll gloves." Beyond the name and some fanciful stories I was told growing up about the foxglove being beloved by fairies, I have yet to find much lore pertaining to the connection between foxgloves and fairies within the Welsh cultural continuum.

Foxglove is a poisonous flower, and I have spoken to many magical practitioners who work with the fairies on the subject of their association with poisonous and psychotropic herbs and plants. The terms discussed previously for fungi, such as bwyd yr ellyllon, are often attributed to mushrooms that are inedible to humans. Fairies do not seem to have the same physical aversion to poison as we do.

I would not recommend working with foxglove if you are inexperienced working with poisonous plants. However, I do know of a few witches and magical practitioners, Welsh and otherwise, who use the juice drawn from the leaves of the foxglove in their ritualistic practice. They do not consume the juice; instead, they draw with it or sprinkle it upon working spaces to draw in the fair folk as magical allies.

Derw—Oak

There is likely no tree more associated with magic and enchantment in Welsh lore than the oak. Steeped in mythology and legend, the oak is a tree of otherworldly influence. Beloved by the ancient Druids and wizards like Merlin, the oak tree is also supposedly the favourite tree of the fairies.

Fairies preferred to dance beneath the shade of great oak trees, and people would often catch a glimpse of them on warm summer nights, just as the sun was setting, dancing beneath these glorious giants.[212] Fairy rings are also most commonly said to appear beneath these trees more so than any other tree.

In the Mabinogion, it is an oak tree where Gwydion eventually finds Lleu after Blodeuedd attempted to murder him. The oak tree he is found in exists in this liminal state, a bridge between our world and the Otherworld itself. Oak trees seem to be the ancient bridge between our world and the Other, and magic seems to happen beneath their branches.

Because of this, the oak tree is a powerful ally for a magical practitioner embarking upon a journey to forge connections with otherworldly forces. A staff or wand made of the branches of an oak could be valuable in deepening and strengthening connections with the fair folk. Working magic on Tuesday or Thursday nights beneath an oak tree is another method of building connections with the fair folk and otherworldly forces.

The oak stands as a guardian, inspiration, and guide for those of us attempting to reach beyond the mists and commune with the Awen—imbued whispers of the Otherworld.

. . . .
212. Sikes, *British Goblins*, 106.

Collen—Hazel

The hazel tree shares a name in Welsh with the seventh-century monk who was said to have vanquished Gwyn ap Nudd and his fairy tribe: Collen. Despite this shared name with a rather vocal banisher of fairies, however, the hazel tree is associated with communing with fairies within Welsh folk magic.

The hazel tree appears in various early modern grimoires in recipes and instruction on how to see the fairies.[213] This tradition of the hazel as a powerful ally in aiding with communication with the fairies trickled its way into the practices of a cunning man from Denbighshire. We will explore the practices of this cunning man in more detail in the next chapter. This cunning man kept a mystic book that contains instructions on how to commune with and summon the Tylwyth Teg.

Amidst these practices is a rite that requires the magical practitioner to make three hazel wands. Upon each wand, they must write the name of the spirit or fairy they wish to summon. The wands should then be buried beneath a hill where the fairies are known to haunt on a Wednesday. On the following Friday, the three wands should be dug up and the ritual to summon them should be performed.[214]

Inspired by that rite, I made my own rite constructing hazel wands, which are to be used in rites concerning Gwyn ap Nudd, the Tylwyth Teg, and the ellyllon.

Exercise
Hazel Communication Wands

Find a local hazel tree and begin building a relationship with it over time. After a relationship has been forged with the tree and you feel the tree is in agreement with you taking three branches to construct wands, cut the best branches for the job and take these branches home.

Allow the branches to dry a little before making them into wands. A rule of thumb I was taught when I initially began making wands was to place the cut branches in a dry, warm place. For every inch of thickness at the thickest part of the branch, it may take upward of one year to fully dry. However, a branch that will become a wand will rarely be very thick. And I do not particularly wait for the branch to dry out entirely

. . . .

213. Boyer, *Under the Witching Tree*, 34–36.
214. Bosse-Griffiths, *Byd y Dyn Hysbys*, 132.

before beginning the carving process. The last hazel branch I carved into a wand took approximately one month to dry, and was no more than half an inch in thickness. I have found that you can speed up the process of drying by placing the branch in warmer areas of the home, such as in cupboards near the water heater or in warm conservatories.

Once adequately dry, remove the bark from the branches and smooth your newly created wands down with sandpaper. Finally, you will need the appropriate tools to carve a different word onto each wand. I tend to use a small whittling knife. Of all the wands I have ever made, I have found that hazel is particularly pleasant to carve and rarely causes any issues.

On one, carve the name Gwyn ap Nudd. On another, carve Y Tylwyth Teg or Bendith eu Mamau. On the third wand, carve the word ellyllon. As an alternative to carving the actual words, if you are someone who likes to work with sigils, you may prefer to create sigils for those three words and carve the sigil onto each wand instead.[215]

Once these words or sigils have been carved onto the wand, you can continue carving or decorating the wands to your preference. Add your own individuality to them while remembering their primary function and purpose to build relationship with fairies.

When they are done, take them on a Wednesday to a place that is associated with fairies. This might be a place known for its fairy folklore or a location that is liminal in nature. Hills, caves, lakes, and deep dark groves are all effective locations.

Once there, bury your wands in the shape of a triangle pointing toward the cardinal direction of north. Once they are beneath the earth, place your palms upon the ground, close your eyes, and recite the following words three times in a whisper. Or, better yet, write your own incantation to use at this point.

Fairy feet that grace this land,
Charge these tools 'neath where you stand,

215. For a guide to creating powerful effective sigils, I recommend the book *Sigil Witchery* by Laura Tempest Zakroff.

Sacred tools, perform your rite,

Gather magic on this night.

Leave the location and do not return until the following Friday. On Friday, dig up the wands and take them home. These wands are now yours to use whenever you are working magic involving Gwyn ap Nudd, the Tylwyth Teg, or the ellyllon.

Fairy Fauna

When we think of the denizens of the Otherworld, we tend to be incredibly humanoid centric. We think of glorious, magical fairy maidens, or liminal, enigmatic kings. The Otherworld is also home to an abundance of animals, just as our world is. In this section, we will explore the animals associated with fairies, from the hunting hounds of otherworldly nobility to the cattle that emerge from the depths of the lakes.

Cŵn Annwfn, the Dogs of the Otherworld

In the first branch of the Mabinogi, the Cŵn Annwfn, hounds of the deep or hounds of the Otherworld, are the first otherworldly beings we come across. Hunting companions of Arawn, lord of Annwfn, these dogs are clearly not of this world. Their fur is a bright, vivid white all over their bodies except for their ears, which are a deep bloodred. Though their appearance in this scene in the first branch of the Mabinogi is likely where folk know them from most, they do appear in later folklore as well.

Dogs and hunting hounds seem a common animal among the fair folk. They are quite obviously present in the court of Arawn and act as hunting companions to Arawn and possibly all the hunters and denizens of the Otherworld. The small, vegetarian fair folk described in the tale of Elidorus are also said to have greyhounds that are adapted to their size.[216]

Interestingly, there are various synonymous names for these hunting hounds that have been collected by writers and folklorists throughout history. As is the case with very many other topics within the Welsh cultural continuum, examining these names can give us a glimpse into the lore and beliefs surrounding them.

. . . .

216. Cambrensis, *The Itinerary Through Wales*, 69.

The most commonly used name for these otherworldly dogs is of course Cŵn Annwfn or Cŵn Annwn, which simply translates to mean "the dogs of Annwfn/Annwn." This indicates to us that they are of the Otherworld, hailing from Annwfn just like Arawn and the other denizens we come across in mythology.

The reverend Edmund Jones recorded that they were also sometimes called Cŵn Bendith eu Mamau, which literally translated means "the dogs of the bless-ings of their mothers."[217] As we have already discussed in earlier chapters, Bendith eu Mamau or Bendith y Mamau are terms used synonymously with Tylwyth Teg to denote the fair family, fairies, or denizens of the Otherworld. This means that Cŵn Bendith eu Mamau can be translated simply to "the dogs of the fair folk."

So far, all these names seem to match quite well with one another, describing these creatures as dogs that come from the Otherworld or belong to the deni-zens of the Otherworld. However, Edmund Jones also noted the usage of another term, cŵn wybir, to describe these dogs.[218] Cŵn wybir is interesting as it trans-lates to mean "sky dogs," which provides us with some insight into the belief that these dogs are aerial in nature, able to hunt through the skies.

We already touched upon the aerial nature of the dogs of the Otherworld in the second chapter of this book, where we discussed who the dogs belong to in various pieces of lore. To quickly recap, the cŵn wybir are perceived to be spectral hounds who hunt the souls of humans upon the wind and in the sky. They are led by various folkloric characters, including but not limited to Arawn, King Arthur, Gwyn ap Nudd, and a mysterious horned creature.

In their aerial spectral nature, they are associated with a Welsh equivalent of the Wild Hunt folkloric motif. Running upon the stormy nights in search of mortal souls, they growl and snarl as they run through the skies. The louder you can hear their barking and howling, the further away they actually are from you.

Some pieces of folk belief state that the pathways upon which they run through the skies are the same pathways a corpse will take route to being buried in a churchyard. This brings us to another name given to these dogs: cŵn cyrff, which translates to mean "corpse dogs," drawing upon the lore surrounding these dogs being death portents.[219]

. . . .

217. Jones, *A Relation of Apparitions of Spirits in the County of Monmouth*, 82.

218. Jones, *A Relation of Apparitions of Spirits in the County of Monmouth*, 82.

219. Jones, *Welsh Folklore and Folk Custom*, 211–212.

The howling of the phantom dogs was believed to be an omen that death would soon follow. Yet another name associated with these dogs is cŵn toili, and this is likely the most mysterious of names given to the phantom otherworldly dogs.[220]

Toili is a word that refers to a phantom funeral.[221] A phantom funeral is a spectral funeral procession that is witnessed by the living. A real funeral will undoubtedly occur following the same route as the phantom funeral in the very near future. It is an omen of a funeral to come, and to see one wandering from your own home toward the churchyard is an omen of a death that will soon occur in the family.

However, what is incredibly interesting about the word toili is that it is related to words such as tolaeth, which refers to an omen of death, but also to words such as tylwyth, as in Tylwyth Teg, meaning "family" or "host." This perhaps offers us an insight into the connection between fairies and the spirits of the dead.

Cŵn toili could therefore be translated to mean "phantom funeral dogs," "death portent dogs," or "dogs of the hosts."

The Cŵn Annwfn are a diverse and mysterious grouping of otherworldly creatures. They range from being simply hunting companions to the nobles of the Otherworld to being fearful phantom hounds who hunt the souls of the dead upon stormy nights. They are indicators that the Otherworld is near, but also omens of death. They run alongside their leader, who can be a variety of folkloric characters associated with fairies and the Otherworld.

Corgis as Steeds of the Fairies

A rather common idea I come across, on a regular basis, is the fanciful idea that Welsh fairies are especially fond of corgis, and that they even ride them as their steeds. This idea has become incredibly popular in online spaces and in Pagan spaces. I cannot seem to deliver a talk or lead a workshop focusing on the fairy traditions of Wales without someone bringing up corgis.

This was not a piece of lore I ever grew up hearing, but then I also did not own a corgi nor know anyone who did. It is possible many who do own corgis might have heard this little piece of lore all their lives. For me, however, I first stumbled upon this whimsical idea online.

· · · · · · · · · · · · · · · · ·

220.   Jones, *Welsh Folklore and Folk Custom*, 211–212.

221.   Rüdiger, *Y Tylwyth Teg*, 33.

A meme was circulating on social media stating that corgis were the preferred method of transportation for Welsh fairies. For obvious reasons, such as the fact that corgis are an adorable small breed of dogs, these memes are often incredibly popular. With upward of thousands of people sharing them, this piece of lore has become a commonly repeated Welsh fairy fact. But where does it come from?

For the longest time, I had no idea where this supposed element of ancient fairy lore originated. As a rather fond lover of folklore, I was surprised that I had never come across one tale or legend that referred to corgis as the steeds of the fairies. Surely the idea must have its roots in some form of older legend, mustn't it?

The mystery surrounding this piece of internet lore was made clear to me when I came across its origin. It might surprise many to learn that the origin of this idea does not stem from older Welsh folk belief or mythology, but instead from a fairly modern poem written by a poet from Dorset, England.

The poem in question is titled "Corgi Fantasy" and can be found in full in *An Illustrated Study of the Pembroke Welsh Corgi Standard*, a handbook published by the Pembroke Welsh Corgi Club of America. The poem is credited as having been first published in 1946, possibly in an older *Welsh Corgi League* handbook. This poem includes all the elements of the lore that circulates the internet today.

The poem tells the origin of corgis, explaining how they came to be in our world. Two children stumble upon puppies with golden coats and faces like foxes playing in a hollow. The children take these puppies home, and the men of the village tell them that they are gifts from the realm of the fairies.[222] Corgis, according to the poem, play a prominent role in fairy society. They pull the coaches of the fairies, they work fairy cattle, they are playmates for fairy children, and they are the steeds for fairy warriors. The poem ends by saying:

> *Should you doubt this ancient story,*
> *Laugh and scoff and call it nonsense,*
> *Look and see the saddle markings,*
> *Where the fairy warriors rode them.*[223]

222.   Biddlecombe, "Corgi Fantasy," in *An Illustrated Study of the Pembroke Welsh Corgi Standard*.

223.   Biddlecombe, "Corgi Fantasy," in *An Illustrated Study of the Pembroke Welsh Corgi Standard*.

A fanciful and whimsical poem from the mid-twentieth century making waves today as it is touted as authentic fairy legend. The fact that this piece of lore is now beginning to circulate as true fairy belief, however, prompts the question: When does something become folklore? We know this poem does not have its roots in the ancient past nor in older folk beliefs. However, it is slowly but surely becoming common corgi lore.

I have, over the years, met many a farmer or corgi owner who will say it is bad luck to kick a corgi, even by accident, because they are favoured by the fairies. Teachers share the lore of corgis as fairy dogs with their students, and it is a fact that I have heard many a Welsh Pagan repeat at gatherings and events.

The word corgi itself lends itself to their fairy nature. The word has its origins in the Welsh language, coming from the Welsh cor meaning "dwarf" and ci meaning "dog." While this name likely comes from their small stature, I have met many today who use this etymology to prove that they are the steeds of the smaller fair folk who dwell in the hills and hollows of this mystical land.

Pigs

Likely not the first animal that comes to mind when one thinks of fairy animals, pigs, nonetheless, have rather visceral otherworldly qualities within Welsh lore. In the Mabinogion, it is revealed to us that pigs arrived upon the Island of Britain from the Otherworld, a gift from Arawn, lord of Annwfn, to Pryderi, son of Pwyll.[224] They seem to be a continuation of the otherworldly gifts sent to the kingdom of Dyfed after Pwyll's adventure in Annwfn in the first branch.

Pigs in Mythology

In the fourth branch of the Mabinogi, Gwydion, a trickster magician, uses his magic to fool Pwyll into giving him these otherworldly gifted pigs. They are desired by Gwydion because they are said to have flesh better than beef. It is mentioned in the text that an old name for pigs is hobeu, but that they are now known as moch, which is, to this day, the word used to describe pigs in the Welsh language.

Later in the fourth branch, Gwydion also follows a sow to find his nephew Lleu, who has transformed into a decaying eagle after Blodeuedd attempted to kill him with help from her secret lover Gronw Pebr. The sow leads Gwydion to

....
224. Davies, The Mabinogion, 48.

a mystical otherworldly oak tree that exists within a seemingly liminal state of being where it is both in our world yet not at the same time. Lleu, as an eagle, is perched in this oak tree and only descends from the tree after Gwydion sings an englyn to call him down.

Another place we find reference to pigs within Welsh lore is in the triads. Triad 26, found in the *White Book of Rhydderch*, references the three powerful swineherds of the Island of Britain.[225] These three powerful swineherds are Drystan, son of Tallwch; Coll, son of Collfrewy; and Pryderi, son of Pwyll, who became known as lord of Annwfn. It is revealed in this triad that Pwyll seemingly brought seven pigs from Annwfn and gave them to Pendaran Dyfed, who in the first branch of the Mabinogi becomes Pwyll's guardian. The pigs are kept in Glyn Cuch, the exact place where Pwyll came upon Arawn in the first branch.

Triad 26, focusing on the swineherds of Britain, is the most informative of all the Welsh triads and is also among the longest.[226]

The presence and stature of pigs, boars, and sows within the Mabinogion and other Welsh texts indicates that these animals were of great importance in our history and culture. Pigs appear as important creatures in tales concerning the Otherworld, such as in the fourth branch of the Mabinogi, where Pwyll is said to have been given pigs from the otherworldly court, but also in Arthurian literature such as in the tale of Culhwch and Olwen.

In the story of Culhwch and Olwen, the titular character Culhwch must hunt down a mystical boar known as the Twrch Trwyth. Beyond this, Culhwch's name features the word hwch, a word usually used to describe a sow in Welsh.

This reverence for pigs as creatures of otherworldly stature continued into later folklore, where pigs are said to have supernatural abilities, such as the ability to see the wind. Spirits and devils often take the physical form of pigs or possess the bodies of pigs as well.[227]

Yr Hwch Ddu Gwta, a Halloween Folk Devil

A great and terrifying sow still to this day plays a prominent role in the lore surrounding Nôs Galan Gaeaf (the eve of winter), the Welsh equivalent to Halloween or Samhain. Growing up, I was warned that if I stayed out too late on Nôs

225.   Bromwich, *Trioedd Ynys Prydein*, 52.
226.   Bromwich, *Trioedd Ynys Prydein*, 54.
227.   Owen, *Welsh Folk-Lore*, 348.

Galan Gaeaf, which fell on the thirty-first of October, then the hwch ddu gwta would capture me and do sinister things to me. I believed throughout my youth that this eerie folk devil in the form of a large, tailless black sow was a creature specific to my village's local lore, but I would discover that the hwch ddu gwta has been part of Nôs Galan Gaeaf lore for centuries.

Nôs Galan Gaeaf was a night of revelry; bonfires were lit and families would gather around the hearth to play games, practice divination, and feast together. In some areas, as people made their way home from being out enjoying the bonfires and such, they would sing verses referencing the tailless black sow, yr hwch ddu gwta.

Adre! Adre, am y cynta'!
Hwch Ddu Gwra a gipia'r ola'!

Home! Home, let each try to be first!
And may the tailless black sow take the hindmost![228]

Horses

Fairy characters often appear, especially in earlier mythology, riding upon their noble steeds. The two most obvious mythical characters with otherworldly motifs surrounding them, Arawn, lord of Annwfn, and Rhiannon make their first appearances upon the backs of horses. The texts in which we learn the stories surrounding these characters take time to describe their horses with clarity.

Arawn appears out of the thicket upon a dapple-grey horse, whereas Rhiannon appears in Pwyll's vision riding upon a gleaming white horse with the magical ability to move faster than anyone pursuing its rider. While many might overlook the colour of these horses as simply being a useful descriptor to bring the story to life, many have theorised the colour of the horse says more to the listener of the story than we might think.

Sioned Davies explored how the colour of a horse would make it more or less sought after, especially by those within nobility. Horses that were pure black or pure white were considered the most sought after within a medieval context, and within a story such as the corpus of the Mabinogion, a gleaming white horse may

....
228. Jones, *Welsh Folklore and Folk Custom*, 157.

indicate nobility and wealth to the contemporary audience.[229] Beyond this, however, we must also consider how white animals are often associated with otherworldly forces. Take, for example, the Cŵn Annwfn in the first branch, with their gleaming white fur and bloodred ears. Or the white boar in the third branch, who leads Pryderi into an otherworldly trap. With this in mind, not only does Rhiannon's gleaming white horse communicate nobility and opulence, but also a supernatural otherworldly quality.

Gwyn ap Nudd is also associated with horses. In the dialogue between Gwyn ap Nudd and Gwyddno Garanhir found in the *Black Book of Carmarthen*, the poem notes how Gwyn is riding upon a white horse who attempts to nudge Gwyn away from the battle he has just witnessed. Once again we see a character who would later become incredibly linked with the fairy tradition riding upon a white horse. In the tale of Culhwch and Olwen, he is also said to ride upon a mystical horse called Du y Moroedd (black of the seas) who can gallop across the waves of the sea.

Du y Moroedd seems to be a magical horse who acts as a bridge between our world and the Otherworld for its rider. The fact that this horse can gallop over the waves of the sea emphasises the liminal and transitory nature of water; it is a conduit between our world and the Other. However, horses seem to be common bridges between our world and the Other as well. While Du y Moroedd carries Gwyn across the waves of the sea, Arawn also rides a horse between the kingdom of Dyfed and Annwfn in the first branch of the Mabinogi. Rhiannon also arrives, supposedly from the Otherworld, on horseback.

Beyond this, horses also appear with fairies in later folklore. The fairies Elidorus encounters in the chthonic fairy world he visits have horses that are around the size of greyhounds in our world, making them the perfect size for the fairy men in that world to ride on.[230]

It seems that, just as we have relied upon and cared for horses as companions in our world, horses play a similar important role for the denizens of the Otherworld too.

. . . .

229. Davies, *Horses in the Mabinogi*, in *The Horse in Celtic Culture*, 121–140.

230. Rüdiger, *Y Tylwyth Teg*, 36.

Ceffyl Dŵr, the Water Horse

Another horse creature that exists within the realm of all things fairy is the ceffyl dŵr, a malevolent spirit who takes the form of a glorious and enticing horse. The ceffyl dŵr usually stalks watery areas such as the shores of lakes. They are so incredibly beautiful and hypnotic to look upon that people feel compelled to walk up to them and climb upon their back. Once they are on their backs, however, they soon regret their choice.

Once a person has climbed upon their back, the ceffyl dŵr begins to gallop across the landscape. In an instant, they begin to rise into the air, taking flight and rising to great heights. They fly toward the sharp rocks of the mountains or above the deep glacial lakes. Suddenly, just as their rider begins to calm themselves at the fact they are on the back of a flying horse, the ceffyl dŵr transforms itself into water vapour, leaving the unsuspecting rider to plummet to their doom.

Ceffyl dŵr literally translates to mean "water horse." They are said to dwell in subaquatic domains and leave their watery homes in order to send mortals to their deaths. The folklorist Elias Owen recorded how there was a belief that magical practitioners would sometimes summon the ceffyl dŵr by shaking a magical bridle over the pools and lakes within which they lived.[231] The reason a magical practitioner would summon such a creature is unknown to me; however, if I were to guess, it would be to curse or cause harm to a victim, perhaps by sending the ceffyl dŵr to deal with them.

Fairy Cattle

While it may be tempting to think only of romantic or fanciful animals in relation to fairies, within our corpus of lore, fairies are often associated with prosperity and opulence, and this opulence is often a by-product of their glorious herds of cattle. Fairy cattle are often seen as incredible symbols of the bounties and prosperity that can come about in unions between fairy and mortals.

Fairy maidens often appear emerging out of lakes, watery gateways between our world and the Otherworld. However, it is not just fairy maidens that cross these portals. In various tales, certain lakes are also associated with cattle that rise from the lakes and graze in the landscape surrounding the lake. One example is the cattle of Llyn Barfog, in Eryri, North Wales.

. . . .

231.   Owen, *Welsh Folk-Lore*, 141.

The Story of the Fairy Cow of Llyn Barfog

Llyn Barfog was purportedly haunted by a group of fairy maidens who would rise out of the lake at dusk on summer evenings and wander the area dressed in glorious gowns of green with their fairy hounds by their sides. Alongside these fairy maidens and their otherworldly hounds, cows would also rise from the lake to graze in the area near the lake. These cows were white as milk, and the local farmers swapped tales about how glorious it would be to capture one.

One day a local farm boy noticed that a gleaming white cow had made its way into his field and was seemingly courting with one of his own bulls. Using the fact that the two kine had fallen in love, he captured the fairy cow. From that day on his luck would only grow, for this cow produced the strongest of calves and the most delicious milk, and from that milk he would make the best cheese and butter. People travelled from far and wide to buy his dairy products or to beg that he sell them one of the calves.

The cow became known as Y Fuwch Gyfeiliorn, the stray cow.

How prosperous his life became, all because of this cow. But being a greedy and feeble mortal, the farm boy grew anxious that the cow would one day grow old and stop producing such amazing dairy. He made a decision, which was only logical in his mind, to fatten the cow and sell her at market as meat.

Being of fairy stock, the cow fattened beyond anything earthly. She was a grand and glorious size, a cow like none had ever seen before. Everyone was excited to see what kind of meat this gift from the Otherworld would become.

The day of slaughter arrived, and a crowd gathered to see the cow be killed by the butcher. When the butcher raised his arm to strike the cow with a fatal blow, however, a shriek echoed through the town. This unearthly shriek caused all the people watching to cover their ears. It pierced through their eardrums and made the inside of their head feel as though it was vibrating.

The cow looked up toward the hills near Llyn Barfog, the lake from which she had arrived into this world. There, stood like a goddess with an ethereal glow, was a woman dressed in a glorious green gown.

She opened her mouth, and a voice like thunder came from her, uttering an incantation that caused the cow to be released from her shackles and follow the fairy maiden back up toward the lake.

From that day on, the people in the towns and villages surrounding Llyn Barfog never again saw the pearly white fairy cows, nor the fairy maidens, nor the otherworldly hounds rise from the depths of the lake to haunt the hills and hollows around it. And the farmer who had kept the cow for many years went from being the wealthiest farmer in the land to living in absolute poverty.[232]

Fairy cattle appear in numerous folktales, including the infamous story of the maiden of Llyn y Fan Fach. In the Llyn y Fan Fach story, as a wedding gift, the fairy maiden's father offers the newly betrothed couple the gift of as many cattle as the maiden can count on one breath. These cattle, just like the fairy cow of Llyn Barfog, offer the couple wealth and prosperity.

When the taboo of the fairy maiden of Llyn y Fan Fach is broken and she returns to her otherworldly home, she takes the cattle with her. As she walks toward the lake, she calls out the names of all the cattle in the fields. Some have theorised that the names she calls out are actually the names of now extinct breeds of cattle, and that the story acts as an explanation for the disappearance of long-lost breeds.[233] Though, many scholars now refute that claim as simply a romanticised euhemeristic idea.

Fairy cattle represent the bounty, opulence, and wealth of the Otherworld from which the fair folk emerge. Having a fairy cow within your ownership leads to great wealth and comfort, but mortals are usually unable to care for them as they should, leading to the gift being taken away and the riches produced from the cow vanishing as well.

Goats

I am particularly fond of goats; there is something about them that simply awakens a part of me that cannot help but squeal in delight. Perhaps it is their vacant yet all-knowing stares, their glorious horns, those cloven hooves, or their shrieking bleats. Imagine my delight when I discovered that, according to Welsh lore, goats were considered rather sacred magical animals.

This little piece of lore came to me via the work of the folklorist Wirt Sikes, who wrote, "Goats are in Wales held in particular esteem for their supposed

232.   A version of this tale titled "The Stray Cow" can be found in Thomas, *The Welsh Fairy Book*, 110–113.

233.   Wood, *The Fairy Bride Legend in Wales*, 61.

occult intellectual powers. They are believed to be on very good terms with the Tylwyth Teg and possess more knowledge than their appearance indicates."[234]

Sikes goes on to explain that fairies are fond of braiding and combing the beards of goats, all the while whispering arcane knowledge into their ears. The idea that goats hold a particularly occult intellect speaks to those of a magical persuasion rather intimately, I would imagine. The image of the goat in relation to transgressive forms of magic is well established. One need only look to the paintings of the witches' sabbaths by Francisco de Goya or at the imagery of Baphomet created by the occultist Éliphas Lévi to realise that the goat has long been associated with magical themes.

The magical nature of the goat is echoed in other folktales, such as the story of "Einion and the Lady of the Greenwood" collected by W. Jenkyn Thomas in *The Welsh Fairy Book*. This story has a fairy maiden in it, known as the Lady of the Greenwood, who has goat-like hooves instead of feet, giving us a hint that fairies can have therianthropic qualities. The Lady of the Greenwood is cunning and mischievous and could be interpreted as acting maliciously toward the protagonist of the tale, Einion, whom she places under a spell and causes to part from his beloved.

Another tale concerning goats is that of Cadwaladr and his goats. Cadwaladr was a goat herder who lived in the mountains of Eryri. One of his goats, Jenny, turns out to be a fairy maiden who has disguised herself as a goat. When Cadwaladr shows affection, care, and kindness to her without knowing she is more than an ordinary goat, she whisks him away to a secret place atop Yr Wyddfa, our tallest mountain, and there he sees a great gathering of spectral goats. These goats have shadowy horns, and their bleats sound so unearthly and supernatural to Cadwaladr's mortal ears.

The spectral shadowy goats who gather atop the mountain have a king, and his voice echoes through the land louder than any church bell. This goat king rushes toward Cadwaladr, sensing him as an outsider, and butts him with his horns. This sends Cadwaladr, as if by magic, back to the land where he herds his goats. He awakens the next morning unsure if it was all a dream or not. One thing, however, is certain: his goat Jenny is nowhere to be seen.[235]

. . . .

234.   Sikes, *British Goblins*, 53.

235.   A version of this tale can be found in Sikes, *British Goblins*, 54–55, and in Thomas, *The Welsh Fairy Book*, 78–79.

Adar Rhiannon—The Birds of Rhiannon

The Adar Rhiannon, or the Birds of Rhiannon, appear in two specific noteworthy texts. First, in the second branch of the Mabinogi, after the terrible events
of the war in the second branch and after Branwen has died, the survivors take
Bran's severed head to Harlech, where they are welcomed by a glorious feast in
their honour.

As soon as they begin to eat, the song of three birds echoes around them.
These birds are the Adar Rhiannon. Under the powerful song spell of the birds,
the survivors and all those present at the feast continue in their festivities and
celebrations for seven years. They feast in a state of bliss. The song of the birds
seems to alter their relationship with time and space.

The birds are said to fly over the sea, far away from the castle within which
they feast. And yet, their song sounds as though they are in the room with them.
There is no description of the birds, such as what kind of birds they are, other
than simply Adar Rhiannon, Birds of Rhiannon. Over the years I have come
across many interpretations of the birds in art and spoken to many people about
how they perceive them. Some see them as blackbirds, crows, ravens, or another
corvid. This might be because of the correlations drawn by some scholars between
Rhiannon and the Morrigan.

Others have interpreted the birds as being unlike any bird that exists in our
world, golden, or some other supernatural colour, glowing and ethereal. This is
closer to how I have envisioned the Birds of Rhiannon since I was a child, like
something entirely unearthly and magical.

Their magical song seemingly places those who listen to it into a liminal state
of existence, where they are not fully aware of how much time has gone by. Here
in the second branch, we do not learn about them at any depth; however, their
appearance in another story might unveil some insights into them.

Another mention of the Adar Rhiannon is found in the tale of Culhwch and
Olwen. The birds are included in a list of things needed for Culhwch to marry
Olwen. Ysbaddaden, Olwen's father, says, "I want the Birds of Rhiannon, they
that wake the dead and lull the living to sleep, to entertain me that night."[236]

. . . .
236. Davies, *The Mabinogion*, 196.

This request shines some light as to the powers of the birds. They wake the dead and lull the living to sleep. This idea echoes ideas surrounding the Otherworld as being a liminal space where the dead and the living are but one and the same. After all, as we have discovered in earlier chapters, the dead are sometimes seen alongside the fairies, and characters such as Merlin exist in a liminal sleep-like death awaiting the time to return to the real world once again.

So perhaps the Birds of Rhiannon break down the gossamer barriers that separate our world from the Otherworld. Like water itself, which they are said to fly over, their song creates a melding place where our world and the Other meet. The birds themselves offer us more of an insight into Rhiannon's otherworldly qualities as well. These magical birds, which can create liminal spaces, are hers, and they likely originate from the Otherworld, like her.

Fairies
and Magic

Today, fairies exist within our modern culture predominately as beings that dwell within the domain of children's stories. The question, "Do you believe in fairies?" would garner a raised eyebrow from many. However, not too long ago, fairies were not only very real, but could also be a threat to your comfort, stability, and safety.

There were, and there are still to this day, special people who possess not only a great knowledge of fairy lore, but who also understand how to seek their counsel, call upon them, placate them, and break their enchantments. They were magical practitioners, those who specialised in understanding the unseen aspects of our world. Within Welsh tradition, some of the names we use to refer to these people are Pobl Hysbys or Cyfarwydd (cunning folk), Swynydd (charmers/enchanters), Dewin (wizard), or Consuriwr (conjurer), to name a few.

The fairies lived in proximity to humans, and so occasionally they influenced the lives of ordinary people. It was imperative that the local magical specialist have a knowledge of the fairies, but also a knowledge of how to deal with them via their magical craft. That way they could better serve their community.

In this chapter, we will explore the ways in which magical practitioners interacted with the fairies. The first part of this chapter will deal with understanding the historical and folkloric landscape of the intersection between magical practice and fairies. The second part will focus more so on how these traditions and practices continue to this day, as I showcase not only the elements of my own personal practice, which are immersed within fairy tradition, but also how I incorporate a relationship with the fair folk into my day-to-day life as a modern-day Swynwraig.

Mortals Dealing with the Fairies

To understand the relationship between fairies and magical practitioners, we must first briefly explore the ways in which ordinary folk interacted with and dealt with the fairies. Ordinary people who had no inclination of learning about the world of magic, spirits, and the Otherworld tended to want absolutely nothing to do with the fairies.

Fairies could be the cause of great misery, misfortune, trauma, and pain for ordinary people. Many a folktale seems to echo the idea that the fairies are not only mischievous and cunning creatures, but also dangerous and frightful.

The fairies could cause you physical harm, as we explored in more detail in the third chapter of this book, as well as trick people, steal babies, and even bestow gifts that would ultimately bring nothing but bad. Some stories of fairies causing harm to mortals seem justified, such as the story of "A Fairy Dog" collected in *The Welsh Fairy Book*.[237] In this story, the fairies left a dog in a place where a mortal girl stumbled upon it. This girl treated the dog with absolute cruelty. The fairies appeared before her and asked her what seemed to be a riddle: "Would you care to travel above wind, mid-wind, or below wind?"

The girl, unsure how to answer, chose below wind. Suddenly, she was snatched off her feet by an unseen force and dragged through bogs, brambles, briars, and swamps. When the unseen hands finally set her free, she had countless cuts and scratches across her body from which her blood poured out.

Stories such as "A Fairy Dog" echoed the idea that one must be careful in seemingly strange situations where odd animals or strange travellers appear before you, because they just might be of the world of fairy.

Ordinary people tried day by day to do all they could to not offend the fairies. We see this in traditions associated with the household fairy, as explored earlier

. . . .
237. Thomas, *The Welsh Fairy Book*, 231–232.

in chapter 4. Keeping the house warm, clean, and tidy, as well as leaving an offering for the household, was important. If these tasks were not performed, then the fairy could retaliate.

To the ordinary people who possessed no knowledge of magic, fairies were feared just as demons or ghosts were. Many folk magical practices attributed to ordinary people, as opposed to learned magical practitioners, were in fact methods of warding or protecting themselves or the household from the mischief and malice of the fairies.

Wards and Protections against the Fairies

The fact that we have evidence within folk culture of wards and protections used to avert the influence of fairies is proof enough that most people wanted nothing to do with them. Some wards against the fairies were discussed in the previous chapter where we explored plants, herbs, and trees associated with fairies. The rowan tree, or as it was more commonly referred to in the past, the mountain ash, was said to be incredibly powerful in keeping fairies at bay.

Rowan branches would be manipulated into rings that were placed either under doorposts or even into the ears of cattle to protect them from the fairies. Canes would be constructed out of the rowan tree to keep above the bed, and the rowan berries were strung, dried, and hung in the household.

Similarly, gorse was also utilised as a protective barrier against the fairies. The fairies would not dare cross a barrier made of gorse.

Iron

Beyond these natural protections against fairies, they are also said to despise iron. Iron is common material fairies are averse to in an abundance of cultures, and the reasons behind their dislike of iron have been discussed by many writers and scholars for decades. The reverend Robert Kirk states in *The Secret Commonwealth of Elves, Fauns, and Fairies* that fairies abhor iron because it reminds them of hell.[238] Morgan Daimler discusses a few theories surrounding iron as a ward against fairies in their book *Fairies*, stating that some believe that, as humans developed iron, fairies were pushed out of our world.[239] Daimler goes on to present their own theory as to the protective virtue of iron, explaining that they

. . . .

238. Kirk, *The Secret Commonwealth of Elves, Fauns, and Fairies*, 51.

239. Daimler, *Fairies*, 205–209.

believe it is down to the idea that iron draws, interferes with, grounds, and dispels magical energy.[240]

Others seem to express the idea that fairies being averse to iron may be more of a metaphor. For example, Kristoffer Hughes in *The Book of Celtic Magic* writes, "One wonders if this is indicative of an actual magical repulsion or if it is metaphoric of the human industrial revolution, a period that greatly advanced our technologies but closed our eyes to wonder and magic."[241]

I have personally spent many years pondering this question and even attempting to divine an answer from the fairies themselves. I have yet to come to a satisfying conclusion. Regardless, one thing I am certain of is that it is true fairies are indeed repulsed by iron. From personal experience, fairies are not at all happy to reside or be near iron. Hence why, when practicing any magic involving them, I tend to avoid wearing or carrying any tools made of iron. My cast-iron cauldron is replaced by cauldrons made of other metals or materials, and I tend to ensure my tools are mostly made of wood or cloth.

Within our Welsh lore, iron even plays a role in versions of the fairy bride motif. In certain versions of the fairy bride legend, the taboo that is placed upon the fairy-mortal betrothal is that the fairy wife must never be struck with iron. Usually in these stories the iron strikes the fairy wife accidentally; for example, in certain stories such as that of the fairy bride of Drws Coed Farm, the fairy wife is struck by the iron on the saddle of her horse.[242] Once the iron has struck the fairy maidens in these stories, they vanish into thin air, returning to their otherworldly home. The idea of an iron saddle bit touching a fairy maiden and causing her to vanish became a motif, as we saw this exact thing happen in the story of the fairy maiden of Nant y Bettws, Caernarfonshire.

Sheathed Knives

Another common protection against fairies was to unsheathe a knife in their presence. Some stories recall how travellers wandering the rural roads at night would be teased by the fairies. The fairies would attempt to frighten them or lead them away from the clearly beaten path into the path of danger. Once they were aware that it was the fairies or some other form of nasty spirit that was influenc-

. . . .

240. Daimler, *Fairies*, 205–209.

241. Hughes, *The Book of Celtic Magic*, 150.

242. Sikes, *British Goblins*, 45.

ing them, the traveller would pull out their knife. The sight of the knife would banish the fairies instantly.[243]

Seeking the Aid of Magical Specialists

As we can see from this section, there were numerous methods of warding away the fairies, but when things became difficult, those under attack would turn to the only people they knew could help. The local cunning man, wisewoman, or wizard would be consulted when matters arose that were difficult for ordinary people to deal with. The magical specialist was an integral part of rural communities across Wales, and you can read more about that in my first book, *Welsh Witchcraft*. One specific role the magical specialist played, however, was dealing with mischief and malice caused by wicked spirits, malefic witches, and, of course, fairies.

Fairies and Magical Practitioners

While fairies could be the cause of misfortune and trauma for ordinary people, for those learned in the ways of the numinous, they were powerful allies. Knowing all that could be learned about the fairies was rather important for any magical practitioner who aided their community via their magical knowledge and skill. People would travel far and wide to seek the help of those learned in the art of magic and conjuration when they were troubled by the fairies. This is echoed in folklore concerning the wise folk.

A story collected by the folklorist Elias Owen details how a Gwr Cyfarwydd (cunning man) was sought out to help deal with a case of a boy who was trapped with the fairies, dancing in a fairy ring.[244] In this story two servants are sent by their master to work in a nearby woodland. In the woods they acknowledge strange rings upon the ground. Having worked hard, they both fall asleep amidst the trees, and one of the servants wakes hours later to find that the other is missing.

The servant and his master spend days searching for the missing boy, until eventually they decide to ask the help of a local cunning man. The cunning man states that the strange rings the servant boy saw upon the ground were fairy rings and were telltale that this place was a local haunt of the fairies.

. . . .

243.   Sikes, *British Goblins*, 51.

244.   Owen, *Welsh Folk-Lore*, 37–39.

The cunning man goes to the woods with the servant boy, and upon reaching the fairy rings, he tells the boy to place his foot just on the border of one of the fairy rings, being careful not to step inside fully. When the boy does this, it is as though he is betwixt and between our world and the Otherworld. Suddenly he can see fantastical creatures dancing inside the rings. Only moments before that they were entirely invisible to him, but now they are revealed. The missing servant boy is there among the dancing fairy beings.

The cunning man explains that once the missing servant boy is close enough to grab, the boy with his foot upon the border of the ring should push him out of the circle. He does this, and the boy is released from the Otherworld. He shakes his head and asks why he had been pushed. He is shocked to discover that it has been days since they last saw him, for to him it feels like mere minutes have gone by since he heard the music and stepped into the ring.

This story reveals how cunning folk were approached to help deal with matters beyond the ordinary people's comprehension and skill. The cunning man in this story was obviously learned of fairy lore and tradition, and in how to deal with the Otherworld and with fairies safely.

Magical practitioners and specialists were consulted for many situations involving fairies, including when it was believed that a child had been swapped with a changeling. The magical specialist would be aware of the methods to be rid of the changeling and to bring the real human baby back.[245] It is clear from these stories that dealing with fairies was one of many tasks placed upon the magical specialist.

Fairies as Magical Allies

Beyond being able to counter the mischief, malice, and magic of the fairies, magical specialists also viewed fairies as powerful magical allies in their craft and trade. Fairies are beings that are not limited by things such as time and corporeality, and therefore could aid the magical practitioner in a variety of tasks.

They could find lost objects, seek out hidden treasures, cure illnesses and distribute remedies for ailments, look into the past and the future, and they had knowledge of things beyond our human sciences. For all these reasons, fairies were considered beneficial allies to the magical practitioner.

. . . .

245.   Jones, *Welsh Folklore and Folk Custom*, 77.

Richard Suggett, one of the leading experts on the history of witchcraft and magic in Wales, has expressed in his writing how, compared to England and other European countries, the idea that witches and conjurers made a pact with the devil or demonic forces was not as common in Wales. In contrast, however, magical practitioners would admit to having worked with or sought the counsel of fairies, even boasting about their relationship with them.[246]

Having a good working relationship with fairies, or being able to subdue them via ceremonial ritual and such, was a mark of a good magical specialist. Some magical practitioners excelled in carrying out their work, which was at its core a trade, via their relationship with fairies. They obtained knowledge from them and could either beseech them or command them to do their bidding.

Seeking the Counsel of Fairies

There is an eighteenth-century Welsh-language tract against witchcraft, conjuration, and popular magic titled *Cas Gan Gythraul* written by an author known only as T. P. This text serves to convince the Welsh folk of the time that seeking the counsel of cunning folk, conjurers, and diviners is an inherently wicked act and should not be done. The tract is interesting for various reasons; for example, it records elements of folk belief and culture relating to magic contemporary to the time of the author and offers us a window into eighteenth-century Welsh magical beliefs.

Beyond this, the author of this tract also references the relationship between fairies and magical practitioners. The text outlines how magical specialists and practitioners would consult the fairies for various needs and reasons.[247] The author himself even recalls a story of how he once knew a man who kept company with the fairies, and he would meet with them once a month on a Wednesday night.[248]

It is via this text we learn not only how the clergy viewed the fairies as wicked spirits akin to demons, but also that those learned in magic would occasionally make pacts or forge relationships with them.[249] This is not the only text that makes reference to the relationship between fairies and magical specialists;

. . . .

246. Suggett, *Welsh Witches*, 33.

247. Tallis, *Cas Gan Gythraul*, 62–63.

248. Tallis, *Cas Gan Gythraul*, 65–66.

249. Tallis, *Cas Gan Gythraul*, 67.

the puritan John Penry also noted how there were swarms of soothsayers and enchanters in Wales who had filled the hearts of the common people with a reverence for the fairies.[250]

It is clear via these accounts, in conjunction with collected folklore, that magical practitioners were known for communing with, making pacts with, and seeking the counsel of the fairies. They sought them out in their own domain, usually in wooded areas and old ruins, and would conduct rites in order to call upon their aid. Some of these rites will be outlined later as we explore the magic recorded in secret books kept by cunning folk.

The fairies were considered powerful magical allies who could aid magicians in their work. However, this would of course be taken advantage of by those wishing to make money from people's naivety and struggle.

Confidence Tricksters

One interesting piece of evidence we have to support the notion that fairies played a role in the magical traditions of Wales is the fact that they are mentioned in witch trials. Trials against those accused of witchcraft were rather uncommon in Wales when compared to England and many other European countries.[251] However, we do have records of some trials involving witchcraft and magic, and occasionally these records refer to the association between magical practitioners and fairies.

In 1635 a woman by the name of Ann Jones was taken to court on accusations of felonious witchcraft.[252] Ann Jones was not her real name; she created a persona in order to forge a sense of anonymity. Her real name was Elen Gilbert, but for the sake of ease I shall refer to her as Ann Jones for the duration of this chapter.

Ann Jones claimed that she had a special relationship with the fairies. She was an enchanter who could charm away ailments and illnesses. She utilised magical ingredients, such as dew gathered in the month of May, to aid in healing people. Ann, however, was unfortunately a con artist. She wandered up and down Wales in search of parents with sick children; she would prey on their suffering and claim that she could convince the fairies to heal the children. To do this, she would need coins from the parents with the saliva of the child upon them to show the fairies, and thus they would be able to heal the child. She promised that she

. . . .

250. Suggett, A History of Magic and Witchcraft in Wales, 64.

251. Tallis, Cas Gan Gythraul, 5.

252. Suggett, Welsh Witches, 123.

only needed the money to show the fairies, and that once she had consulted with them, she would return it.

Unfortunately for the parents, Ann would then run away with the money, and they would never see her again. Eventually one of the parents she promised to help tracked her down and she ended up in court for her actions.

While Ann was certainly a confidence trickster, she was obviously drawing upon established belief that there were indeed magical practitioners who had a relationship with the fairies and could petition their help. For example, she claimed to utilise dew gathered in the month of May, which indicates that she was tapping into common folkloric beliefs.

Dew gathered in May has long been associated with bountiful magical virtue in numerous cultures.[253] Specifically in Welsh lore, dew gathered in May was said to be imbued with the power to bring good fortune, vitality, and protection.[254] The month of May in and of itself is also deeply associated with fairy lore. Calan Mai, the first of May, is one of the three Ysbrydnos, or spirit nights, of the year, and it is also the time when Gwyn ap Nudd, king of fairy, takes part in an annual battle in Welsh mythology.

Ann was not the only confidence trickster who operated in this manner. Just one year after Ann Jones's court case, a man named Harry Lloyd was also taken to court after he convinced people that he could persuade the fairies to heal the sick, as well as aid the poor in making their fortune.[255] Despite being a con man and trickster, however, Lloyd was well known as a cunning man who was learned in the art of fortune-telling and spirit conjuration.[256] Perhaps some of these con artists were genuine magical practitioners as well, and truly believed they had a working relationship with spirits and fairies.

Despite these confidence tricksters, we do also have historical records that show fairies did indeed play a role in magical practice. One example is the Llyfr Cyfrin, a mystic or secret book that belonged to an unnamed cunning man from Denbighshire.

. . . .

253.   Opie and Tatem, *A Dictionary of Superstitions*, 245–246.

254.   Rhŷs, *Celtic Folklore: Welsh and Manx*, 309.

255.   Suggett, *Welsh Witches*, 126–133.

256.   Rüdiger, *Y Tylwyth Teg*, 187–188.

Y Dyn Hysbys o Sir Dinbych–
The Cunning Man of Denbighshire

In the late 1970s, the writer and scholar Kate Bosse-Griffiths published a book in the Welsh language titled *Byd y Dyn Hysbys* (*The World of the Cunning Man*). In this book she explains how a Llyfr Cyfrin, which belonged to an anonymous nineteenth-century cunning man or conjurer, landed in her lap.[257] It was held at the time by the special collections at Swansea University.[258]

The book itself was a small thing, around two hundred pages long, and all handwritten. Of the two hundred pages, at least a dozen of them were written in the Welsh language. The book included information on charms, geomancy, and magic, which echoed what could be found in older grimoires or books on occult philosophy.

This mystic book belonged to an unknown magical practitioner from Denbighshire, and thus has been given the name *Llyfr Cyfrin y Dyn Hysbys o Sir Dinbych* (*The Mystic Book of the Cunning Man from Denbighshire*).

One incredibly interesting element of the book itself is that at least one tenth of the book provided instructions on how to call upon "yr Ysbrydion a elwir y Tylwyth Teg," the spirits we refer to as the Tylwyth Teg.

Unfortunately, the book itself is currently missing. A friend of mine, Andrew Phillip Smith, has been attempting to track it down for a while. And Andrew has also published a book that explores the Llyfr Cyfrin in more depth, as luckily Kate Bosse-Griffiths recorded quite a good amount of what could be found within its pages. His book is titled *Pages from a Welsh Cunning Man's Book*. Welsh readers may wish to track down the hard-to-find book by Kate Bosse-Griffiths, *Byd y Dyn Hysbys*. However, Andrew's book acts as an alternative for those who cannot read Welsh, or who cannot find the Welsh text.

What was recorded by Kate Bosse-Griffiths, however, provides us with an insight into how magical practitioners of the nineteenth century perceived the fairies and worked with them magically. Conjurers seemed to believe that fair-

. . . .

257. Llyfr Cyfrin translates to mean "secret book," though the word Cyfrin in the Welsh language can also mean "esoteric" or "mystic." Therefore, "esoteric book," or "mystic book," would also be an appropriate translation.

258. Bosse-Griffiths, *Byd y Dyn Hysbys*, 43.

ies were a sort of middle ground between angels and demons. They are easier to commune with and more sociable than infernal or celestial beings.[259]

The Tylwyth Teg in the Llyfr Cyfrin are ruled over by a king and a queen, namely Oberion and Meiob or Meicob. The name Oberion is one many readers may be familiar with, as it is indeed the same Oberon who is king of the fairies in Shakespeare's *A Midsummer Night's Dream*. However, Oberon's origins far predate this play. In fact, references to an entity that is likely the origin of this Oberon figure extend at least as far back as the thirteenth century, and there are numerous early modern magical manuals that describe methods to conjure a spirit named Oberon, whereas Meiob/Meicob is the queen of fairies, known under the name Micol—the work of William Lilly.[260]

To read more about Oberon and Meiob/Micol/Meicob, I recommend reading the introductory material to *The Book of Oberon* by Daniel Harms and Joseph H. Peterson. But suffice to say, this king and queen have their origins in older folklore that extends beyond the confines of Wales.

The book also gives specific mention to seven fairy sisters who are conjured in order to aid in magical tasks. These sisters are under the rulership of the king and queen of fairies, and yet they must be of high status because they are also said to rule over legions of spirits of their own. The sisters' names are as follows: Sibia, Reflilia, Forta, Folla, Affrita, Julia, and Benula.

It should be rather obvious by their names that these seven sisters do not have their origin in Welsh lore. In fact, the seven sisters are a common motif found in various magical traditions across Northern Europe. In most traditions they are considered demons associated with fevers, and their names change from culture to culture.[261] The seven sisters have been found in magical traditions across Germany, England, and parts of Scandinavia.[262]

Here, however, in this Welsh text, they are not demons associated with fevers. Instead, they are fairies who have knowledge of hidden treasures, and who have command over legions of spirits.

The book goes on to instruct various methods of how to conjure and commune with the Tylwyth Teg. The methods seem like a simpler version of ceremonial forms

. . . .

259.   Bosse-Griffiths, *Byd y Dyn Hysbys*, 130.

260.   Harms, Clark, and Peterson, *The Book of Oberon*, 21–24; Rüdiger, *Y Tylwyth Teg*, 194.

261.   Rüdiger, *Y Tylwyth Teg*, 195–200.

262.   Rüdiger, *Y Tylwyth Teg*, 195–200.

of magical practice, such as that found within the grimoire traditions. They are rit-ualistic and precise, yet not too inaccessible. Sometimes the methods call upon the need for the blood of a white hen or black cockerel, but for the most part the meth-ods simply call for cleanliness and offerings of things such as cream and pure water.

One method asks that the magician ensure the space where they are conduct-ing the rite be exceptionally clean. A circle must be drawn on the ground. A cloth must then be placed onto the ground or onto a short table, no more than around a foot off the ground. Atop the cloth, offerings must be placed, such as a roasted chicken or another roasted bird. As well as chicken or roasted bird, an offering of pure, clean drinking water must also be given in a bowl. Finally, an offering of cream in a dish must be placed upon the cloth. These offerings are said to make the fair folk more amiable or pleasant to deal with.

The text is very clear that numerous rules must be followed to ensure the effi-cacy of this rite. The magician must be clean; so, too, must the space; the offerings must not leave the circle at any time. If the instructions are followed, the magician must then call the names of the seven sisters and ask them, as well as the queen and king, Meicob and Oberion, to aid them in their bidding.[263]

Once conjured, the fair folk can aid the magician in seeking hidden treasure, seeking hidden knowledge, or finding cures for ailments and solutions to their clients' problems.

All that we have explored up to this point in this chapter showcases how fairies have always been a prominent aspect of the Welsh magical tradition. Whether it be common folk enacting magical wards or carrying charms in order to pro-tect themselves from the mischief and malice of the fairies, or cunning folk and conjurers beseeching them, conjuring them, and working in tandem with them to reach their goals, a relationship with, and a knowledge of, fairies has always been an imperative and important aspect of being a magical practitioner within a Welsh cultural context.

. . . .
263.   Bosse-Griffiths, *Byd y Dyn Hysbys*, 122–134.

Building a Working Relationship with Fairies

Now that we have explored the historical and folkloric context for working magic with the fairies, I thought it worthwhile to introduce some of the components of my own personal practice, which involves working with fairies.

A disclaimer before I continue. Things I will express in the following pages are merely elements of my own practice. Much of that practice is inspired and influenced by the fact I was born and raised within this culture, have been mentored by those who were also born and raised within this culture, and have spent many years of my life delving into traditional magical lore and practice. While much of what I am about to outline has a historical and cultural basis, it is tailored to work specifically for me. The same can be said of all the exercises that have been detailed in this book to this point. I recommend that if you are to incorporate any of these elements into your personal practice, you spend time altering them to suit your needs.

I was always taught by my fabulous mentors that the most important thing about magic is that it works. It matters not what others think, how pretty it looks, nor whether it fits the narrative fed to us by academics or armchair occultists. What matters is that the methods used wield real results. Everything I will outline here has wielded real results for me. If they do not for you, I invite you to play with them. Journal your process, experiment, and find what works.

And finally, obviously there are certain elements to my own craft and practice that are too personal for me to reveal publicly. What I share here is simply what I am happy to share. My hope is that this provides a framework or guide for those who wish to begin paving their own way but have no idea where to start.

Why Build a Relationship with Fairies?

The magic of my culture is undoubtedly deeply connected to the magic of the Otherworld. The very concept of Awen itself is entirely entrenched in lore concerning the Otherworld and the ways in which that world influences our own. It is my personal opinion that attempting to connect to the magical expression of this culture, without building a working knowledge and working practice with those otherworldly forces, is impossible.

When we open ourselves up to those otherworldly forces, we will undoubtedly make ourselves known to the denizens of that Otherworld, and the liminal entities that reside betwixt and between our world and the Other. To ignore those otherworldly and liminal entities would be foolhardy.

Beyond this, there is also a wealth of magic that will open up to you if you do take the time to dedicate yourself to understanding and forging relationships with the Otherworld. Embarking upon this work will be incredibly rewarding and eye-opening, though not in any way easy.

There is a tendency among people today to view fairies in a strict binary manner. Fairies are either twee beings of love, light, and positivity that bestow wonderful gifts to those who appease them, or they are terrifying monsters. The truth is somewhere in the middle, I find. It is important to establish a clear understanding of the difference between the whimsical fairies of pop culture and the very real numinous beings that are part and package of our cultural expression of magic.

Just as we see in the lore of old, fairies can be dangerous. To the inexperienced and the uninformed, they can cause devastation, misery, and misfortune. It is important, before committing to building a relationship with fairies, to first consider whether you are truly prepared. It is a commitment, and it will at times be challenging if done correctly. You will get things wrong and will suffer the consequences.

My advice is to take as much time as you can truly immersing yourself in the study of fairy lore, first and foremost. Do not stop at this book. Read widely and take your study beyond the page and into real life. If possible, speak with elders in communities about their views on these topics. I am fortunate in that I grew up in a Welsh-speaking community and spent many years talking to a variety of people about beliefs that persist to this day regarding the fairies. Some may think that fairy lore is a thing of the past, but in some corners, among some people, the fairies are still very much real and part of daily life. We live in an age of scepticism and logic, yet you would be surprised how many people I have known who are the farthest thing from a modern-day Pagan but will say, "Of course I don't believe in fairies! But ... I did experience something strange once."

Building a relationship with fairies and with otherworldly forces will provide you with a new perspective on life, as well as a new mode of practice. The methods I will outline in the next section are but simple, introductory methods of including a nod to the fair folk within your magical practice. In times of old, chance encounters with the fairies were far more common than actually summoning them. Summoning them was the domain of the cunning folk, the conjurers, and the ceremonial magicians. Because of this, many of the basic techniques listed below are inspired and informed by that very cunning tradition.

fairy Magic from a Welsh Witch's Grimoire

Adapted from the magical practices, rites, and spells in my own Llyfr Cyfrin, the following practical approaches to magic involve seeking the counsel of or building relationship with fairies. I invite the reader to trial these workings for yourself and adapt as you see fit so that they might work for you. Most of what is recorded here is inspired and informed by historical, or folkloric, sources. Some were methods taught to me by past mentors that I have adapted over many moons. All are personal to me, and all work for me.

Exercise
Cleansing Rite

Cleanliness is a common motif found in various elements of fairy lore. The fair folk seem to value cleanliness, and reward those who routinely ensure that their home or their person is clean. For example, household fairies rewarded women who kept the house warm, clean, and tidy.[264] The rituals contained within the Llyfr Cyfrin belonging to the unnamed cunning man from Denbighshire, which call upon the Tylwyth Teg, also emphasise the importance of the location of any ritual involving them being clean as well as the magician being well bathed.[265]

For these reasons, cleansing is a vital part of my personal devotional and magical relationship with the fair folk. The rite, as I will outline below, can be performed once a month or as and when needed, such as prior to a ritual or working. Personally, I conduct this rite at least once a month when the moon is new, and I tend to perform it if I am to undertake a ritual or working that I believe is incredibly important.

The rite is split into three parts: emotional cleansing, physical cleansing, and spiritual cleansing.

....

264. Sikes, *British Goblins*, 30.
265. Bosse-Griffiths, *Byd y Dyn Hysbys*, 123.

Emotional Cleansing

The purpose of cleansing oneself on an emotional level is to attempt to bring forth a clear, calm mind into the work that this rite precedes. This is not a method of purging our emotions, nor bypassing the need to confront and work with our emotions, but rather a method of accepting them for what they are and mindfully acknowledging all that you are feeling.

I perform this task by taking myself into a dimly lit room, somewhere I know I will not be disturbed for an hour or so, putting on some music that aligns with how I am feeling, sitting at a table with a journal before me, and spending twenty minutes or so in a meditative state, breathing, feeling, and doing whatever comes naturally. If during this time I feel the desire to laugh, cry, or scream, I allow myself to do just that. Then, when I feel ready, I journal my thoughts and feelings.

Perhaps this method would work for you too, or perhaps you can think of a better way. The point is to partake in an activity that will allow you to not only feel all that you are feeling at that moment, but to also work through it and reach a stage where your mind is calmed and your feelings have been met.

Once this is done, I will move on to the next step.

Physical Cleansing

This is as simple as it sounds: cleansing oneself physically. For me this includes taking a bath or a shower and scrubbing my body with sweet-smelling lotions, herbal concoctions, and lovely soaps. While doing so I visualise that any emotions or residual energies that have built up around me since I last performed a cleansing are being washed away by the waters. To finish, I dry myself before applying a body oil that smells sweet and fresh, anointing my body in preparation for the work I am to carry out.

Spiritual Cleansing

The entirety of this cleansing rite will be inherently personal. Only you know the best method to cleanse yourself on an emotional and physical level. The same can be said of spiritual cleansing. For me, I use a mixture of smoke cleansing and sound cleansing, along with visualisation, to cleanse myself energetically.

Arogldarthu is the word I like to use for smoke cleansing. Arogldarth is the Welsh word for incense, and so Arogldarthu is the verb of that word. It literally means "to incense" or "to scent with fragrant smoke." I burn dried rosemary in a small metal bowl upon some charcoal, flood a room with the smoke, and simply sit there, allowing the smoke to envelop my body. In Welsh herbal lore, rosemary is said to be imbued with the power to release people from imprisonment.[266] While in folklore this was carried out literally, to aid in prison escapes, I take on this folkloric quality metaphorically. I like to believe that the smoke of the rosemary as it flows over my body, and as I breathe it in, releases me of the shackles of my own anxieties and personally placed barriers.

Within my practice, I do not "use" herbs, but work with them as spiritual allies. Therefore, during this rite, I am calling upon the very spirit of the rosemary plant to aid me in my work, to help cleanse my body and spirit in preparation for the work ahead.

And finally, as the rosemary smoke begins to dissipate and the charcoals have burnt out, I ring a bell three times to dispel any leftover stagnant energies.

After undertaking these three methods of cleansing, you will feel prepared to carry out the work needed, assured of the fact that you are clean and appropriate to be in the presence of the fair folk.

Exercise
Basic Ritual Outline

This ritual can act as a basic framework or outline that you can alter and adapt to suit any magical work. To craft this ritual outline, I drew inspiration from three primary sources: first, from lore pertaining to fairies and their interactions with human enchanters; second, from the rituals and workings outlined in the Llyfr Cyfrin of the unnamed Denbighshire cunning man; and last, from my own magical experiences.

This outline calls upon and draws forth otherworldly forces and the presence of the fairies to your work. It includes offerings to be left for them

. . . .

266. Owen, *Welsh Folk-Lore*, 273.

and invocations directed to them. Whether you wish to simply connect to those otherworldly forces or to ask the aid of those forces in a magical working, this ritual outline can be used for either.

After cleansing yourself and choosing the location to work your magic, take yourself to that location with the following items:

+ A white cloth
+ Two small bowls
+ A bottle of fresh spring water
+ Fresh cream or a home-baked good such as a small cake, cookie, or similar
+ A wand made of hazel or oak wood

If you are conducting the ritual indoors, ensure that the room is well cleaned, dimly lit or dark, and that it is flooded with a sweet scent produced either by incense or an oil burner. If outdoors, choose a location that is associated with fairies, such as beneath the branches of an oak tree, in a liminal place such as the shore of a lake, or in an ancient ruin.

Carry out your usual ritual needs. For example, if you usually call to the four elements or the three realms or you cast a circle, do that first before moving forward with the next steps.

Take your wand of hazel or oak and hold it in both hands, as if presenting it to someone, and recite the following words from a Welsh poem titled "Cân y Tylwyth Teg," ("Song of the Fair Folk").

O'r glaswellt glan a'r rhedyn mân,
Gyfeillion dyddan dewch,
E ddarfu'r nawn, mae'r lloer yn llawn,
Y nôs yn gyflawn gewch.
O'r Chwarae sydd ar dwyn y dydd i'r dolydd awn ar daith.
Nyni sydd lon, ni chaiff gerbron,
Farwolion ran o'n gwaith.[267]

....
267. Owen, *Welsh Folk-Lore*, 87–88.

From grasses bright and bracken light,
Come, sweet companions, come.
The full moon shines, the sun declines,
We'll spend the night in fun.
With playful mirth we'll trip the earth,
To meadows green let's go.
We're full of joy, without alloy,
Which mortals may not know.[268]

Place your white cloth on a table or upon the floor. In each top corner, place the two empty bowls. Recite the following:

Cyfarchaf i yr Tylwyth,
Y rhain o dan reolaith Gwyn ap Nudd,
a'i frenhines fonheddig.
Derbyniwch yr offrymau yma.

I call to the fair folk,
The hosts under rulership of Gwyn ap Nudd,
And his noble queen.
Accept these offerings.

At this moment, pour the fresh spring water into one of the bowls, and the fresh cream or baked good will go into the other bowl. Next, take your wand into your left hand and hold it up to the sky. At the same time, point your right index finger to the ground. Recite the following:

O Dylwyth Teg, O deulu bonheddig yr arallfyd,
Rhowch aed i mi heddiw yn fy ngwaith.
Clywch pob gair, clywch pob swyn,
Fel fydd hi yn y deyrnas uwchlaw,
Felly fydd hi yn y deyrnas islaw.

. . . .
268. Translation from Owen, *Welsh Folk-Lore*, 87–88.

O Fair folk, O regents of the Otherworld,

Aid me in my work upon this day,

Hear every word, aid every spell,

As they shall be uttered above,

So they shall take form below.

And with this done, go forth and carry out your work, whether it be a devotional ritual, a celebration of the season, or a magical working. Move forward with the knowledge that the denizens of the Otherworld hear all that is said and see all that is done. Under their watchful eye they may choose to aid you in your work.

As your ritual comes to a close, ensure that you tidy the area and leave no trace that you have been there. Before you leave the space, recite the following.

Gwyn a dy frenhines,

Gwyn a dy dylwyth,

Diolchaf ti am fod yma heddiw.

Gad i ni adael mewn heddwch.

Gwyn and his queen,

Gwyn and his host,

I depart and bid farewell,

Allow us to leave in peace.

Walk away from the ritual ground without looking back. Over the next few days, take note of any strange occurrences and note them in your journal. You may experience strange dreams or notice that you have a sudden desire to leave offerings at your altar to Gwyn and his tribe more often than usual.

Exercise
Sensory Deprivation Trance Journeying

Receiving knowledge, inspiration, and wisdom from the Otherworld is a common theme found in prophetic and magical traditions within a Welsh cultural context. The bards of old believed that Awen, the very force of divine inspiration, flowed into our world from the Otherworld itself.[269] The Awenyddion or "inspired ones" were people who would glean prophetic wisdom and insight by entering trance-like states.[270]

Allowing the very wisdom and insight from the Otherworld to flow through us is an integral part of a practice that involves fairies, in my belief. The method I personally use to enter trance involves sensory deprivation, the idea being that we limit sensory input to enhance extrasensory input and ease the ability to journey, via a form of spirit flight, to the Otherworld.

One of the rituals mentioned in the Llyfr Cyfrin from Denbighshire, which conjures the fairies to assist a magical practitioner, asks that the practitioner enter a room that is devoid of light and flooded with sweet scents: "Mewn ystafell ddirgelaidd o oleuwch ac ynddi arogl peraidd, y mae'n gymwys gwneud y gwaith hwn. A room where all light is obscured and in it there is a sweet scent is an appropriate place to carry out this work."[271]

While that specific ritual is one to discover lost objects, as opposed to journeying or receiving wisdom from the Otherworld, I draw inspiration from the idea of a room flooded with sweet-smelling incense and kept in darkness to enable a trance-induced state of journeying.

Find a place where you will not be disturbed and where you can block out as much light and sound from the outside world as possible. Earplugs and blindfolds may be used to reduce as much sensory input as possible.

In this room, burn an incense that will smell sweet. It may be useful to burn certain herbs that will aid you in reaching a trance-like state. I

....

269.   Haycock, Legendary Poems from the Book of Taliesin, 114.

270.   Cambrensis, The Itinerary Through Wales, 179–183.

271.   Griffiths, Byd y Dyn Hysbys, 130.

tend to burn pine resin alongside rose petals and dried mugwort when carrying out this working. Ensure the incense is burning in a firesafe container, away from anything that could catch on fire.

Sit in the room and acknowledge the scent of the incense for a while. Recite these words:

Llen rhwng pob teyrnas, llen rhwng pob byd.
Agorwch y drws i'm dewiniaeth a'm hud.

Veils that divide, I ask you now part.
Open the ways for my oracular art.

If necessary, use blindfolds, face masks, or earplugs now. Lie or sit down in a comfortable position. Take a few moments to allow your body to adjust to being in complete darkness and complete silence. Steady your breathing. At this stage I like to employ a 4-7-8 method of breathing. Lift the tongue to the roof of the mouth, close the mouth, and breathe in through the nose for four seconds. Hold the breath for seven seconds, before finally exhaling for eight seconds.

The fact that my mind is actively counting and acknowledging my breath enables me to enter a state of calm, and the counting itself can sometimes aid in entering a trance state.

When your breath is stable and you feel calm, allow yourself to drift away from the burdens of day-to-day life. Allow your mind to open up to anything that may come your way. Nothing that appears in your mind at this point is random; make a mental note of any imagery, sounds, or words that come to mind. If mundane thoughts spring to mind, simply acknowledge them and move on.

When you awaken from this state—which might happen naturally or you could set an alarm to bring you back after an allotted time— spend some time writing about your experiences. Journal what you saw, what you felt, what words or visuals appeared to you.

While being in this state, I have experienced rather transcendental and visceral visions. I have journeyed to places beyond my imagination and received messages regarding all manner of things. It can take a while to find a method that works for you, so if this specific method does not work, I encourage you to attempt to find a trance method that suits you. Some people I know like to recite a verse to induce a trance state, others like to fiddle with something in their hands, and some rock back and forth. Find your method, experiment, and do not stress about it. Enjoy a period of experimentation.

Exercise
Crystal Scrying

Just as with entering trance states, scrying is a method of obtaining oracular visions, either from external sources or via the agents of our own unconscious minds. While scrying into a crystal may not seem at first glance to be a practice relating to fairies in any context, there is a specific Welsh connection to crystal scrying that ties the practice with fairies.

Scrying as an occult practice has been utilised for centuries by magicians, even the infamous John Dee, a sixteenth-century mathematician and confidante of Queen Elizabeth the First, practiced the art of crystal gazing with help from scryers.[272]

In an entry in the autobiography of the seventeenth-century astrologer William Lilly, we get a glimpse into a crystal scrying method that involves the fairies. Lilly was mentored in his craft by a Welsh man named John Evans, and John had a daughter named Ellen who was a scryer. It is noted in Lilly's autobiography that whenever Ellen Evans prepared to scry within her crystal, she would recite an invocation to the queen of the fairies: "O Micol, O tu Micol, regina pigmeorum veni! O Micol, O you Micol, queen of the fairies, come!"[273]

The queen of the fairies was invoked to aid in the scrying method. Fairies are, after all, said to be unrestrained by time and body, therefore they are aware of all things past, present, and future, and have knowledge of things beyond our understanding. With this in mind, they are powerful allies to aid in any divinatory practice.

. . . .

272. Wolley, *The Queen's Conjuror*, 167–169.

273. Lilly, *William Lilly's History of His Life and Times from the Year 1602 to 1681*, 229.

I have been practicing the art of scrying since my late teens, and it is something that connects me to my late paternal grandmother. In my first language, we refer to our grandmothers as Nain; my siblings and I would affectionately refer to my paternal grandmother as Nain Mŵ-Mŵ' (Grandmother Moo-Moo) because she lived on a farm surrounded by fields filled with cattle. My Nain Mŵ-Mŵ was a sweet woman who mostly kept to herself and went to chapel every Sunday. However, she also had an interest in divination.

Nain Mŵ-Mŵ was known locally for her talent at reading tea leaves. What intrigued me more so than her love for tea leaves, however, was her crystal ball. I never actually saw Nain Mŵ-Mŵ using her crystal ball, but she did sometimes joke about how she could see all things in it. The crystal she used was a sphere of glass with a few bubbles and colours at the centre, an unassuming thing that would sit on a table in the farmhouse. Family lore says she acquired all manners of visions and insights from her divinatory techniques. It was also said that she once saw something so terrible while divining that she packed up the practice altogether, hiding the crystal ball in a box and refusing to read anyone's leaves. I have always wondered what was so terrible to lead her to do this.

Nain Mŵ-Mŵ died when I was quite young, but her magical qualities continued to inspire me. When I became interested in witchcraft and magic, one of the first things I did was save up to buy a crystal ball of my own to carry on the tradition of scrying.

This is my own method of crystal scrying that I have developed over many years.

Before you start, you will need a crystal to scry in. This does not necessarily need to be a sphere, nor does it really need to be made of crystal. The important thing is that the crystal itself can sit on a table and that it is made of a reflective material. I have used flat pieces of crystals such as obsidian or quartz, glass crystal balls, and even mirrors to carry out this method.

My current favourite crystal to scry in is a sphere of clear quartz with hematite structures in the middle. The sphere is mostly clear, but with specks of red surging through the centre. Some prefer a completely clear sphere; the choice is entirely up to your preferences.

Preparing the Crystal

Once a suitable scrying crystal has been found, it is time to prepare it for the work. First, gather water from a lake. Lakes are often seen as liminal spaces that can act as doorways into the Otherworld. If possible, gather water from a lake associated with a fairy story or legend. As you gather the water, leave an offering for the lake itself. This could be anything from a few picked flowers from your garden to a poem or song you have written with it in mind. Give it in thanks.

Wait for the new moon to pass, and as the moon grows, once a week on a Thursday night, wash the crystal with the water gathered from the lake, all the while keeping in mind that you are imbuing the crystal with the liminal otherworldly qualities of the lake itself. Repeat this once a week until the next full moon. On the night of the full moon, soak the crystal in the lake water overnight.

The next night, remove the crystal from the water and dry it. Prepare a room so that it is dark and quiet. Try to block all light sources, except for the light of one lit candle. Place the crystal on a table, preferably with a black cloth beneath it. Place the candle somewhere behind you so that its light can gently illuminate the crystal, but so that the reflection of the flame is not visible in it.

Bring to the table two small bowls. Fill one with fresh, clean, drinkable spring water. In the other, place an offering in the form of a baked good, a picked flower, a poem written by hand, or something meaningful that you are willing to give to the queen of fairies. Say these words.

Offrymaf rhain i ti, Frenhines Annwfn.

I give these offerings to you, Queen of Annwfn.

Place your hands on the crystal and recite this invocation.

Frenhines Annwfn, cyfarchaf ti,
Dewch, ymunwch â mi, rhowch aed i mi yn fy newiniaeth heno.

Queen of Annwfn, I call to you,
Come, join with me, aid me in my oracular work this night.

Light some incense and recite the same invocation used in the journeying exercise.

Llen rhwng pob teyrnas, llen rhwng pob byd.
Agorwch y drws i'm dewiniaeth a'm hud.

Veils that divide, I ask you now part.
Open the ways for my oracular art.

Now stare at the crystal and allow yourself to sit there and gaze upon it for as long as you feel is necessary. You may not see images appear in the crystal itself, as often happens on television, but instead images will appear in your mind, words will come to you, and messages will come through.

Once you feel your time crystal gazing is over, pick up a journal or piece of paper and record all that came to you in your session. Keep the crystal in a safe place, perhaps with fabric draped over it or in a lovely box, only to be taken out for scrying sessions in the future.

Exercise
Crossroad Counsel

Crossroads have long been considered a liminal space where spirits dwell and where visions of extraordinary things can occur. In Welsh lore, fairies were often seen gathering at crossroads at midnight during liminal times of the year.[274]

This next working draws upon the lore of the crossroads but is not for the faint of heart. This working can be somewhat frightful and should only be carried out in a location where you are unlikely to be disturbed by living people.

. . . .
274. Thomas, *The Welsh Fairy Book*, 61–62.

Find a crossroads, where four roads or paths meet, in an obscure location where you are unlikely to come across another human being for a good while. Take a blindfold with you. Go to this location on a special day, such as one of the three spirit nights of the year: Calan Mai (May 1), Nôs Galan Gaeaf (October 31), or Gwyl Ifan (the summer solstice). This working is best carried out either at sunset or at midnight.

When you arrive at the crossroads, hail and welcome the spirits of the place and leave them an offering you deem fitting for the location. Sit somewhere near the crossroads where you can see all four roads meet. If possible, sit somewhere you will be concealed but can still see the roads or paths before you. Utter out loud your intentions for the evening. At this place, on this special day, at this special hour, you can, if you so desire, learn of things that would otherwise be unknown to you. If you have a specific question, utter the question to the winds. If not, simply say these words: "Reveal to me that which I should know."

Then, as the sun begins to set, or the clock strikes midnight, place the blindfold on your eyes. Now sit in this place for as long as you are able and listen. Listen to the voices carried by the winds. Listen to the sounds of the liminal spirits of the crossroads. Listen well, and you should be able to decipher messages. Visions may also flood your mind.

When you feel the working is over and you have learned all you need, remove the blindfold, utter a thank-you to the winds, and leave the place. As you walk home, do not turn around to look at the crossroads again. When you arrive home, journal your experiences. That night, sleep with a piece of iron under your bed or pillow or a piece of the rowan tree near you.

Conclusion
fairies Today

The interest and allure of fairies continues to inspire people today. The very fact that you have read this far is proof of that. It is easy to decide that fairy beliefs are a thing of the past, a relic of a world long lost. However, fairies are alive and well in the modern world. Whether they exist purely as characters in children's media, or as sensual protagonists in urban fantasy, or whether they play a significant role in modern spiritual and religious beliefs, the fairies are here to stay.

As we come to a close on this exploration of Welsh fairies, I thought it worthwhile to briefly explore what role fairies play in modern Paganism, and specifically how Welsh fairy traditions continue to grip people's imaginations across the world. I would also like to touch upon what role fairies play beyond the world of Paganism and witchcraft. Do people still encounter the fairies atop the mountains and near the lake shores of Wales? Or have they all but fizzled out into mere characters of fiction and fantasy?

fairies in Modern Paganism

One need only take a glance at any good section dedicated to Neopaganism, witchcraft, magic, the occult, and Paganism in a bookstore today to realise that fairies have a prominent place in modern occulture.

How did fairies become such a staple of modern-day Paganism and witchcraft? An obvious answer to that question would of course be that Pagans and witches are deeply inspired by the beliefs of the past that have their roots firmly in a reverence for the natural world. Fairies are part and package of the folkloric cultures of the past, so of course they play a role in Paganism today. However, we must also look at the expression fairies take within modern Paganism.

In the late nineteenth and early twentieth century, folklorists liked to attach euhemerization theories to fairy beliefs. One example of this happening within a Welsh context is with the folklorist Sir John Rhŷs.

Euhemerization is essentially an attempt by people to explain mythology and folklore by theorising that said myths and lore were inspired by real, historical events or people. In terms of fairies, euhemerization usually takes the form of fairies being theorised to be a memory of real, secretive, and mysterious races of people living alongside the dominant culture.

In Sir John Rhŷs's case, he theorised that the fairies of Welsh folklore were, at one point, a race of people who had survived from the Stone Age by living in mounds and in general obscurity and secrecy from general society.[275] Rhŷs believed that a cultural memory of these strange, underground-dwelling peoples who did not use iron weapons and had a culture that was inherently "other" to the standard cultures of contemporary society at the time eventually made its way into stories, which transformed into fairies.

Why is this relevant at all to how fairies came to be perceived in modern Paganism and witchcraft? Well, some of the leading figures in the development of Neopaganism latched onto these styles of euhemerization theories and even developed them further.

Margaret Murray was an Egyptologist and historian in the latter half of the nineteenth century and the early part of the twentieth century. She is most well known among Pagans and witches today as being the author of the 1917 book *The God of the Witches*. This book suggested a theory in which the people who

. . . .
275.   Rhŷs, *Celtic Folklore: Welsh and Manx*, 683.

were persecuted as witches in the early modern period were actually members of a secretive pagan cult that practiced devotion to a Horned God figure and a goddess in secrecy on the outskirts of broader society.

Margaret Murray delved into fairies within this book, stating that fairies of older folklore were in fact also outcasts, surviving pagan societies that had been mythologised over time into fairies.[276] Essentially, she conflated fairies with the members of her theorised witch cult.

Gerald Gardner, father of modern-day Wicca, firmly believed in Murray's theories and incorporated many of these ideas into his tradition of witchcraft.[277] In Gardner's 1954 book *Witchcraft Today*, which has a foreword written by Margaret Murray, there is an entire chapter dedicated to "Little People." In this chapter, it is clear that Gardner genuinely believed that the fairies were indeed a real race of people at one point in history. He describes the race of people who inspired the fairies as "small people bullied by their bigger neighbours and driven out of the best lands into the hills and woods and other inaccessible places."[278]

Gardner's belief in this theory, coupled with his addition of certain elements of fairy tradition into his witchcraft, had an ongoing effect on later iterations of witchcraft. To this day I meet Pagans who insist that fairies are in actuality a memory of "ancestors" who once dwelled in inaccessible places and had practices and beliefs that we would consider a form of magic today.

Gardner also specifically included elements of the Welsh tradition into his tradition, such as the inclusion of Gwyn ap Nudd as an epithet of the god of the witches.[279] The fact Gwyn ap Nudd, who is so intrinsically linked with fairy tradition, was given so much credence as a British expression of the god of the witches, and as guardian of the mound, emphasises how important older fairy and folkloric traditions were in setting the foundations for much of Neopaganism.

Welsh fairy beliefs would continue to inspire movements with a Pagan expression well into the latter half of the twentieth century. The goddess movement, in particular, tended to draw upon elements of Arthurian lore, which was in turn inspired by earlier Welsh mythology.[280] To this day there are numerous Pagan

. . . .

276. Murray, *The God of the Witches*, 35–40.

277. Rüdiger, *Y Tylwyth Teg*, 253.

278. Gardner, *Witchcraft Today*, 63.

279. Gardner, *The Meaning of Witchcraft*, 158.

280. Rüdiger, *Y Tylwyth Teg*, 254–257.

groups across the world who draw upon the mythology of Avalon, and Arthuriana, and in turn Welsh tradition, to inform their practices. The Lady of the Lake, who likely has a connection to the lake maidens of the Welsh fairy tradition, is revered by many a Pagan and witch today.

All of this has led us to today, where there are numerous groups who incorporate an element of the Welsh fairy tradition into their personal philosophies, cosmologies, and worldviews. Whether it be overt, such as in the case of groups like the Church of the Tylwyth Teg, or it be simply a part of their broader beliefs, as is the case with many streams of modern Druidry, the fairy tradition is there.

Fairies within a Pagan context take, from what I have experienced, three primary expressions. Modern-day Pagans perceive the fairies to either be, as Murray and Gardner as well as earlier folklorists suggested, euhemerized beings who have their origins in real history. If not that, then fairies are perceived in a very Paracelsian worldview, as elemental beings and spirits of the natural world. The elemental nature spirit approach is incredibly popular among theosophists and occultists, I have found. Or, finally, fairies may also be perceived as real, liminal, otherworldly entities as they are portrayed in older folk beliefs.

I fit into the latter category. Fairies to me are not necessarily *the* spirits of the natural world, nor are they a memory of some hidden race of people who lived alongside humans. I view the fairies as something inherently "other," denizens of an Otherworld that I truly believe to exist. Alternatively, they could also be understood to be entities that exist in this same world as ours, but on the periphery, beings we may never truly be able to fully define conclusively.

Fairies as they are perceived in modern-day Paganism, as well as various other streams of spirituality, take on a diverse set of roles. They can be beings of pure light, adorning oracle decks and being called to in spiritual healing sessions. Alternatively, they can be viewed as dangerous entities akin to demons. Pick up a variety of books written on the subject of fairies within a modern spiritual context and you will discover that they have taken on a diverse, broad expression today.

Fairies in Broader Culture

The fairy traditions of Wales have gripped the entire world within a Pagan or spiritual context. Entire spiritual groups or magical traditions have been founded as far away as the United States, Canada, Australia, and elsewhere, which draw inspiration from the fairy beliefs of Wales. But what of broader culture in Wales today? How do fairies and fairy beliefs exist among the people in Wales to this day?

One of my favourite memories from my late teens was riding on a bus from my village of Aberffraw to the town of Caergybi where my boyfriend lived. At the time, I was a few years into practicing magic and was, as always, utterly obsessed with all things fairy. There was a young child on the bus travelling with an older woman, whom I knew to be her grandmother. I was reading a book at the time and was completely oblivious to the world around me. That is, until I heard the phrase Tylwyth Teg uttered by the older lady.

I continued the ruse that I was reading my book but secretly began to eavesdrop. We were passing a lake called Llyn Maelog, which was situated right on the road between the villages of Llanfaelog and Rhosneigr on the bus journey. The grandmother started telling the child a story in Welsh about fairies, and that story has stayed with me to this day. It went a little something like this:

Do you see that lake over there? Well, not too long ago, the Tylwyth Teg who live in another world used to visit our world. Their world was under the lakes, and so they would come up out of the water to explore our world. When I was little, my mother had a friend called Bela, and she was the most beautiful woman I had ever seen. She dressed in the most beautiful dresses and had golden curly hair that went down to her bum.

Bela would give me the most amazing presents: handmade dresses, the most delicious home-baked goods, and books filled with pressed flowers. She smelled like roses, and she would hum to herself all the time in the loveliest singing voice. She was like a princess.

One summer day, Mother and I were sat in the garden enjoying the sunshine. I was playing with paper dolls on the grass. Bela came to visit and sat with my mother. I remember turning around after a while and seeing them hug each other and crying. That was the last time I ever saw my mother's friend Bela. Whenever I asked my mother where Bela had gone, she just said that she'd moved back to live with her family far away.

Years later, when I was much older, my mother told me the truth. Bela was a fairy who had come out of that lake, Llyn Maelog, to visit our world for a bit. She had fallen in love with a man from Aberffraw and decided to stay longer than she'd originally planned. But that summer day, her marriage with that man came to an end. And so, she went back home, through the lake, back to her fairy kingdom. And that is why I never saw Bela again.

This story absolutely delighted me, and it also delighted the woman's grandchild, who asked countless questions once the story was over. From that day on, whenever I passed Llyn Maelog on the bus, I thought of Bela the fairy woman who married a man from Aberffraw.

It intrigued me that this story seemed to follow the standard fairy bride motif: a fairy woman ascending from a lake and marrying a mortal man, before eventually having to return to the Otherworld. I always wondered if this story was true, or if it was just something the older lady made up to entertain her grandchild, drawing inspiration from older folklore.

Either way, I have come to realise that this story was evidence that the stories of fairies continue to hold the imagination of people across Wales. Hearing this woman recite this tale to a child, in the native Welsh language, and seeing the child being so captivated by it gave me hope that our folkloric storytelling traditions are still alive and well.

It is not only people from Wales who are captivated by our fairy stories, however. Tourists flock in the thousands to places such as the Eryri National Park, and specifically to places like Ffos Anoddyn near Betws-y-Coed, which is known in English as "fairy glen." Every tourist attraction in Wales that has a gift shop seems to carry books on our folktales and myths, and there are more books on these subjects available today than ever before.

In an earlier chapter of this book, we discussed the fairy beliefs that now surround the Pembroke corgi. This belief is a fairly modern one, that corgis are the steeds of the fairies, and yet it is one that has gripped all of Wales, despite originating in a poem written by a woman from Somerset, England. I have met farmers who own corgis and swear they are fairy dogs. This is evidence of how the fairy tradition is not only alive and well, but evolving.

Even if it only inspires stories told from grandmother to grandchild, quirky beliefs about dog breeds, and modern-day urban fantasy and fiction, it is undoubtedly true that fairies continue to hold a prominent place in the hearts and minds of the people of Wales.

fairies and Aliens

A question I am always asked whenever I discuss fairy folklore is whether fairy abductions, sightings, visitations, and experiences, as outlined in various older folktales, are still a regular occurrence in Wales. While you do get the occasional news websites sharing stories of fairy sightings in certain places, this doesn't seem to be as common as folklore would lead us to believe.

However, is it possible that fairy experiences have simply taken on a new identity? In a world of scientific thought, atheism, logic, reason, and scepticism, is it possible that people who do experience what could once have been classed as "fairy experiences" are simply labelling these experiences differently?

A man named Mr. Thomas went for a walk near the town of Castell Martin in Pembrokeshire, South Wales, in 1952. While out on this walk, Mr. Thomas would come across something incredibly strange. Amongst the sand dunes, he came across a strange, metallic-looking object. He attempted to get closer to the object, when suddenly he was confronted by two otherworldly beings. These beings warned Mr. Thomas not to come any closer, lest the object harm him. The two entities warned Mr. Thomas that humans were on a path of self-destruction and should change their ways. They then went on to recount to him how they had been visiting his world for centuries. Mr. Thomas eventually left the scene, unable to recall every detail of this strange encounter.[281]

One could easily reword this story to fit within the fairy tradition, and yet this is recorded as a mid-twentieth century encounter with aliens. The lore concerning aliens and UFOs seems to fit quite well with many fairy encounters. Abductions, visits to other worlds, objects unlike anything from our world, people who look somewhat human yet a little different, strange lights, lost time, loss of memory: these are all motifs common in both folktales concerning fairies and modern UFO and alien abduction stories.

Many people have noted these similarities over the years, though with the conclusion usually being that perhaps the fairy sightings and experiences of the past were simply encounters with aliens, altered to suit the sensibilities and beliefs

. . . .
281. Richards, *UFO Wales*, 38.

of the time. I, however, pose the opposite argument: What if the encounters being recorded to this day with aliens and UFOs are encounters with fairies and the Otherworld?

Nowadays, if I were to admit to being abducted by fairies, not many would take me seriously. And yet, if I changed the word fairy to alien, suddenly the believability of my story would rise. I would still, obviously, raise a few eyebrows, but in our modern society aliens seem more plausible than fairies.

The same could be said for ghost stories. I cannot begin to explain how many times a friend has opened up to me about a ghostly encounter that has left me thinking, *Could that have been a fairy encounter?* After all, how would one be able to tell the difference between a poltergeist and an angry household fairy? Or a ghostly apparition of young children dancing in a rural part of the country versus fairies dancing in a ring?

The fact that fairies predominately reside within children's stories within a sanitised, whimsical expression today leaves many believing that the belief in fairies is nothing but silly. Ghosts and aliens are easier to believe and are simply part and package of the High Strangeness territory popular today. Luckily, however, I believe things to be changing slowly.

In 2019, a documentary series titled *Hellier* was released on YouTube and Amazon Prime. The series followed Greg and Dana Newkirk, along with other paranormal investigators, who begin exploring strange goings-on that seem to pull them toward a place called Hellier in Kentucky. The series explores themes such as goblin sightings and the connection between fairy lore and, later, strange encounters with aliens and the paranormal.

Among the group is Dana Newkirk, a practicing witch who not only uses divinatory techniques as part of the paranormal investigations, but also leaves offerings to the potential entities they are interacting with.

This series has opened people's eyes to the intersection between High Strangeness and folkloric beliefs of the past. It is becoming clear that stories concerning strange interactions with the Otherworld are not a thing of the past, but perhaps today in our highly sceptical society, it is less likely we will label these encounters as "fairy."

Moving forward

And with that, we end our exploration and investigation into fairies within a Welsh context. My hope is that this will not be the final book you read on this subject. I encourage those of you who either live in Wales today or who have ancestors who hail from here to look at your specific region of Wales and delve into how fairies have shaped the folkloric landscape.

For those of you who read this book in hopes of incorporating fairy beliefs into your spiritual and magical life, I hope the book provided a theoretical underpinning to that ongoing process. Involving otherworldly forces and fairies in your spiritual and magical life is neither an easy nor quick process. Look to the suggested reading and bibliography of this book and continue on your journey.

I am glad that this topic is receiving more attention as of late. My only hope is that the fairy tradition continues to inspire people, and that more books and work in this field are published. I hope that this, my contribution to this field, will be a helpful guide and window into this tradition and culture I care so deeply about.

Bendithion Swynol,

Mhara Starling
Summer 2023

Guide to Welsh Pronunciation

Here you will find a glossary of various prominent words and terms mentioned in this book and their meanings. The words featured here are words from my native Welsh language, and I have provided a guide to the phonetic pronunciation for those who do not speak Welsh. I have also created a YouTube video alternative to this glossary, which can be found on my YouTube channel (*Mhara Starling*), so that you can hear these words as they are meant to be pronounced.

A note: the Welsh alphabet consists of most of the same letters as the English alphabet but excludes some letters and includes others.

The Welsh Alphabet

a, b, c, ch, d, dd, e, f, ff, g, ng, h, i, l, ll, m, n, o, p, ph, r, rh, s, t, th, u, w, y

Welsh Vowels

A rather ignorant and tired joke that is often flung at the Welsh language is the idea that we "have no vowels." English speakers often bemoan the difficulty of understanding how some words seemingly have no vowels at all. However, what they forget when they make these comments is that Welsh is an entirely different language, and as such we also have a different vowel system. In fact, Welsh has more vowels than English! The Welsh vowels are:

a, e, i, o, u, w, y

And they are pronounced as such:

A = *Ah*, as in *apple*.

E = As in the *e* in *bed*, never as in *be*.

I = *Ee*, as in the double *ee* in *tree*.

O = *Aw*, as in the *o* in *from*.

U = A slightly difficult one for non-Welsh speakers; essentially an *ee* noise, as in *tree*, but with the tongue rolled into the shape of a *u*.

W = *Ooh*, as in the noise the double *o* makes in *food*.

Y = This is one of the only Welsh letters that can change depending on context. For the most part, *y* is pronounced *uh*, as in the sound *u* makes in English in words such as *turn*, or like the noise *e* makes in words such as *the*. However, sometimes, usually in multisyllabic words, the *y* becomes more of an *ee* sound, more or less indistinguishable from the Welsh *u*. The best word to showcase this difference in pronunciation is *ysbyty*, the Welsh word for *hospital*, which has three *ys*. The first two *ys* are pronounced *uh*, whereas the final *y* is pronounced more so as an *ee* noise. *Uss-BUTT-ee*.

Welsh is a phonetic language, and therefore once you learn how to pronounce each letter in the alphabet, it is fairly easy to deduce how a word should sound. For example:

The Welsh word for *apple* is *afal*. If you know that in the Welsh alphabet *a* is pronounced *ah*, *f* is pronounced like an English *v*, and *l* is pronounced similar to *l* in English, as in *lake* or *little*, then all one need do is put those letters together. *Ah, v, ah, l… ahvahl… afal!*

Find an easy guide to the Welsh alphabet online and listen to how each letter is pronounced. Practice these pronunciations and your Welsh will improve greatly in no time at all! It is only in very rare circumstances a letter might be pronounced differently to how it is pronounced in the alphabet, such as with *y*, or in situations where there is a circumflex above a vowel.

A letter with a circumflex above it (â, ê, ŷ, ŵ) implies that the vowel is extended. So a word such as *mon*, if spelled without a circumflex, would be pronounced *mohn*; *môn* is pronounced more like *mawn*. The *o* is extended into more of an *aw* noise.

A non-native speaker, or someone unfamiliar with Welsh, may find themselves stumped at the additional letters of *ch, dd, ff, ng, ll, ph, rh*, and *th*.

To those whose first language is English, it may seem strange to consider what seemingly appears to be two letters together as one singular letter. However, individual letters they are. Each of these letters creates a specific sound:

ch—A throaty sound emanating from the back of the throat. Similar to how a Scottish person would pronounce the *ch* in *loch*. It is not an *s* sound, nor a sound similar to the *ch* in English words such as *cheek*.

dd—The sound of this letter comes from the front of the mouth. Similar to the sound *th* in English words such as *there, them*, and *this* but not like the *th* in English words such as *thick* and *thin*.

ff—This is a hard *f* sound as in the English words *fight, freedom*, or *full*. The singular *f* in Welsh is a *v* noise as in *video*.

ng—Think of *ng* as the same sound found at the end of English words such as *thinking, listening*, or *singing*.

ll—The double *l* letter is one of the most complex Welsh letters. There is no English counterpart. It is a sound similar to that of a hiss.

ph—Pronounced similarly to the *ph* in the English word *phrase*.

rh—Very similar to a rolling *r* sound when used within words. Roll your *r* and then exhale or sigh while doing so.

th—Pronounced as the *th* in the English words *thick* and *thin*.

For a more in-depth guide to Welsh pronunciation, please look to my You-Tube channel. Simply search *Mhara Starling* on YouTube. And now for a glossary of the common words, names, and place-names found within this book. The phonetic method of pronouncing them is in brackets, though I have left the *ll* and *dd* as they would be in Welsh due to a lack of equivalent English sounds.

Welsh Glossary

Adar Rhiannon (*Ah-DARR Rhee-ANN-on*)—The Birds of Rhiannon. Magical birds that have the ability to wake the dead and lull the living into a sleep-like state. They appear in the second branch of the Mabinogi and in the tale "How Culhwch Won Olwen."

Afon (*Ah-VON*)—The Welsh word for *river*.

Annwfn (*Ann-OO-vuhn*)—Also spelled *Annwn* (*ANN-oon*); the Welsh Otherworld where fairies are said to come from and where all inspiration is born.

Arallfyd (*Arr-All-vid*)—Literally "Other World"; another way of denoting the Otherworld. *Arallfydol* (*Arr-All-VUD-all*) would be a way to say *otherworldly*.

Arawn (*AR-ow-n*)—Lord of Annwfn, the Otherworld, in the first branch of the Mabinogi. One of many otherworldly kings from Welsh lore.

Arianrhod/Aranrhod (*Ah-ree-ANN-rod/Ah-RAN-rod*)—A goddess from the fourth branch of the Mabinogi; sister of Gwydion.

Arogldarth (*Ah-ROG-uhl-darth*)—Incense.

Awen (*AH-when*)—Blessed, holy gift of inspiration. A force that flows from the Otherworld like a river or a gentle breeze, and we make form of it.

Barclodiad y Gawres (*Bar-CLOD-yad Uh GOW-ress*)—Literally "Giantess's Apronful," a name given to various ancient monuments across Wales. Folklore states the megalithic monuments were formed when a giantess dropped an apronful of stones onto the ground. *Gow* sound in *Gawres* rhymes with *cow* not *toe*.

Bendith y Mamau (*Ben-DEETH Uh MAM-eye*)—Literally "the mother's blessing," a term used to describe the fair folk, especially in regions of South Wales.

Bendithion (*Ben-DEETH-ee-on*)—Blessings.

Blodeuedd (*Blaw-DAY-edd*)—A woman conjured from flowers in the fourth branch of the Mabinogi. She was made purely to be a wife to Lleu Llaw Gyffes (*Llay llOW Guff-ess*), and when she attempted to murder Lleu, she was transformed into an owl by Gwydion, and thus became Blodeuwedd (*Blaw-DAY-whedd*).

Brân (*Br-AH-n*)—A giant and king of Wales in the second branch of the Mabinogi. Also known by the epithet Bendigeidfran (*Ben-dee-GAYD-vrahn*), meaning "Brân the Blessed."

Branwen (*BRAHN-when*)—Brân's sister, who was married to the Irish king in the second branch of the Mabinogi. The abuse she suffered under the hand of the Irish caused a war between the Irish and the Welsh.

Brenin Llwyd (*BREH-neen Ll-OO-id*)—Literally "Grey King" or "Monarch of the Mist"; a folkloric character who haunts mountain ranges.

Brwyn (*BROO-in*)—Rushes, common rush; a type of plant that grows usually in wetland habitats.

Buchedd Collen (*Bee-chEdd CAW-ll-ehn*)—"The Life of Saint Collen," the lore of the life of a seventh-century monk who was said to have interacted with Gwyn ap Nudd atop Glastonbury Tor.

Bwbach (*BOO-Bahch*)—A household fairy or spirit; maidens would keep houses clean and warm to appease the bwbach.

Bwgan (*BOO-gahn*)—A generic word to describe a variety of frightful spirits and creatures from Welsh lore. A monster, bogie beast, or terrifying folk devil.

Bwyd yr Ellyllon (*BOO-id Uhr Ell-Uhll-ON*)—Literally "food of the ellyllon"; a term used to describe fungi, mushrooms, toadstools. In particular poisonous mushrooms inedible to humans.

Caer Siddi (*KYRE See-thee*)—One of the many forts of Annwfn in "*Preiddeu Annwn*," a poem about a journey to the Otherworld. Caer Siddi can be roughly translated to mean "otherworldly fort." The word *siddi* is theorised to have its root in the Irish *sidh*.

Calan Mai (*KAH-lann Mye*)—The "calend of May," literally the first day of May. One of the three spirit nights of the year. An annual celebration of the start of the summer season; a time of divination and magic.

Cantre'r Gwaelod (*KAN-tray-uhr GWAY-lodd*)—A region of Wales that, according to myth, sank beneath the waves of the sea.

Canwyll Corff (*KAH-noo-eell KOR-ff*)—A corpse candle; an omen of death that expresses itself as a glowing orb of spectral light. They travel the path the coffin of the soon-to-be-deceased will take on its way to be buried.

Cas Gan Gythraul (*KASS Gahn GUTH-rye-uhl*)—Literally "The Devil's Aversion," the title of a seventeenth-century tract against seeking the counsel of conjurers, diviners, and cunning folk.

Caws Llyffant (*COW-ss Ll-uh-phant*)—Literally "frog's cheese," another folk term used to describe mushrooms. Sometimes given as an offering to fairies.

Ceffyl Dŵr (*KEH-phil DOOH-uhr*)—A water horse, a frightful fairy creature.

Cerddinen (*Kare-ddIN-ehn*)—Rowan, the rowan tree, and rowan berries, which are said to protect from the mischief and malice of fairies.

Cerridwen (*Kerr-ID-when*)—Witch, Goddess, and Mother; she who brewed a potion of pure Awen in order to help her son overcome his utter ugliness.

Cewri (*COW-ree*)—Giants, the singular for giant being *cawr* (COW-er).

Chwedlau (*Ch-WED-lie*)—Folktales or fables.

Cnocars (*Kuh-KNOCK-ars*)—An alternate name for *coblynnau*; fairy-like beings who dwell in mines and under the earth.

Coblynnau (*Cob-LUNN-eye*)—Fairy-like beings who dwell in mines and under the earth.

Consuriwr (*Con-SEER-yew-uhr*)—A conjurer, a type of magical practitioner who conjures spirits.

Corach (*KORR-ah-ch*)—The modern Welsh term for earth-dwelling, fairy-like beings similar to dwarves or gnomes, though not necessarily found much in traditional Welsh lore.

Creiddylad (*Krey-THULL-add*)—A character from Welsh mythology said to be one of the most beautiful women in all of Britain. Gwyn and Gwythyr fight for her hand every May Day.

Criafol (*Kree-AV-all*)—An alternate name for rowan, the rowan tree, and rowan berries, which are said to protect from the mischief and malice of fairies.

Cŵn Annwn/Annwfn (*COON ANN-oon/Ann-OO-vn*)—The hounds of the Otherworld; beings that have pure white fur everywhere on their bodies except their ears, which are bloodred.

Cŵn Wybir (*COON Wee-BEER*)—Sky dogs; an alternate name for the hounds of the Otherworld. Cŵn Wybir tend to appear more frequently in folklore as terrifying hounds that howl and growl in the skies as an omen of death.

Cylch Cyfrin (*KILL-ch Kuv-REEN*)—A secretive magical group that operated on the Isle of Anglesey in the late nineteenth and early twentieth centuries.

Derw (*DEH-roo*)—Oak, as in the oak tree.

Dewin (*DEH-ween*)—The Welsh word for *wizard*.

Du'r Moroedd (*DEE'r MORE-oy-dd*)—Black of the Seas; a horse that can gallop upon the waves of the sea.

Dyfed (*DUH-ved*)—In Welsh history, a region in the southwest of Wales. In mythology, the kingdom ruled over by Pwyll, who went on to marry Rhiannon.

Dyn Hysbys (*DEEN Hus-BISS*)—A Welsh term for a cunning man or male magical specialist. A feminine equivalent would be *Gwraig* (*Gooh-RYE-guh*) *Hysbys*.

Dynion Bach Teg (*Duhn-ee-ON Bah-ch TEGG*)—Literally "small fair men," an alternate name for fairies in some regions of Wales.

Eithin (*Ey-THEEN*)—The Welsh word for the plant gorse, which is said to ward away fairies.

Ellyll (*Ehll-Eell*)—A fairy-like creature that haunts the landscape and the ruins of old places.

Ellyll-Dân (*Ehll-Eell DAHN*)—Elf fire; a glowing spectral orb that leads travellers astray in old lore.

Emrys (*Em-RISS*)—The name of a boy in Welsh lore who would later be used as inspiration for the infamous wizard Merlin. Essentially an earlier Welsh version of Merlin.

Englyn (*Eng-LEEN*)—A type of Welsh poem form that involves syllabic counting and rigid rules about rhymes and half rhymes. Often Englynion are seen as a form of song-spell in Welsh mythology.

Eryri (*Eh-RURR-ee*)—Wales's largest national park. A mountainous region filled with mythology and lore.

Ffos Anoddyn (*Foss ANN-odd-in*)—A rocky, tree-lined ravine near the village of Betws-y-Coed in North Wales. Referred to in English as "fairy glen," it is a place abundant with folklore and attracts numerous visitors seeking inspiration.

Ffynnon (*Fuh-NON*)—The Welsh word for *well* or *spring*.

Gorsedd Arberth (*Gorr-SETH Arr-BEAR-th*)—A significant hill in Welsh mythology where Pwyll sees Rhiannon for the first time.

Grug (*GrEEg*)—Heather, a plant the fairies are said to dance upon in the summer months in Welsh lore.

Gwendol Wrekin ap Shenkin ap Mynyddmawr (*Gwen-DOLL Ree-KIN app Shen-KIN app Muhn-ith-mah-oohr*)—A giant who was responsible for creating the Wrekin, a hill in Shropshire.

Gwenhudwy (*Gwhen-HID-wee*)—A mermaid from older Welsh sources said to be the "shepherd of the waves."

Gwrach (*GOO-rach*)—In modern Welsh, a term used to describe witches, though etymologically a term that implies something disgusting or a haggard old woman.

Gwragedd Annwn/Annwfn (*GOO-rag-eth ANN-ooh-vunn*)—The wives of the Otherworld, a term often given to describe the fairy maidens who marry mortal men.

Gwyddno Garanhir (*Gweeth-NO Garr-ANN-here*)—The ruler of a sunken land off the coast of Wales known as Cantre'r Gwaelod (*KANN-treh-'r GWAY-lodd*).

Gwydion (*Gwee-dee-ONN*)—A mischievous magician from Welsh mythology.

Gwyl Ifan (*GOO-eel Eve-ANN*)—Also known as Gwyl Ganol Haf (*GOO-eel GANN-all Have*), it is the celebration of Midsummer in Wales. One of the three spirit nights within the Welsh calendar.

Gwyn ap Nudd (*Goo-WIN app Neath*)—A mythical character who is regarded as being king of fairies and leader of the Wild Hunt.

Gwythyr ap Greidol (*Gwee-THERE app Gray-DOLL*)—A nemesis to Gwyn ap Nudd. Every May Day Gwyn and Gwythyr battle in an annual fight that will continue until the end of time itself.

Hafgan (*Hav-GANN*)—A king in the Otherworld who fights with Arawn.

Hud (*Heed/Hid*)—The Welsh word for *magic*.

Kat Godeu (*Cat God-ay*)—A mysterious and enigmatic medieval poem that features Gwydion, a magician from Welsh lore, as he summons via his magic an army of trees.

Llên Gwerin (*LI-ENN Goo-WHERE-een*)—The Welsh term for *folklore*.

Llwyd ap Cilcoed (*LIOO-id app Kill-COYED*)—A mischievous character in the third branch of the Mabinogi who is likely otherworldly in nature.

Llyfr Cyfrin (*Llee-VUHR CUV-reen*)—Literally translates to "mystic" or "secret book"; a term applied to the journals and books that once belonged to conjurers, magicians, and magical specialists of the past.

Llyn (*LI-IN*)—The Welsh word for *lake*.

Llyn y Fan Fach (*LI-IN Uh Van VAH-ch*)—A lake located in the south of Wales where, according to folklore, a fairy maiden once rose out and married a mortal man in the area.

Mabinogi (*Mabb-ee-NOGG-ee*)—The four branches of the Mabinogi make up what is considered the primary corpus of Welsh mythology. You will often see it spelled *Mabinogion*, which is believed to be a scribal error. *Mabinogion* is, however, used today in academia to denote the four branches of the Mabinogi and the non-Mabinogi tales often placed with the Mabinogi in translations.

Maen Awenyddol (*Mine Ah-WHEN-uth-all*)—Literally "inspiring stone," a stone we created in an exercise in this book.

Mallt y Nôs (*MAH-llt UH noss*)—A folkloric character who is said to ride upon stormy nights, gathering the souls of the dead.

Matholwch (*Mah-THAWL-ooh-ch*)—The king of Ireland in the second branch of the Mabinogi.

Melltith y Mamau (*Mehll-TEETH uh MAH-my*)—A possible earlier version of Bendith y Mamau, where instead of being the blessings of the mothers, the fairies were the curses of the mothers.

Menyg Ellyllon (*Meh-NEEG Ehll-UHll-onn*)—A folk name for the foxglove flower in Welsh. It literally translates to mean "the gloves of the elves/ellyll."

Môr-Forwyn (*More VORR-win*)—A mermaid; literally translates to "sea-maiden." A term applied to the fair folk of the seas.

Myrddin (*MUHrr-theen*)—An older name for Merlin in Welsh.

Niwl (*New-UHL*)—The Welsh word for *mist*.

Nôs Galan Gaeaf (*Noss Gah-LANN Gay-av*)—The eve of winter, Halloween, October 31.

Pair Dadeni (*Pah-eer Dah-DEN-ee*)—A mystical cauldron in the second branch of the Mabinogi that can bring the dead back to life.

Plant Annwfn (*Plant ANN-Ooh-vuhn*)—An alternate name for fairies in Wales, which means "the children of the Otherworld/lower worlds."

Plant Rhys Dwfn (*Plant RHEESE dooh-vuhn*)—An alternate name for fairies in Wales, which means "the children of Rhys the Deep"; Rhys the Deep was said to be a ruler of a land beneath the waves.

Plant yr Is-Dwfn (*Plant uhr EES-dooh-vuhn*)—An alternate name for fairies in Wales, which means "the children of the lower/deeper worlds."

Plentyn Newid (*Plehn-TIN neh-weed*)—A changeling, a fairy creature left in the place of a mortal baby who was stolen away by the fairies.

Pobol Gyfarwydd (*Poh-BOLL Guv-ARR-with*)—A term applied to cunning folk, wisewomen, and magical specialists in Wales, literally meaning "those who are familiar."

Pobol Hysbys (*Poh-BOLL Huss-BISS*)—As above, another term used to describe magical specialists in Wales.

Preiddeu Annwn (*PREY-they Ann-oon*)—"The Spoils of Annwn," a middle-Welsh poem found in the Book of Taliesin that outlines a journey to the Otherworld.

Pwca (*Pooh-KAH*)—A mischievous goblin-like being from Welsh lore who haunts ancient monuments and can cause trouble for humans.

Pwyll (*PWEE-ll*)—The prince of Dyfed, and later named the chief of the Otherworld in the first branch of the Mabinogi.

Rhaffau'r Tylwyth Teg (*Rhah-FIRE Tuhl-WITH Tehg*)—Literally "the ropes of the fairies," a name given to gossamer that gathered on marshy land.

Rhamanta (*Rhah-MAN-tah*)—A form of divination maidens would partake in to seek information about their future lovers.

Rhedyn (*Rheh-DINN*)—The Welsh word for *ferns* or *bracken*.

Rhiannon (*Rhee-ANN-onn*)—An otherworldly character who marries Pwyll, prince of Dyfed. Known today as a goddess to Pagans and witches.

Rhitta Gawr (*Rhee-TAH GOW-er*)—A notorious giant who battled with numerous British kings and made a cape out of their beards. His grave is said to be atop the tallest mountain in Wales.

Swyn (*SOO-in*)—The Welsh word for *charm* or *spell*.

Swyngyfaredd (*SOO-in-GUHV-are-eth*)—The art of enchantment, the native form of magic or enchantment.

Swynwraig (*SOO-in-wry-guh*)—Literally meaning "spell wife" or "magic woman," it is the feminine word for a woman who practices enchantment and is specifically learned in the art of charming. The masculine version would be *Swynwr* (*SOO-in-ooh-uhr*).

Swynydd (*SOO-in-ith*)—A generic, gender-neutral term for *Swynwraig*; a person learned in enchantment, magic, and the art of charming.

Taliesin (*Tahl-EE-ess-inn*)—The greatest poet and prophet in Welsh legend and lore.

Twrch Trwyth (*TOOR-ch TROO-ith*)—A great boar hunted in the story of Culhwch and Olwen.

Tylwyth Teg (*Tuhl-WITH Tehg*)—Literally "the fair family"; the most common term used to describe fairies in Welsh.

Y Teulu (*Uh TAY-lee*)—Literally "the family"; an alternate term given to describe fairies in Welsh.

Ymenyn y Tylwyth Teg (*Uh-menn-in Uh Tuhl-WITH tehg*)—The butter of the fairies; a type of oil that appears on rocks.

Ynys Enlli (*UHN-iss En-llEE*)—Bardsey Island, an island off the coast of North Wales.

Ynys Gwales (*UHN-iss Goo-AL-ess*)—An island in Welsh mythology where time and grief had no effect on those upon the island.

Ynys Môn (*UHN-iss MAWN*)—The Isle of Anglesey, a large island in northern Wales.

Ynys Wydryn (*UHN-iss WID-rinn*)—An old Welsh name for Glastonbury, which literally translates to "the glass island."

Yr Hen Ogledd (*Uhrr HEHNN OGG-laydd*)—"The old north"; a term applied to a once Brythonic region in the southernmost part of Scotland and northernmost part of England.

Yr Hwch Ddu Gwta (*Uhrr WHO-ch Thee GOOH-tah*)—The black tailless sow, a Halloween folk devil.

Yr Wyddfa (*Uhrr WITH-vah*)—The tallest mountain in Wales.

Ysbaddaden (*Uss-bah-THAH-den*)—A giant found in Welsh mythology who is said to be the chief of all giants.

Ysbryd (*UHSS-breed*)—The Welsh word for *spirits*.

Ysbrydnos (*UHSS-bruhd-noss*)—Literally "spirit night." There are three spirit nights in the year: May Day, Midsummer, and Halloween.

Ystoria Taliesin (*UHSS-torr-ee-ah Tahl-EE-ess-inn*)—The story of the birth of Taliesin, which involves Witch Goddess Cerridwen.

Bibliography

Manuscripts Consulted

The National Library of Wales has many manuscripts available to view digitally via their website: www.library.wales/discover/digital-gallery/manuscripts/

Peniarth MS 1. Designated *Llyfr Du Caerfyrddin* (*Black Book of Carmarthen*). Circa thirteenth century. National Library of Wales.

Peniarth MS 4. Designated *Llyfr Gwyn Rhydderch* (*White Book of Rhydderch*). Circa fourteenth century. National Library of Wales.

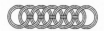

Bevan, Gareth, and Patrick Donovan, eds. *Geiriadur Prifysgol Cymru* (*A Dictionary of the Welsh Language*). Cardiff: University of Wales Press, 2004.

Biddlecombe, Anne G. "Corgi Fantasy." In *An Illustrated Study of the Pembroke Welsh Corgi Standard*. Ed. The Illustrated Standard Committee of the Pembroke Welsh Corgi Club of America, Inc. Place Unknown: The Pembroke Welsh Corgi Club of America, Inc., 1975.

Bosse-Griffiths, Kate. *Byd y Dyn Hysbys: Swyngyfaredd yng Nghymru*. Talybont: Y Lolfa, 1977.

Boyer, Corinne. *Under the Witching Tree: A Folk Grimoire of Tree Lore and Practicum*. London: Troy Books, 2016.

Briggs, Katharine. *Abbey Lubbers, Banshees & Boggarts: A Who's Who of Fairies*. London: Butler & Tanner Ltd., 1979.

Bromwich, Rachel, ed. *Trioedd Ynys Prydein: The Triads of the Island of Britain*. Croydon: University of Wales Press, 2014.

Brooke, Stopford A. *The History of Early English Literature*. London: Macmillan & Co, 1899.

Burne, Charlotte Sophia. *Shropshire Folk-lore: A Sheaf of Gleanings*. London: Trübner & Co, 1883.

Cambrensis, Giraldus. *The Itinerary Through Wales*. London: J. M. Dent & Co. 1908.

Classen, Albrecht, ed. *Handbook of Medieval Culture: Fundamental Aspects and Conditions of the European Middle Ages, Vol. 1*. Berlin: Walter de Gruyter GmbH, 2015.

Conran, Tony. *Welsh Verse: Fourteen Centuries of Poetry*. Bridgend: Seren, 1967.

Daimler, Morgan. *Fairies: A Guide to the Celtic Fair Folk*. Croydon: Moon Books, 2017.

Daimler, Morgan. *A New Dictionary of Fairies: A 21st Century Exploration of Celtic and Related Western European Fairies*. Hampshire: John Hunt Publishing, 2020.

Davies, Sioned. "Mythology and the Oral Tradition: Wales." In *The Celtic World*, edited by Miranda J. Green, 785–91. New York: Routledge, 1995.

Davies, Sioned, and Nerys Ann Jones, eds. *The Horse in Celtic Culture: Medieval Welsh Perspectives*. Cardiff: University of Wales Press, 2022.

Davies, Sioned, ed. *The Mabinogion*. New York: Oxford University Press, 2008.

Evans, Hugh. *Y Tylwyth Teg*. Liverpool: Gwasg y Brython, 1935.

Evans-Wentz, W. Y. *The Fairy Faith in Celtic Countries*. First published in 1911. Facsimile Ed. Glastonbury: The Lost Library, 2016.

Fardd, Myrddin. *Llên Gwerin Sir Gaernarfon*. Caernarfon: Y Genedl Gymreig, 1909.

Fernandez, Carles-Enric. "Legends of the lakes of Wales: Thematic classification and analysis." PhD diss., University of Wales Trinity Saint David (United Kingdom), 2012. Accessed July 8, 2023. https://repository.uwtsd.ac.uk/id/eprint/381/1/CARLES%20FERNANDEZ.pdf

Ford, Patrick K. *The Mabinogion: And Other Medieval Welsh Tales*. Oakland, CA: University of California Press, 2019.

Gardner, Gerald B. *Witchcraft Today*. Essex: Jarrolds Publishers (London) Ltd., 1968.

Goodrich, Jean N. "Fairy, Elves and the Enchanted Otherworld." In *Handbook of Medieval Culture: Fundamental Aspects and Conditions of the European Middle Ages, Volume 1*, edited by Albrecht Classen, 431–63. Berlin, Germany: De Gruyter, 2015.

Graves, Robert. *The White Goddess*. London: Faber and Faber Limited, 1999.

Gruffydd, Elis. *Tales of Merlin, Arthur, and the Magic Arts: From the Welsh Chronicle of the Six Ages of the World*. California: University of California Press, 2023.

Harms, Daniel, James R. Clark, and Joseph H. Peterson. *The Book of Oberon: A Sourcebook of Elizabethan Magic*. Woodbury, MN: Llewellyn Publications, 2015.

Hartland, E. Sidney. "Robberies from Fairyland. Elidorus: The Luck of Eden-hall." In *The Archaeological Review 3*, no. 1 (1889): 39–52. Accessed June 12, 2023. http://www.jstor.org/stable/44243835.

Haycock, Marged. *Legendary Poems from the Book of Taliesin*. Aberystwyth: CMCS publications, 2007.

Heselton, Philip. *Gerald Gardner and the Cauldron of Inspiration*. Somerset: Capall Bann Publishing, 2003.

Hughes, Kristoffer. *Cerridwen: Celtic Goddess of Inspiration*. Woodbury, MN: Llewellyn Publications, 2021.

Hughes, Kristoffer. *The Book of Celtic Magic: Transformative Teachings from the Cauldron of Awen*. Woodbury, MN: Llewellyn Publications, 2014.

Hutton, Ronald. *Finding Lost Gods in Wales*. A Presentation for Gresham College. Accessed June 14, 2023. https://www.gresham.ac.uk/sites/default/files/transcript/2023-04-26-1800_Hutton-T.pdf

Hutton, Ronald. *The Pagan Religions of the Ancient British Isles: Their Nature and Legacy*. New Jersey: Wiley, 2010.

Hutton, Ronald. *The Triumph of the Moon: A History of Modern Pagan Witchcraft*. Oxford: Oxford University Press, 1999.

Hutton, Ronald. "The Wild Hunt in the Modern British Imagination." In *Folklore*, 130(2), 175–191, 2019. Accessed June 15, 2023. https://research-information.bris.ac.uk/ws/portalfiles/portal/145138643/FolkloreWH.pdf.

Huws, Daniel. *Medieval Welsh Manuscripts*. Cardiff: University of Wales Press, 2002.

Huws, John Owen. *Straeon Gwerin Ardal Eryri: Cyfrol 1*. Llanrwst: Gwasg Carreg Gwalch, 2008.

Huws, John Owen. *Straeon Gwerin Ardal Eryri: Cyfrol 2*. Llanrwst: Gwasg Carreg Gwalch, 2008.

Ifans, Dafydd a Rhiannon. *Y Mabinogion*. Ceredigion: Wasg Gomer, 2007.

Isaac, Evan. *Coelion Cymru*. Aberystwyth: Cambrian News, 1938.

Jenkins, D. E. *Bedd Gelert: Its facts, fairies, & folk-lore*. Portmadoc: Llewelyn Jenkins, 1899.

Jones, Edmund. *A Relation of Apparitions of Spirits in the County of Monmouth, and the Principality of Wales*, 1813. Facsimile reprint. Milton Keynes: Lightning Source UK.

Jones, Evan John, and Doreen Valiente. *Witchcraft: A Tradition Renewed*. Suffolk: Robert Hale Limited, 1990.

Jones, Gwyn, and Thomas Jones. *The Mabinogion*. Southampton: J. M. Dent & Sons Ltd., 1949.

Jones, T. Gwynn. *Welsh Folklore and Folk Custom*. First published 1930. Reprint, Cockatrice Books, 2020.

Kirk, Robert. *The Secret Commonwealth of Elves, Fauns, and Fairies*. First Published in 1815. Reprint, Dover Editions, 2008.

Lecouteux, Claude. *Phantom Armies of the Night: the Wild Hunt and the Ghostly Processions of the Undead*. Rochester, VT: Inner Traditions, 2011.

Lilly, William. *William Lilly's History of His Life and Times: From the Year 1602 to 1681*. London: Charles Baldwyn, 1822.

Lindahl, Carl, John McNamara, and John Lindow, eds. *Medieval Folklore: A Guide to Myths, Legends, Tales, Beliefs, and Customs.* New York: Oxford University Press, 2000.

Lindahl, Carl, John McNamara, and John Lindow, eds. *Medieval Folklore: A Guide to Myths, Legends, Tales, Beliefs, and Customs.* New York: Oxford University Press, 2002.

Lloyd, D. M., and E. M., eds. *A Book of Wales.* Great Britain: Collins, 1954.

Lynch, Frances. *Prehistoric Anglesey: The Archaeology of the Island to the Roman Conquest.* Llangefni: The Anglesey Antiquarian Society, 1970.

Narváez, Peter, ed. *The Good People: New Fairylore Essays.* Kentucky: University Press of Kentucky, 1991.

Opie, Iona, and Moira Tatem, eds. *A Dictionary of Superstitions.* New York: Oxford University Press, 1989.

Owen, Elias. *Welsh Folk-Lore: A Collection of Folk-Tales and Legends of North Wales.* First published 1896. Facsimile edition by Llanerch Publishers, 1996.

P. G. *A most strange and true report of a monsterous fish, who appeared in the forme of a woman, from her waste upwards, 1604.* Library of Wales. Accessed July 23, 2023. https://www.library.wales/discover-learn/digital-exhibitions/printed-material/monsterous-fish.

Parry, Thomas, ed. *Gwaith Dafydd ap Gwilym,* Caerdydd: Gwasg Prifysgol Cymru, 1952.

Parry, Thomas. *Gwaith Dafydd ap Gwilym.* Gwasg Prifysgol Cymru, 1963.

Parry-Williams, T. H., ed. *Rhyddiaith Gymraeg: Y Gyfrol Gyntaf: Llawysgrifiau 1488–1609.* Caerdydd: Gwasg Prifysgol Cymru, 1954.

Rhŷs, John. *Celtic Folklore: Welsh and Manx.* Oxford, London: Clarendon Press, 1901.

Rhŷs, John. *Studies in Arthurian Legend.* Oxford, London: Clarendon Press, 1891.

Roberts, Tony. *Myths and Legends of Pembrokeshire.* Fishguard: Pembrokeshire Handbooks, 1975.

Rowland, William. *Straeon y Cymry.* Aberystwyth: Gwasg Aberystwyth, 1935.

Rowlands, William. *Chwedlau Gwerin Cymru.* Rhydychen: Gwasg Prifysgol Rhydychen, 1923.

Rüdiger, Angelika. *Y Tylwyth Teg. An Analysis of a Literary Motif.* Bangor University (United Kingdom), 2022. Accessed June 3, 2023. https://research.bangor.ac.uk/portal/files/40328713/2021_R_diger_AH_PhD.pdf.

Shack, Joseph. *Otherworld and Norman 'Other': Annwfn and its colonial implications in the first branch of the Mabinogi.* In *Proceedings of the Harvard Celtic Colloquium,* 172–186. The Department of Celtic Languages and Literatures Faculty of Arts and Sciences, Harvard University, 2015. Accessed July 11, 2023. https://www.jstor.org/stable/24893610.

Shakespeare, William. *Macbeth.* Wordsworth Editions, 1992.

Sikes, Wirt. *British Goblins: Welsh Folklore, Fairy Mythology, Legends and Traditions.* London: Sampson Low, Marston, Searle & Rivington, 1880.

Sims-Williams, Patrick. *Irish Influence on Medieval Welsh Literature.* New York: Oxford University Press, 2011.

Singer, Rita. "Of Mermaids and Fairies | Môr-forynion a'r Tylwyth Teg." *Ports, Past and Present.* Accessed July 24, 2023. https://portspastpresent.eu/items/show/564.

Smith, Andrew Phillip. *Pages From a Welsh Cunning Man's Book: Magic and Fairies in Nineteenth-Century Wales.* Barry, Wales: Bardic Press, 2023.

Starling, Mhara. *Welsh Witchcraft: A Guide to the Spirits, Lore, and Magic of Wales.* Woodbury, MN: Llewellyn Publications, 2022.

Stephens, Meic, ed. *The Oxford Companion to the Literature of Wales.* New York: Oxford University Press, 1986.

Suggett, Richard. *A History of Magic and Witchcraft in Wales.* Gloucestershire: The History Press Ltd., 2008.

Suggett, Richard. *Welsh Witches: Narratives of Witchcraft and Magic from 16th and 17th Century Wales.* St. Asaph, Wales: Atramentous Press, 2018.

Tallis, Lisa, ed. *Cas Gan Gythraul: Demonology, Witchcraft and Popular Magic in Eighteenth-century Wales.* Newport: South Wales Record Society, 2015.

Thomas, Gwyn. *Y Traddodiad Barddol.* Dinbych: Gwasg Prifysgol Cymru, 1976.

Thomas, W. Jenkyn. *The Welsh Fairy Book.* Cardiff: University of Wales Press, 1995.

Thorpe, Lewis, ed. *The History of the Kings of Britain.* London: Penguin Books, 1966.

Trevelyan, Marie. *Folk-Lore and Folk Stories of Wales*. London: Elliott Stock, 1909.

"Was it a Mermaid?" In *The Pembrokeshire Herald and General Advertiser*, September 16, 1910. Accessed July 24, 2023. https://newspapers.library.wales /view/3065248/3065251/39/.

Wilby, Emma. *Cunning Folk and Familiar Spirits: Shamanistic Visionary Traditions in Early Modern British Witchcraft and Magic*. Eastbourne: Sussex Academic Press, 2013.

Williams, Mark. *The Celtic Myths That Shape the Way We Think*. London: Thames & Hudson, 2021.

Wood, Juliette. "The fairy bride legend in Wales." In *Folklore 103*, no. 1, 56–72, 1992. Accessed July 9, 2023. https://www.tandfonline.com/doi/abs/10.1080 /0015587X.1992.9715829?journalCode=rfol20.

Woolley, Benjamin. *The Queen's Conjuror: The Life and Magic of Dr Dee*. London: Flamingo, 2002.

Index

A

Adar Rhiannon, 168, 213

afterlife, 40

alien, 205, 206

animal(s), 11, 12, 16–18, 20–24, 34, 38–42, 46, 48, 53, 55, 58, 63, 70, 72, 76, 83, 92, 98, 119, 123, 125, 127, 129, 137, 140, 146, 156–167, 172, 174, 204, 214–216, 221

Annwfn, 8, 10–17, 22–28, 30, 36, 37, 40, 41, 43–45, 47, 51, 54–57, 60, 63, 64, 73, 79–82, 86, 90, 113, 124, 129, 156–158, 160–163, 195, 196, 213, 215, 216, 218, 219

Arawn, 10, 12–16, 20, 21, 51, 54, 56–58, 66, 120, 122, 156, 157, 160–163, 213, 218

Arianrhod, 121, 213

Arthur, King, 22, 41, 43, 54, 57, 60, 142, 157

Arthurian tales, Arthurian, 22, 38, 40, 55, 60, 161, 201

ash tree, 138, 173

Australia, 59, 202

Awen, 9, 26–31, 90, 153, 183, 191, 214, 215

B

baby, babies, 71, 76, 82–85, 148, 172, 176, 220

Barclodiad y Gawres, 103, 141, 142, 214

Bardic Tradition, the, bard, bards, 9, 13, 25–28, 30, 36, 38, 122, 126, 133, 134, 136, 139, 191

Bardsey Island, 132, 221

Belenos, 121

Bendigeidfran, 143, 214

birds, 8, 19, 40, 128, 168, 169, 182, 213

Birds of Rhiannon, 8, 19, 168, 169, 213

Blodeuedd, 153, 160, 214

Brân, 18, 19, 97, 121, 143, 214

Branwen, 18–20, 168, 214

Britain, British, 19, 25, 34, 42–44, 53–55, 59, 60, 76, 100, 103, 105, 107, 115, 131–133, 135, 142, 147, 153, 160, 161, 167, 174, 175, 185, 201, 216, 220

Bronze Age, 111

Brothers Grimm, 115

Brythonic, 121, 221

Bwgan, 8, 108, 109, 215

C

Caer Fanddwy, 40

Caer Siddi, 27, 215

Calan Mai, see also May Day, 34, 42, 43, 60, 74, 179, 197, 215, 216, 218, 221

Canada, 59, 202

Cantre'r Gwaelod, 39, 138, 215, 218

Canwyll Corff, 103, 104, 215

Cas Gan Gythraul, 177, 178, 215

cauldron(s), 18, 28, 29, 59, 140, 174, 219

cave(s), 10, 24, 33, 34, 52, 70, 102, 111, 113, 116, 155

Caws Llyffant, 151, 152, 215

Ceffyl Dŵr, 164, 215

Celtic, Celts, Celt, 2, 11, 28, 29, 35, 37, 39, 40, 48, 54, 60, 74, 77, 80, 86, 89, 97, 100, 129–131, 139, 163, 174, 179, 200

ceremony, ceremonial, 13, 177, 181, 185

Cerridwen, 26, 28–31, 48, 121, 122, 215, 221

changeling(s), 82–85, 176, 220

children, child, kid, kids, youth, young, 85

Christian, Christians, Christianity, 24, 48, 49, 73, 75, 88, 89, 101, 121

chthonic, 9, 13, 17, 27, 32, 33, 163

Clan of Tubal Cain, 61

Coblynnau, 65, 111–113, 115, 117, 216

Cochrane, Robert, 38, 61

Collen, St., 43–48, 54, 63, 73, 97, 154, 214

conjuring, conjurer, conjure, conjuration, 1, 2, 9, 26, 30, 85, 96, 171, 175, 177, 179–182, 185, 215, 216, 218

corgi(s), 158–160, 204

Cornish, 105, 111, 112

cow(s), 34, 83, 165, 166, 214

Creiddylad, 42, 43, 51, 60, 216

crystal, 193–196

cunning, 2, 5, 10, 82, 85, 88, 123, 154, 167, 171, 172, 175–180, 182, 185, 187, 215, 217, 220

cunning folk, 5, 88, 171, 176–178, 182, 185, 215, 220

Cŵn Annwfn, 37, 54, 55, 57, 156–158, 163

Cylch Cyfrin, 130, 152, 216

D

dance, dances, dancer, dancers, dancing, 31, 46, 52, 71–73, 77, 78, 96–99, 145, 153, 175, 176, 206, 217

death, 7, 15, 18, 23, 25, 40, 43, 55–59, 61, 83, 87, 88, 96, 103, 104, 112, 115, 116, 133, 135, 137, 157, 158, 168, 169, 213, 215, 216, 219

Dee, John, 193, 216

deity, 48, 54, 62, 74, 120–125, 131, 138, 148

demon(s), demonic, 24, 38, 41, 43–45, 47, 49, 54, 88, 99–101, 105, 173, 177, 181, 202

devil, 2, 38, 47, 48, 99, 101, 161, 162, 177, 215, 221

divination, 114, 148, 149, 162, 194, 215, 220

dog, 11, 12, 16, 20, 39, 53, 55, 58, 156–160, 172, 204, 216

Druids, 55, 89, 153

Du y Moroedd, 41, 137, 163

Dyn Hysbys, 154, 180–182, 185, 191, 217

Dynion Bach Teg, 81, 82, 217

E

Elidorus, 32, 33, 66, 72, 86, 91, 156, 163

Ellyll-Dân, 103–105, 217

Ellyllon, 96, 97, 99–103, 115–117, 150, 152–156, 215, 219

elf, 67, 97, 99, 100, 173, 217, 219

England, 39, 59, 132, 133, 135, 159, 177, 178, 181, 204, 221

English, 5, 6, 35, 40, 51, 52, 58, 59, 92, 99–101, 103, 113, 115, 134, 142, 204, 209–212, 217

Eryri, 132, 143, 164, 167, 204, 217

F

fairy bride, 32, 73–79, 82, 124, 136, 166, 174, 204

fairy cattle, 76, 159, 164, 166

fairy ring (see also fungus, mushroom), 145, 146, 150–153, 175, 176, 215

fall, 71, 75, 103, 132, 151, 175

familiar(s), 31, 56, 88, 100, 105, 106, 110, 111, 181, 220

Farrar, Stewart and Janet, 59

fern(s), 145, 148, 150, 151, 220

fog (see also mist), 2, 5, 10, 20–22, 33, 37, 58, 62, 63, 68–70, 87, 115, 119, 124, 153, 214, 219

folklore, 2–11, 13–20, 22–24, 27, 28, 30–38, 40, 42–44, 47–51, 53–58, 60–63, 65, 66, 69–80, 82, 84–91, 96, 97, 99, 100, 102–113, 115, 116, 120–124, 126, 127, 129–143, 145–148, 150–153, 155–168, 171, 172, 174–179, 181, 183–185, 187, 194–196, 200, 201, 203–206, 213–221

forest, 11, 16, 21, 22, 37, 49–52, 60–62, 78, 89–91, 99, 132, 140, 175, 176, 201

foxglove, 152, 153, 219

fungus (see also fairy ring, mushroom), 145, 146, 150–153, 175, 176, 215

G

Gaul, Gauls, Gaulish, 121

Gardner, Gerald, 38, 59, 61, 201, 202

Gardnerian Witchcraft, 61

Germany, 59, 181

Ghost(s)(also spectre, phamtom, spectral entity), 37, 38, 44, 53, 54, 86, 87, 89, 95, 96, 99–101, 103–109, 112, 113, 139, 157, 158, 167, 173, 206, 215, 217 giant, giantess, 18, 22, 41, 102, 103, 119, 120, 134, 140–143, 153, 214, 215, 217, 220, 221

goat(s), 98, 166, 167

goblin(s), 34, 54, 55, 76, 86, 95, 99, 100, 103, 105, 107, 111, 114, 115, 135, 147, 153, 167, 174, 175, 185, 206

gorse, 147, 148, 150, 173, 217

Gorsedd Arberth, 16, 17, 20, 126, 127, 217

Graves, Robert, 38, 59–61

Green Islands, 35

Grimm, Jacob, 53

Gwenhudwy, 138–140, 218

Gwrach, 113–117, 218

Gwragedd Annwfn, 82, 218

Gwyddno Garanhir, 39, 43, 138, 139, 163, 218

Gwyl Ifan, 197, 218

Gwyn ap Nudd, 6, 23, 24, 27, 37–40, 42–61, 63, 64, 68, 69, 71, 73, 86, 87, 92, 97, 113, 120, 122, 123, 136, 137, 154–157, 163, 179, 189, 201, 214, 218

Gwythyr ap Greidol, 218

H

Hafgan, 12–16, 218

Hafren (the river)(Severn), 74

Hafren (goddess)(Sabrina), 74

hag(s), 84, 115, 116

Halloween, 108, 114, 148, 161, 197, 219, 221

hazel, 83, 154, 155, 188

heather, 72, 150, 151, 217

hell, 24, 27, 45, 47–49, 61, 73, 89, 173

Horned God, the, 55–57, 61, 157, 201

Horse (also steed, water horse)(see also animal), 12, 16–18, 20, 23, 38–42, 46, 63, 70, 72, 76, 119, 123, 125, 127, 129, 137, 158–160, 162–164, 174, 204, 215, 216

horseshoe(s), 85

hunt, 11, 12, 15, 16, 20, 38, 41, 53–58, 61, 63, 77, 87, 156–158, 161, 218, 221

Huntsmen (Huntsman), 53–55

Hwch Ddu Gwta, 161, 162, 221

I

Iarlles y Ffynnon, 22, 140

Ireland, 17, 18, 27, 35, 44, 59, 80, 105, 214, 215, 219

iron, 49, 74, 78, 83–86, 89, 91, 102,
    111, 140, 142, 146, 173, 174, 197,
    200
Iron Age, 74, 86, 102, 142

island, 9, 10, 18, 19, 27, 31, 34–36,
    42, 74, 80, 100, 108, 111, 132, 135,
    139, 147, 160, 161, 221

J

Jesus Christ, 44, 47, 89
Jones, Evan John, 16, 23, 33, 35, 59,
    61, 70–72, 76, 79, 86, 87, 100,

105–107, 134, 136, 138, 139, 157,
    158, 162, 176, 178, 179
justice, 129

K

king, 2, 3, 6, 8, 10, 12–16, 18, 22,
    37–39, 41, 43–51, 54, 56–58,
    60–65, 68, 71, 87, 119, 120, 124,

129, 131–133, 137–139, 142, 143,
    156, 157, 167, 179, 181, 182, 213,
    214, 218–220

L

lake, 9, 33–35, 73–77, 82, 84, 85, 89,
    91, 119, 130, 135, 152, 155, 156,
    164–166, 188, 195, 199, 202–204,
    210, 218, 219
liminal, liminality, 7, 9–11, 15–18,
    29, 33, 35, 37, 40, 52, 59, 61, 64,
    88–91, 113, 115, 124–127, 130,
    134, 141, 153, 155, 156, 161, 163,
    168, 169, 183, 184, 188, 195–197,
    202
Lleu Llaw Gyffes, 121, 214
Llwyd ap Cilcoed, 21, 218
Llyfr Cyfrin, 179–181, 185, 187, 191,
    218

Llyn, 28, 29, 34, 35, 74, 76, 77,
    164–166, 203, 204, 218, 219
Llyn Barfog, 34, 164–166
Llyn y Fan Fach, 34, 76, 77, 166, 219
lore, 2–9, 27, 32, 36, 38, 40, 42, 51,
    53–56, 58, 60–63, 65, 66, 72–75,
    77, 79, 80, 82, 85, 89, 90, 96, 100,
    103–107, 109, 111, 112, 115, 116,
    120, 121, 129–134, 136, 137, 139,
    142, 143, 145–148, 150–153,
    156–162, 164, 166, 171, 174, 176,
    179, 181, 183–185, 187, 194, 196,
    200, 201, 205, 206, 213–218, 220,
    221

M

Mabon, 121

Mabinogi, 9–12, 14, 16–18, 20, 22–25, 27, 31, 35, 40–42, 51, 54, 56, 57, 66, 73, 121, 123–125, 127, 129, 131, 140, 143, 153, 156, 160–163, 168, 213, 214, 218–220

Mabinogion, 9, 11, 12, 14, 16, 17, 22–24, 40–42, 54, 56, 57, 66, 123, 127, 131, 140, 153, 160–162, 168, 219

Four Branches of the, 10, 18, 20, 22, 31, 219

First Branch of the, 10, 12, 20, 23, 51, 56, 73, 124, 125, 127, 156, 161, 163, 213, 220

Second Branch of the, 18, 27, 35, 143, 168, 213, 214, 219

Third Branch of the, 22, 218

Fourth Branch of the, 22, 129, 160, 161, 213, 214

magic, 1–5, 8–11, 13, 15–25, 29, 31, 32, 34–36, 38, 41, 48–52, 59, 62, 65, 69, 71, 80, 85, 88, 90, 99, 105, 106, 110, 113–116, 119, 120, 123–127, 129, 130, 133, 134, 136, 138, 140, 142, 145, 146, 148–154, 156, 160, 162–164, 166–169, 171–185, 187, 188, 190, 191, 194, 200–203, 207, 213, 215–218, 220, 221

May Day (see also Calan Mai), 34, 42, 43, 60, 74, 179, 197, 215, 216, 218, 221

Mallt y Nôs, 57, 58

Maponos, 121

medieval, 10–14, 16, 17, 31, 38–40, 42, 47, 49–51, 54, 55, 57, 61, 66, 97, 102, 121, 124, 132, 135, 162, 218

Menyg Ellyllon, 152, 219

Merlin, 131–134, 153, 169, 217, 219

mermaid(s), 8, 97, 119, 120, 129, 134–140, 218, 219

mist (see also fog), 2, 5, 10, 20–22, 33, 37, 58, 62, 63, 68–70, 87, 115, 119, 124, 153, 214, 219

Môr-Forwyn, 134, 136, 219

mounds, 16–18, 27, 47, 52, 61, 63, 97, 102, 140, 141, 143, 200, 201

Murray, Margaret, 200–202

mushrooms (see also fairy ring, fungus), 145, 146, 150–153, 175, 176, 215

music, 35, 62, 97, 98, 102, 176, 186

N

Native tales, 10

Neopaganism, 200, 201

Nôs Galan Gaeaf, 148, 161, 162, 197

O

oak, 60, 83, 85, 153, 161, 188, 216

occult, 3, 167, 180, 183, 193, 200, 202

Otherworld, 2–6, 8–29, 31–41,
    43–45, 48, 49, 51, 53–63, 65, 66,
    68, 71–74, 79–82, 85–92, 96, 98,
    101–104, 106, 108, 113–117,
    119, 120, 122–125, 129, 130, 133,
    134, 137–139, 141, 146, 148, 153,
    156–158, 160–169, 172, 174–178,
    183, 184, 187–191, 195, 200–207,
    213–216, 218–220

Owen, Elias, 33, 38, 55, 56, 73–75,
    79, 82, 85, 86, 89, 92, 93, 100,
    136, 137, 148–150, 161, 164, 175,
    187–189

P

pagan, 3–5, 28, 37, 38, 40, 48, 54, 55,
    58–61, 74, 101, 120–123, 125,
    140, 158, 160, 184, 199–202, 220

Pair Dadeni, 18, 219

pig(s), 20, 21, 41, 129, 160–163, 221

Plant Annwfn, 73, 79, 113, 219

Plant Rhys Dwfn, 67, 73, 80, 81, 219

Plant yr Is-Dwfn, 220

plant, 4, 63, 67, 73, 79–81, 113, 126,
    145–148, 150, 152, 153, 173, 187,
    214, 217, 219, 220

Pobol Gyfarwydd, 220

Pobol Hysbys, 220

poem, 25–27, 29, 30, 39–41, 53, 68,
    69, 92, 93, 96, 100, 101, 116, 126,
    132, 139, 145, 152, 159, 160, 163,
    188, 191, 195, 204, 215, 217, 218,
    220

pre-Christian (see also pagan), 48, 55,
    120, 121

Preiddeu Annwn, 215, 220

psychopomp, 40, 43, 54, 87

Pwyll, 10–17, 20, 25, 123, 124, 126,
    127, 129, 160–162, 216, 217, 220

R

raven, 40, 168

Rhaffau'r Tylwyth Teg, 150, 220

Rhamanta, 148, 220

Rhiannon, 8, 17, 19–21, 66, 120–128,
    162, 163, 168, 169, 213, 216, 217,
    220

Rhitta Gawr, 142, 220

Rhŷs, John, 35, 38, 40, 55, 74, 77, 79,
    86, 89, 179, 200, 209

rowan, 85, 91, 148–150, 173, 197,
    215, 216

S

sabbath, 167

Scotland, 39, 105, 132, 211, 221

scrying, 193–196

sea (also ocean), 7–9, 18, 27, 28, 35, 38, 39, 41, 42, 79, 80, 130, 134–140, 163, 168, 215, 216, 219

Shakespeare, 104, 105, 113, 181

Sikes, Wirt, 34, 38, 54, 55, 76, 100, 103, 105, 107, 115, 134, 135, 147, 153, 166, 167, 174, 175, 185

soul(s), 30, 37, 38, 40, 55, 58, 76, 84, 87, 101, 104, 114, 157, 158, 219

spirits of the land, 17, 114

spring, 1, 67, 126, 179, 188, 189, 192, 195, 197, 215, 217

Stone Age, 89, 200

Suggett, Richard, 1, 114, 177–179

summer, 127, 148, 150, 153, 165, 197, 203, 204, 207, 215, 217

Swyn, 189, 220

Swyngyfaredd, 114, 220

Swynwraig, 3, 114, 148, 172, 220, 221

Swynydd, 114, 171, 221

T

taboo(s), 19, 35, 70, 76, 77, 166, 174

Taliesin, Book of, 26, 27, 40, 41, 191, 220

Traditional Witchcraft, 59, 61

transition(s), 11, 16, 48, 59, 61

tree(s), 47, 52, 60, 62, 63, 83, 85, 92, 97, 131, 138–140, 145, 146, 148–150, 153, 154, 161, 173, 175, 188, 197, 210, 215, 216, 218

Twrch Trwyth, 41, 43, 161, 221

Tylwyth Teg, 1, 6, 13, 21, 24, 34, 35, 42, 49, 50, 55, 63, 66–69, 71–74, 79–81, 83–87, 89–92, 100–102, 113, 116, 129, 137, 139, 145, 150, 152, 154–158, 163, 167, 179–181, 185, 188, 201–203, 220, 221

U

UFO(s), 205, 206

United States, 59, 202

W

winter, 55, 108, 161, 219

wand, 4, 153–156, 188, 189

warrior, 37–41, 43, 61, 97, 159

White Book of Rhydderch, 14, 40, 161

Wizard of Oz, the, 115

Wicca, 59, 201

Wild Edric, 77

Wild Hunt, the, 38, 41, 53–58, 61, 77, 87, 157, 218

witch(es), 1–3, 5, 7, 8, 24, 28, 37, 43, 54, 59, 61, 106, 113–117, 120, 121, 125, 148, 153, 154, 167, 175, 177–179, 185, 200–202, 206, 215, 218, 220, 221

witch trial(s), 115, 178

witchcraft, 28, 38, 58–61, 114, 124, 130, 132, 175, 177, 178, 194, 199–201

White Goddess, the, 38, 59, 60

Ynys Enlli, 132, 139, 221

Ynys Gwales, 18, 221

Ynys Môn, 3

Yr Hen Ogledd, 39, 132, 221

Yr Wyddfa, 142, 143, 167, 221

Ysbaddaden, 41, 143, 168, 221

Ysbryd, 221

Ysbrydnos, 179, 221

Ystoria Taliesin, 133, 221

To Write to Mhara Starling

If you wish to contact the author or would like more information about this book, please write to the author in care of Llewellyn Worldwide Ltd. and we will forward your request. Both the author and the publisher appreciate hearing from you and learning of your enjoyment of this book and how it has helped you. Llewellyn Worldwide Ltd. cannot guarantee that every letter written to the author can be answered, but all will be forwarded. Please write to:

Mhara Starling
℅ Llewellyn Worldwide
2143 Wooddale Drive
Woodbury, MN 55125-2989
Please enclose a self-addressed stamped envelope for reply,
or $1.00 to cover costs. If outside the U.S.A., enclose
an international postal reply coupon.

Many of Llewellyn's authors have websites with additional information and resources. For more information, please visit our website at http://www.llewellyn.com.